eat-(Burg.)

SPENSER STUDIES
III

SPENSER STUDIES
A Renaissance Poetry Annual
III

EDITED BY

Patrick Cullen AND *Thomas P. Roche, Jr.*

UNIVERSITY OF PITTSBURGH PRESS

SPENSER STUDIES:
A RENAISSANCE POETRY ANNUAL

edited by Patrick Cullen and Thomas P. Roche, Jr.

is published annually by the University of Pittsburgh Press as a forum for Spenser scholarship and criticism and related Renaissance subjects. Manuscripts ordinarily should be from 3,000 to 10,000 words in length, should include an abstract of 100–175 words, should conform to the *MLA Style Sheet,* and should be submitted *in duplicate.* They will be returned only if sufficient postage is enclosed (overseas contributors should enclose international reply coupons). Manuscripts and editorial correspondence should be addressed to Thomas P. Roche, Jr., Department of English, Princeton University, Princeton, N.J. 08544.

Within the United States, *Spenser Studies* may be ordered from the University of Pittsburgh Press, Pittsburgh, Pa. 15260.

Overseas orders should be addressed to Feffer and Simons, Inc., 100 Park Avenue, New York, N.Y. 10017, U.S.A.

Published by the University of Pittsburgh, Pa., 15260
Copyright © 1982, University of Pittsburgh Press
All rights reserved
Feffer and Simons, Inc., London
Manufactured in the United States of America

ISSN 0195-9468
Volume I, ISBN 0-8229-3408-6
Volume II, ISBN 0-8229-3433-7
Volume III, ISBN 0-8229-3457-4

Contents

The so-called quantitative movement in Elizabethan poetry, like Renaissance prosodic thinking in general, derive from (1) a quasi-religious conception of speech supposed to have been uttered instinctively by the earliest men and everwhere informing the Hebrew scriptures; and (2) a rigorous mathematical description of this speech (called *rhythmos*) gleaned from ancient Greek sources and passed on by St. Augustine, notably in his *De musica* (ca. 387). In the Renaissance, the long and short syllables of classical verse were thought to embody this mystical, mathematical speech, so that writing vernacular quantitative verse was tantamount to linking one's national poetry with "original" poetry. Against this background, the technical minutiae in the documents I examine take on significance. The first, a set of letters exchanged by Edmund Spenser and Gabriel Harvey in 1579–1580, comprises the English quantitative movement's earliest detailed treatise. This correspondence illustrates the phonological uncertainities troubling not only Spenser and Harvey, but also experimenters like Richard Stanyhurst (1582), William Webbe (1586), and George Puttenham (1589), while many of the dicta in the last, belated tract in the series, Thomas Campion's *Observations in the Art of English Poesie* (1602), are simply codified versions of Spenser's earlier gropings. Finally, I trace in Campion's "Rose-cheekt Lawra" a complex pattern of Pythagorean mathematical operations mixed with biblical numerology.

There is strong structural and thematic evidence that *The Faerie Queene* was shaped partly by Spenser's sympathetic familiarity with the *Georgics*. In such crucial passages as the proems to Books I and VI, the first edition's ending of Book III, and the introduction to the Pastorella episode in VI, Vergilian motifs call our attention to the georgic themes of cultivation and effort applied to the world's complexity. Spenser's treatment of these themes reflects his view of his own responsibilities as a writer, and his view of his characters' responsibilities in the world of action.

73
"Pourd out in Loosnesse"
HAROLD L. WEATHERBY

An anonymous English translation of St. John Chrysostom's homilies on Ephesians, published in London in 1581, contains remarkably exact parallels, both thematic and verbal, to passages in Book I, canto vii of *The Faerie Queene*. Chrysostom, like Spenser, exploits the Pauline metaphor of Christian armor in Ephesians 6, and also like Spenser he develops puns based on the etymologies of "dissolute" and "loose." For the former (*diakechymenos*), Henri Estienne's lexicon (1572) offers *effusi, soluti,* "poured out" and "loose"; Red Crosse, having discarded his Pauline armor, is described as "pourd out in loosnesse." A synonym of Chrysostom's for *diakechymenos,* the Greek *hugros,* yields by way of Estienne's etymologies the association of sloth and lust with a flowing stream, which Spenser develops in considerable detail. Chrysostom's word for "loose" (*chaunos*) entails the sexual innuendo attaching to Orgoglio's alteration between tumescence and flaccidity as well as Arthur's role as the *megalopsychos,* the magnanimous deliverer. Such resemblances suggest the influence upon Book I of both Chrysostom and Estienne. They also sustain A. C. Hamilton's case for Spenser's delight in words and especially in etymological puns.

87
Isis Versus Mercilla: The Allegorical Shrines in Spenser's Legend of Justice
DONALD V. STUMP

In recent studies of Spenser's concept of justice in *The Faerie Queene,* most critics have regarded the Temple of Isis as the primary "house of instruction" and the Palace of Mercilla as a secondary locus in the allegory. Yet the evidence suggests that the Christian palace, not the pagan temple, represents Spenser's ideal of justice. In position and in function, it is similar to earlier houses of instruction in Books I and II, and it represents all the traditional parts of justice, of which the equity of Isis is but one. Throughout cantos vii and ix, the poet contrasts the two shrines through the symbols of silver and gold, moon and sun, darkness and light, and paganism and Christianity. His purpose in creating two allegorical shrines was probably twofold. First, he wished to contrast two periods in Queen Elizabeth's career. Canto vii, with its many allusions to Catholicism, represents Elizabeth in her weakness under the oppressive rule of Mary Tudor. By contrast, canto ix represents Elizabeth in her later strength as the defender of English and European Protestantism. Second, Spenser wished to distinguish classical equity from Christian mercy, as he does elsewhere. The trial of Duessa is an instance of equity, and the

Contents

tears of Mercilla at its conclusion are an instance of mercy. In this case, weeping is the only expression of Christian mercy that is defensible. Mercilla's reign represents a return to the ideal justice of Astraea. From the Brass Age, represented by the harsh justice of Artegall early in the book, Spenser leads us to the Silver Age in the Temple of Isis and finally to the Golden Age in the Palace of Mercilla.

When used in the practical context of a work like Spenser's *View,* certain conventional metaphors of Elizabethan political theory reveal their ontological weaknesses. Such apparently innocuous and seemingly illustrative or ornamental devices function in fact as a strategy of justification for the colonial enterprise. But the actual behavior of these metaphors under the kind of pressure exerted by their practical context reveals their insupportability as argument, so that Spenser must at intervals abandon their figurative language for the unambiguous discourse of fact (which in turn gives rise to problems which are simply ignored). The failure of this metaphorical language even in the hands of such a sophisticated employer implicitly invalidates a culturally sanctioned way of talking about (and justifying) one kind of political experience—that of colonial aggression.

Shakespeare's reading of Roman history informs the development of one of his major metaphors: the microcosmic view of an individual as besieged city or household, resisting an alien host but darkly longing to be possessed by it. Livy's treatment of early Roman history, which receives its fullest and most direct treatment in *The Rape of Lucrece,* describes patterns of civil strife which are also intensely intrafamilial and suggestive of psychic ambiguities in names: Tarquins banish other Tarquins. Livy's internalized Roman cityscape, together with the habit of parallelism exemplified so fully by Plutarch, provided Shakespeare with names and imagery which recur throughout his oeuvre, deepening and darkening the implications of the overtly Roman plays and stimulating much of the elaborate linguistic byplay in early works such as *Romeo and Juliet,* where received versions of the feud are reshaped toward the internal psychological drama of man and woman, Protestant England and Catholic Italy, wayfaring pilgrim and the shrine at the end of his journey. Thus the dream of reconciling warring households which links *Romeo* to *Antony and Cleopatra* may share with the later play a common origin in the reading of the young Shakespeare: Livy, Plutarch, and Vergil.

In the reign of Queen Elizabeth, being out of favor often meant leaving court, whether because the queen formally denied someone the grace of her presence or because the courtier thought it best to disappear until the storm blew over. In 1580, after Elizabeth had banished the Earl of Leicester and others from court, Philip Sidney retired to the country, where he probably composed most of the original *Arcadia*. In that romance, he figured himself in the conventional character of a melancholy shepherd, Philisides, exiled in Arcadia for love of a cruel fair, Mira. Love is a common allegorical vehicle for politics in Elizabethan poetry, and the agreement between the misfortunes of Sidney and Philisides suggests that Mira may figure the queen. The first Philisides poem in the Fourth Eclogues describes the mythological dream in which Mira first appeared to him, and the imagery of this vision confirms the connection between the poet's political problems and Philisides' complaints.

This essay suggests a reading of Sidney's *Astrophil and Stella* that sees Astrophil in his role as unrequited lover not as a heroic figure but as a figure of man's obsessive concerns with his own desires, man creating for himself his own private hell, in which his every hope brings him closer and closer to the despair that engulfs the conclusion of the sequence. I read the poem as a negative example of how to go about the business of love. The first section analyzes the imagery of blackness, perversely presented as light, the equally perverse imagery of the uniqueness of his star, which becomes his sun and finally two black stars, and the relation of this imagery to the Morpheus sonnet (32). The next two sections deal with Homeric parallels, bawdy puns and blasphemous metaphors first in the sonnets and then in the songs, the latter never having been treated as an integral part of the sequence. The last section attempts to determine the structural principles of the sequence on the basis of numerological analyses of the placement of the sonnets and the songs to substantiate the earlier analysis of Fowler and Benjamin.

These postprandial remarks at the Spenser Society luncheon in Houston, 1980, address the general problem of Spenserian influence, or the lack of it, in modern

Contents

American literature in order to introduce a backward glance at the mode of Spenserianism manifested in many of Nathaniel Hawthorne's tales. Many of these are not only allusive of Spenserian *topoi,* but seem to base their form of prose romance on *The Faerie Queene*'s episodic structure. A little-known story, *A Select Party,* singled out by Herman Melville as being particularly Spenserian, is invoked as an interesting and curious example of a Spenserian pageant.

SPENSER STUDIES
III

SETH WEINER

Spenser's Study of English Syllables and Its Completion by Thomas Campion

I. The Quantitative Movement in the Context of Renaissance Prosodic Thinking

THIS ESSAY contains a study of some letters exchanged by Edmund Spenser and Gabriel Harvey, samples of experimental verse from these letters and from a translation of Vergil by one Richard Stanyhurst, and a numerological analysis of Thomas Campion's lyric, "Rose-cheekt Lawra." These disparate elements relate all to one movement—an attempt by certain Elizabethan intellectuals to impose on English poetry the quantitative meters of ancient Greece and Rome. Judged against the age's poetic output, the experiments produced by this enterprise seem negligble: they comprise a small corpus of poems, of which a handful are delightful, a few competent, and the rest either dull, banal, or bizarre. Yet in the prosodic treatises of the period, this tiny eddy in the mainstream of poetry receives just as must attention as native, accentual verse. It is, moreover, a fact strange but true that the Elizabethans made their most sustained first efforts at hard thinking about the phonetic realities of English syllables in the very process of trying to adapt the foreign system of syllabic duration to their stress-based vernacular. Judged against the age's prosodic theory, then, the quantitative enterprise is central.[1]

The first to write on quantitative poetry was Roger Ascham in his *Toxophilus* (1545) and again in *The Scholemaster* (1570). Ascham's concerns are general: he tells of the movement's inception at St. John's College, Cambridge, in the 1530s and writes a sort of manifesto for it. The first *detailed* analysis of English quantities is found in the series of "wittie" and "commendable" letters that passed between Edmund Spenser and Gabriel Harvey in 1579–80.[2] These letters are a "first" by default: Sir Philip Sidney was the real impetus behind the movement in the late 1570s, but he published no treatise on the subject. For better or for worse, then, the Spenser-Harvey correspondence occupies an important position in the history of Elizabethan prosodic thought: the quantitative movement was, at least in theory, a communal effort, and later treatises returned quite often to problems that had been posed in earlier ones. In the end, the movement seems to come full circle: many of the *dicta* in Thomas Campion's *Observations in the Art of English Poesie* (1602; entered 1591), a rather belated tract in the series, answer issues that Spenser had raised more than ten years before. The structure of the present essay reflects something of that circular progress: the elaborate numerological study of Campion's "Rose-cheekt Lawra" with which it ends is meant to show how Campion completed what Spenser and Harvey had begun.

We can appreciate the details of the quantitative movement only if we have a general sense of its goals. The impulse to classicize is, of course, obvious. Theorists from Ascham to Campion expressed the wish to rescue English poetry from the fiddlers and tailors who huddled up ale-house ballads, to strip it of its jingling rhymes, and to make it "artificial"—that is, sophisticated, orderly, and above all, learned. What method could be more direct than forcing English verses to behave like the Latin ones so familiar to the community of educated men? But for these educated men of the Renaissance, imitating the ancients meant more than copying their forms: it meant, among other things, recapturing what those forms embodied. Since the structures of classical verse were felt in some vague way to contain the whole wisdom of the ancients, one can scarcely hope to describe the subject adequately in a few sentences. Yet some of the large ideas can and must be stated, at least approximately.

The chief idea, to which all others were tributary, was a deeply felt, musical conception of speech.[3] Speech was the expression of that heavenly harmony intrinsic to the human soul. Renaissance theorists of poetry, music, and oratory refer frequently to the earliest men who perceived the ordering of nature with a primal insight and remembered their other life, which was celestial. By instinct, they incarnated their wisdom in songs of praise that moved according to fixed rhythmic laws and obeyed strict proportions. The ancient Hebrews were supposed to have practiced this inspired art, and many writers in the Renaissance followed St. Jerome (who had followed Josephus and Philo Judaeus) in believing that parts of the Bible were written in Hebrew quantitative verses that could be compared to those written later by Greek and Latin poets. Indeed, the passing of quantitative measures from Hebrews to Greeks, and finally to Romans, was part of the *translatio studii* by which ancient wisdom had moved from one culture to another. For men of the Renaissance, to write quantitative verse in their vernacular was tantamount to linking their national poetry with "original" poetry.

This mystical notion of speech coalesced with and was supported by the ancient Greek science of rhythmics that St. Augustine had codified and passed on to the Latin culture of Western Europe in his *De musica* (c. 387). To a modern reader, the one thing conspicuously absent from *De musica* is music. The treatise appears, rather, to be entirely about Latin meters. But St. Augustine's concern is to show that these meters are in fact instinct with music—not necessarily with the "obvious," audible kind, but with a theoretical music much loftier and far more important. The syllables comprising classical feet consist of long and short units of time, and all those feet that have traditionally pleased the ear, are found to have their long and short times in certain fixed proportions. These turn out to be the very same ratios in terms of which the Pythagorean philosophers of ancient Greece had described the perfect harmonic intervals of the fourth, the fifth, and the octave (*diatesseron, diapente,* and *diapason*)— those harmonies that inform not only heard melodies but also the orderly courses of the universe.[4] It is little wonder that Renaissance prosodic theorists looked back on the masters of classical poetry with awe: for them, the ancient poet, musician, orator, divine, and philosopher were one and inseparable: in speech pronounced by such a magus with due regard for number, weight, and measure, was heard an echo of the Word that moves planets, changes seasons, and numbers every hair and leaf-fall. Antonio Lullo, author of *De oratione libri septem* (1558), a seven-part oratorical treatise based on Hermogenes, coined a nice phrase when he referred to the mystical, musical, mathematical speech that inhered in ancient meters as the dark and secret power of pronunciation.

Such, stated roughly, is the weighty lore behind the minutiae that fill the Spenser-Harvey correspondence. Every detail there is invested with significance: the middle syllable of the word *carpenter* can become something of a *cause célèbre* if one's goal is nothing less than to translate the dark and secret power of pronunciation into English. From ancient times to the Renaissance, prosodic theory, of which the science of rhythmics and the idea of impassioned speech were branches, had pertained chiefly to Latin quantities. The project of foisting the whole system onto English naturally involved elaborate argumentation over the effect of stress on the duration of syllables. Spenser and Harvey will seem far less silly and petty than they otherwise might, if we keep their grandiose *ends* in mind while examining their indecisive yet urgent squabbling over *means*.

These last considerations point up the need to discuss terminology before anatomizing the quantitative experiments, for no Elizabethan prosodist ever wrote the word *stress*. The word they used was *accent*, which can, and often should, be thought of as stress, though it should *not* be limited to that sense. *Accent* translates Latin *accentus*, which is based on Greek *prosodia*, the word used to denote that wide-ranging concept of speech that has been just described. In the Renaissance, *accent* had two related meanings, both reflecting its ancient lineage. The first, stemming from the fact that impassioned speech was musical, referred to variation in pitch: raising the voice produced an *acute accent* and lowering it, a *grave accent*. The other meaning signified the total phonetic quality of pronunciation—something like what we mean today when we speak casually of an Irish or a southern or a Brooklyn accent. The reason it so often makes sense to substitute our word *stress* for the Elizabethan *accent* follows naturally from the fact that stress is the most notable feature of English phonology. But every time we make this substitution, we miss the connotations associated in the Renaissance with *accent*. Besides, the substitution, as we shall see by and by, does not always work. The arguments mentioned above, then, over the role of *stress* in determining English quantities are, more properly speaking, arguments over how syllabic quantities should reflect English *accent*. And by the same token, the modern propensity to distinguish *quantitative* from *accentual* verse, while convenient, is not quite accurate, for the term *accent*, in several of its Renaissance guises, enters freely into Elizabethan discussions of *quantity*.

Renaissance theorists of prosody—especially those writing on the subject in musical treatises—often distinguish three kinds of accent: the grammatical, the rhetorical, and the musical. The Elizabethans we shall examine do not use these exact terms, though their works are everywhere informed by the concepts behind the terms. More importantly, the three accents are useful for describing Elizabethan experiments in quantitative verse because the terminology of accent suits the context of Renaissance prosodic thinking so much better than does that of stress. A particularly full and coherent description of the three kinds of accent can be found in book 8, chap. 13 of the *Sopplimenti musicali* (1588), the last treatise by

Gioseffo Zarlino, a musical theorist of monumental stature in the sixteenth century.[5]

All three accents are modes of pronunciation. The grammatical accent reflects a poem's metrical structure; in Zarlino's words, it "follows the long and short time in the quantity of the syllables." In English, the fact of stress (even if unnamed in the Renaissance) obscures the perception of syllabic quantity, so producing an audible grammatical accent became a major problem for the quantitative experimenters. The problem was compounded since no one really heard the quantities in the Latin models either: Elizabethans generally pronounced Latin like English, and the grammatical accent meant (then as now) a stressed-ictus reading—that is, the first long syllable of each foot gets emphasized. The rhetorical accent, as Zarlino explains it, follows the primary and secondary emphases of ordinary speech, regardless of metrical structure. But a good practitioner of rhetorical declamation also controls his breathing in a special way, now lingering over a syllable, now making his voice swell, and generally ornamenting his recitation so that it bodies forth the meaning of whatever poem or speech is being read. The musical accent is simply a stylized imitation of the rhetorical, transmuting the continuous movement of the voice through a range of pitches to an intervalic motion from one pitch to another.

Zarlino's description of the three kinds of accent blends technical details and illustrative scansions of lines from the *Aeneid* with arcane lore about ancient divines and philosophers, Hebrew poetry, rabbinical explanations of scriptural cantillation marks, Greek rhythmics, Pythagorean ideas of world harmony, and much else that pertains to the Renaissance conception of musical speech. With that conception in mind, and with some sense of Renaissance prosodic terminology, we may plunge into the heap of detail amassed by the Elizabethan metrists involved in the quantitative enterprise.

II. The Spenser-Harvey Correspondence

We will begin with a short piece by Spenser named *Iambicum trimetrum* (Smith 1.90–91) after the classical meter the poet was trying to reproduce. Gabriel Harvey, Spenser's friend and mentor at Pembroke Hall, Cambridge, made some sketchy but astute remarks about this poem that almost amount to a scansion of a few scattered lines. We shall proceed by scanning a few lines of *Iambicum trimetrum* and comparing our results with Harvey's. The virtue of this exercise is that it forces us to confront, with near-brutality, the chief problems besetting the various quantitative theorists and experimenters. As we meet each problem, we shall give it as much attention as seems necessary, discussing and trying to understand the relevant passages from the writings of those other Elizabethans who also struggled with it.

In the first letter, Spenser makes much of the fact that his experiments have the blessing of Sir Philip Sidney and Sir Edward Dyer who were at that time heading some sort of academic society referred to jocularly in the correspondence as the Areopagus.[6] Spenser claims his quantities are based on rules relayed personally to him by Sidney. These were set down originally by one Thomas Drant (the portly Archdeacon of Lewes, then recently deceased) but "enlarged [the rules, that is] with M. Sidneys own iudgement" (Smith 1.99). (Spenser hastens to add the inevitable note of confusion and uncertainty: the rules, he says, were also "augmented with my Obseruations"—whatever these were.) Harvey had not seen the rules; yet, in the course of the letters he criticizes them roundly, basing his objections on inferences that are true but somewhat unfair to the total purport of what Drant had to say. In any event, it is clear that we shall have to take Thomas Drant into account in trying to decipher Spenser's intent and Harvey's response.[7]

The usual pattern for *Iambicum trimetrum* is ⸗‑˘˘|⸗‑˘˘|⸗‑˘˘. In addition to the spondaic substitutions indicated, various others—dactyllic (‑˘˘), anapestic (˘˘‑) and tribrachic (˘˘˘)—are allowed in the first iamb of each dipody. In the more licentiate versions (and Harvey calls Spenser's lines a "mixte and licentious IAMBICKE") the substitutions are permitted anywhere except in the very last iamb. The catalectic line in this meter (that is, the line lacking one syllable at the end) runs as follows: ⸗‑˘˘|⸗‑˘˘|⸗‑˘. With these patterns[8] in mind, we shall attempt to scan the first three lines of Spenser's poem (for convenience of reference, syllables are assigned Arabic numbers, and lines, Roman numerals; thus, for example, "II, 10" means the tenth syllable of the second line):

$$
\begin{array}{l}
\quad\;\;{\scriptstyle 1\;\;2\;\;3\;\;4\;\;\;\;\;5\;\;6\;\;7\;\;\;\;8\;\;\;\;\;9\;\;10\;\;11\;\;\;\;12\;\;13} \\
\text{I. V\u{n}h\=app\u{i}e V\=erse,}\,|\,\text{th\u{e} w\=itn\=esse \=of}\,|\,\text{m\=y \u{v}nh\=app\u{i}e st\=ate,}
\end{array}
$$

$$
\begin{array}{l}
\quad\;\;{\scriptstyle 1\;\;\;\;2\;\;3\;\;\;\;4\;\;5\;\;\;\;6\;\;\;\;\;7\;\;\;\;8\;\;9\;\;\;\;10\;11} \\
\text{II. M\=ake th\=y s\u{e}lfe fl\u{u}tt\u{r}ing w\=ings \=of th\=y}\,|\,\text{f\=ast fl\=y\=ing}
\end{array}
$$

$$
\begin{array}{l}
\quad\;\;{\scriptstyle 1\;\;\;\;\;2\;\;\;\;\;3\;\;4\;\;\;\;5\;\;6\;\;\;\;7\;\;8\;\;\;\;\;9\;\;10\,11\;12\;\;\;13\;\;\;14} \\
\text{III. Th\=ought, \=and fl\=y f\=orth}\,|\,\text{\u{v}nt\u{o} m\u{y} L\=oue, wh\=ers\u{o}\u{e}u\=er sh\u{e} b\=e.}
\end{array}
$$

(Smith 1.90)

Drant's first rule is the time-honored one of position: "Consonant before consonant allwayes longe, except a mute and a liquide (as 'rĕfrayne') suche indiffrent." This accounts for the lengthening of the following syllables:

> I. 2, 4, 6, 7, 8, 11
> II. 4, 5, 6, 7, 9, 11
> III. 2, 4, 5, 9, 12

Position is not *necessarily* reinforced by anything phonetic in these syllables: there is no consistent correlation with stress (I. 7, 8; II. 5, 7; III. 2, 12 are unstressed) nor is any heed given to vowel quality. Here lies one of the chief difficulties with Elizabethan quantitative verse: syllabic length by position, as Derek Attridge shows us time and again, was more a matter of the eye than of the ear. John Hollander, with a sort of good-natured contempt, dubs the scanning of this poetry "decoding" and separates this clearly from the "audible poem" (which, in the case of *Iambicum trimetrum* "is in a free meter that any twentieth-century poet might employ, and that no Neoclassical poet would dare use, either (1) because it has no Classical basis, or (2) because it is a debased, limping form of one of the acceptable analogues of a Classical meter, the accentual-syllabic six-beat line showing French influence.")[9]

The rule of length by position was obviously subject to the "abuse" of doubling consonants or canceling one of a pair in order to secure a desired quantity. Spenser is not a gross offender here; yet, neither is he above taking occasional advantage of orthographic possibilities. In line 12 of *Iambicum trimetrum,* for instance, he must insure that the last syllable of the final iamb be scanned long:

> Sāy thāt lămēntĭng Lōue mărrēth the Mūsĭcāll.

Gladys Willcock, outraged at such complete and complacent ignoring of English phonetics, dismissed this practice as "the farce of manipulating the spelling."[10] Farce it may have been, but no more grotesque a performance than when an Elizabethan scanned a poem in the magisterial Latin tongue itself. In his painstaking reconstruction of Elizabethan reading and scanning habits, Attridge reveals the nearly complete divorce between what was seen in scanning (a series of typographical configurations) and what was heard in reading (a pronunciation following Latin word accentuation and employing English vowel qualities).[11] Under circumstances such as these, it was natural for English *literati* to feel that something like the orderly system imposed on Latin verse could likewise be foisted onto English: in neither case did pattern have to conform to sound. Bolstering this attitude was the humanistic discovery that Roman poets like Vergil and Horace had with purpose and deliberateness adapted Greek measures to a preexisting native tradition. Why could not Englishmen follow suit? Roger Ascham aired this idea in *The Scholemaster* (1570), and subsequent theorists repeated it often:

> And therfore, euen as *Virgill* and *Horace* deserue most worthie prayse, that they, spying the vnperfitnes in *Ennius* and *Plautus,* by trew Imitation of *Homer* and *Euripides* brought Poetrie to the same perfitnes in *Latin* as it was in *Greke,* euen so those that by the same way would benefite their tong and contrey deserue rather thankes than disprayse in that behalfe. (Smith I.33–34)

T. S. Omond makes the rather startling observation that there was no a priori reason to assume that quantitative laws could not work in English.[12] One might indeed expect an easy victory for a rule as purely mechanical as that of length by position, if only there had been complete consensus on the relative importance of the eye and the ear in reading. But consistency, even within the writings of a single theorist, is not the hallmark of Renaissance prosodic thinking. Coexisting with the attitude that quantity need only be visible was the contrary attitude that it must be audible. (Common sense dictates that there should have been no contest here, but we must concur with Attridge that, at times, common sense has little to do with this whole subject.) Thus, in the essay prefixed to his translation of *Aeneid* 1–4 (1582), Richard Stanyhurst feels obliged to follow each of his rules where spelling blatantly determines quantity with statements such as "Althogh I would not wish thee quantitie of syllables too depend so much vpon thee gaze of thee eye as thee censure of thee eare" or "albeyt, as I sayd right now, thee eare, not ortographie, must decyde thee quantitye as neere as is possible" (Smith 1.146). We shall peruse a sample of Stanyhurst's wild production by and by. In practice, he is one of the worst offenders against English sound and is, perhaps, simply protesting too much in the qualifiers noted above. The reverse of Stanyhurst on this point is George Puttenham (*The Arte of English Poesie,* 1589), who follows a clear and full account of how the native ear must determine English quantities according to stress (our most *audible* feature) with protestations on behalf of position and orthography.¹³ But upon examination, Puttenham's rule of position turns out to be a mixed and licentiate version of the ancient law: he tries to bestow the eye's empire on the ear with the assertion that difficult consonant clusters take time to pronounce. Other theorists, notably Campion, follow suit. We shall consider the whole issue more carefully in examining Harvey's famous argument with Spenser over the length of the middle syllable of the word *carpenter*. For now, the point is simply that Elizabethan readers could interpret those of Spenser's syllables that are long by position in two rather different ways. Some would have read them normally without worrying about how to match sound with meter. (Given that sixteenth-century Latin prosodies, like modern ones, never heeded the way people actually read, but were nonetheless full of traditional references to sound values in classical meters, there were probably many who read Spenser's lines normally and *fancied* they heard durational differences between longs and shorts.) The second group (probably Spenser among them, as we shall see) very likely made a special effort to suffer through the difficult consonant clusters, thereby pronouncing the poem differently from ordinary speech.

Anything approaching this last alternative would involve perforce *some* consciousness that reading and scanning practices for English quantitative meters had to differ somewhat from the habitual ways of dealing with the Latin verses that were being copied. Of course, the level of awareness varies from theorist to theorist, yet everyone shows at least a flicker. Puttenham makes the most sustained statement on this subject and, in his remarks, carries us far beyond the confinements of position to which we have thus far constrained the discussion. His Elizabethan ear tells him that Latin (with which he unceremoniously lumps Greek) is inconsistent in matching phonetics with meter. Syllables long by position might actually sound long because of consonant clusters, but they might also sound short, especially if they are swallowed up in the wake of a primary stress. Syllables long and short "by nature" have nothing whatever to do with phonetics: they were established by the often whimsical ears of the very earliest poets whose authority had become traditional (the doctrine of preelection of the first poets—see Smith 2.123). Puttenham concludes:

The quantitie of a word comes either by preelection, without reason or force as hath bene alledged, and as the aunciett

Grekes and Latines did in many wordes, but not in all; or by
election, with reason as they did in some, and not a few.

(Smith 2.126)

On balance, Latin meters are not *consistently* related to sound, and it
makes sense, therefore, to scan them visually by authority and by
position. But this need not be the case in English, where the fund of
preelected syllables dates back only to the 1530s, when the first quantitative verses were penned at St. John's College, Cambridge, and is
therefore piddlingly small. The would-be reformers thus become
elected poets in their own right, and Puttenham feels they can quite
easily base their quantities on phonetic realities (mostly stress with a
small and occasional admixture of position).[14] Puttenham's views
skew the humanistic equation enunciated by Ascham, to wit, that
Elizabethan poets can do in English exactly what Vergil and Horace
did in Latin. The English predicament is only roughly analogous to
the Roman: the formula "just as . . . so" does not really work. In
fact, Puttenham's sense of uniqueness of circumstance and hence of
imitation as analogy rather than as facsimile, is so advanced that to
discuss it would take us beyond the purlieus of the quantitative
movement. What is relevant here is his insistence that English quantities, unlike those in Latin, always and not just sometimes be ac-
commodated to pronunciation. How does this attitude reflect on
Spenser's *Iambicum trimetrum?* We have mentioned briefly and shall
discuss in greater depth the occasional attempts at making position
phonetic. But what of those syllables *not* covered by position—the
cases where Spenser would have found himself playing elected poet?
We must find what rational means, if any, he used in measuring such
uncharted bits of sound.

The Sidney/Drant rules suggest that Spenser's "rational means"
was vowel quality (what we moderns loosely refer to as the long or
the short form of each vowel). "Single consonantes comonly shorte"
says Drant, but not "suche as the vowell before dothe produce longe
(as 'hāte', 'debāte')." We can easily associate Spenser's *stāte* (I.13) and
māke (II.1) with this exception to the single-consonant precept. But
quality is not usually so safe a guide. It is the firm conviction of E. J.
Dobson, after the herculean task of compiling a systematic phonology for early modern English, that one can approach the whole
subject sensibly only if recognizing that "there were many variant
pronunciations, many levels and styles of speech, co-existing at any
time."[15] In other words, Spenser and other experimenters would

have had to establish a consistent line of choices among the welter of available possibilities if the quantitative enterprise were to flourish. The confusion was too great and failure was inevitable: Omond is largely correct in citing as one of the causes of the movement's downfall an overly lax view of quantity determined with regard to vowel quality.[16] Yet "lax view" is not really adequate. A better formulation would be "heroic yet hopeless effort to determine quantity with regard to vowel quality." For an illustration, we may look at the last syllable of *Ŭnhāppiĕ* (I.3, 12). In unstressed position (as it stands in Spenser's line), it was pronounced variously as [əI][17] or as [I] = *i* as in *city*.[18] Spenser chooses the short form without comment, but about a decade later, we find Campion essaying an explanation of this very class of word:

All words of two or more sillables ending with a falling accent [by which Campion means a sliding away of the voice after primary stress—a lowering of pitch, one might almost say] in *y* or *ye*, as *fāirelĭe, dĕmurelĭe, beawtĭe, pittĭe* . . . are naturally short [that is, short by nature] in their last sillables.   (Smith 2.354)

The consistency between Spenser and Campion is indeed impressive, and we shall see other instances where Campion's treatise elaborates or explains, or "realizes," as it were, an inchoate point in Spenser's. Indeed, there are many examples suggesting a sort of communal and cumulative effort among the theorists writing in the 1580s and 1590s: they focused often on the same problematic words or types of words and tried manfully to work out solutions.[19] But someone usually disagreed. In the case under scrutiny it was William Webbe (*A Discourse of English Poetrie*, 1586). "Words ending in *y* I make short without doubt," he writes, and though his dictum is rather extreme, we expect general agreement with Spenser. Then he makes the following exception:

I haue marked . . . one difference which they [presumably previous respected experimenters—probably including Spenser] vse . . . that is to make it [the final *y* ending] short in the ende ⁓ of an Aduerb, as *gladly,* and long in the ende ⁓ of an Adiectiue, as *goodly:* but the reason is, as I take it, because the Adiectiue is or should be most commonly written thus, *goodlie.*
(Smith 1.282)

Webbe probably had in mind the following line of Spenser's (from letter 3 in Smith's reprint, though Webbe saw it not in the correspondence published by Harvey, but rather, as he says, in E. K.'s gloss to "May"):

Ās fŏr⏐thōse mănў̆⏐gōodlў̄⏐māttērs⏐lēaft Ĭ fŏr⏐ōthērs.

(Smith 1.99)

He actually scans this line and changes the spelling of *goodly* to *goodlie,* in accordance with his own rule. Spenser leaves us no hard evidence to explain the difference between *vnhappĭe* and *goodlў̄.* Perhaps, in context, the end of *vnhappie* seemed to slide away more quickly, to have more of what Campion would call a "falling accent" than did the end of *goodlў̄.* Perhaps Spenser simply nodded: the one thing he tells us about this line is that he composed it "*ex tempore* in bed" (Smith 1.99). In any event, Webbe saw fit to base a law on some indeterminate combination of what he heard and what he saw as the practice of authoritative poets. For him the last syllable of Spenser's *vnhappie* (an adjective with the long sound supposedly indicated by final *ie*) would have been scanned long rather than short. He was obviously involved in the same cumulative enterprise to be taken up later by Campion. Of course, it might be tempting to ignore Webbe's "contribution" because his notion that earlier quantitative poets consistently scanned *y* long at the end of adjectives shows poor observation and because, compared with Spenser and Campion, he had the ears of Midas. We cannot, however, discount Webbe's ears or his powers of observation, for they demonstrate the very impossibility of reaching the necessary agreement on the question of which syllables were to be long or short by nature. On the single surviving leaf of a treatise called *Certen observations for Latyne and English versyfyinge* (1589), one H. B., the author, laments "the uncertaine and variable judgement of the eare."[20] Stanyhurst (Smith 1.147) ends his introduction with the apt observation that his rules are "priuat preceptes" and that others among the learned "may franckly vse theyre owne discretion wythowt my direction" when they attempt like experiments in classical meters. Puttenham, with a sort of yeomanly good will, asserts that his stress-rule for determining quantity should be perfectly serviceable so long as "your eare be not to daintie" (Smith 2.125). References of this sort could be multiplied. The point is that pronunciation was quite fluid, that the sense of some standard amid the variability was not nearly so strong as it is today, that therefore everyone could do what was right in the judgment of his own ear, and that as a result the limits of consensus on how to scan syllables by vowel quality could not be tightly enough drawn. These are the causes of some of the difficulties Harvey had when he read Spenser's *Iambicum trimetrum*. The two men were close university friends; they shared much in the way of general outlook and intellectual goals, and they both sought from the quantitative movement that theoretical union of words and music implicit in the conception of pronunciation outlined at the beginning of the present essay. But when it came to actual practice, their ears were tuned somewhat differently.

The syllables that will concern us here are *my* (I.9), *thy* (II.2, 8), the first half of *flying* (II.10), and *fly* (III.3). It is, of course, impossible to produce a perfect reconstruction of Spenser's scansion of these syllables, but fate has obliged us with one or two helpful hints. The first, as usual, comes from Drant:

> Bicause our tonge being full of consonantes and monasillables, the vowell slydes awaye quicklier then in Greeke or Latin, which be full of vowells and longe wordes; yet are suche vowells longe as the pronounciacon makes longe (as 'glōry', 'lādy'), and suche like as seeame to have a dipthonge sownde (as 'shōw', 'blōw', 'dȳe', hȳe').

The question we must answer is: which of the syllables listed above (*my, thy*, and the rest) would Spenser have chosen to pronounce long as the dipthong [əI], matching that in Drant's *dȳe* and *hȳe*, and which would he have chosen to read short as the monophthong [I] = *i* as in *city?*[21] The hint here comes from Spenser himself: "I dare warrant," he writes of his licentiate iambics, that "they be precisely perfect for the feete (as you can easily iudge) and varie not one inch from the Rule" (Smith, 1.90). No one has had an easy time judging. Harvey dismissed Spenser's claim lightly, while twitting him good-humoredly for his presumption. But what if we take Spenser seriously and assume that *he*, at least, found some way of construing his lines so that they conformed exactly to the laws governing *Iambicum trimetrum*? One result would be that the second syllable of line II, *thy*, would have to be long, because a trochee is not permitted in the first foot of an iambic verse.[22] Yet Harvey immediately judged the syllable to be short. Donning his familiar motley, he took Spenser elaborately to task for a supposed initial trochee, going so far as to narrate a tale from

SETH WEINER

Laurentius Abstemius' *Fabulae nuper compositae* in which a trochaically lame man with one leg long and the other short is roundly ousted from the seat at the highest end of a feasting table:

> whereas TROCHEE sometyme presumeth in the firste place, as namely in the second Verse, *Make thy,* whyche *thy* by youre Maistershippes owne authoritie muste needes be shorte, I shall be faine to supplye the office of the Arte Memoratiue, and putte you in minde of a pretty Fable in ABSTEMIO the Italian . . . etc. (Smith 1.95)

What is noteworthy here is that Harvey seems quite conscious that *thy* can be read long with the [əI] diphthong, or deemphasized and pronounced short as [I]. Presumably, the short way sounds better to him, but he cannot be sure that Spenser also found it preferable. In fact, as we saw, Spenser did not. At any rate, faced with uncertainty, Harvey's recourse is to invoke the rule of preelection of the first poets: Spenser himself established the syllable as short. Unless Spenser conveyed this information to Harvey informally or in a missive now unknown, we can only assume that Harvey has made an analogy with the short syllable *my* in line I (I.9).[23] But if Spenser's meter is to work, it is apparent that *he* made no such analogy, reading *my* short in line I and *thy* long in line II. We cannot say exactly what guided him: perhaps because *my* in line I is more clearly in an unstressed position than *thy* in line II, Spenser's native ear told him that the first was "slipper" (as an Elizabethan would say), while the second could receive some oratorical emphasis. In any event, Spenser and Harvey would have recited line II somewhat differently and were thus unable to scan it the same way.

Uncertainties of this sort abound. Thus, Spenser would no doubt have scanned his third verse so that it had three dipodies, or six feet, as it does in our scansion above. But Harvey, somehow, managed to find seven feet in the line: "the thirde," he writes, "hathe a foote more than a LOWCE (a wonderous deformitie in a righte and pure SENARIE)" (Smith 1.95).[24] Of course Harvey leaves no clue as to how he proceeded. Perhaps he lengthened the second syllable of *whērsŏĕuēr,* allowing a "long" *o* to override the vowel-before-vowel rule.[25] This would yield the following:

Thoūght, ānd flȳ fōrth v̄ntŏ mȳ Loūe, whērsŏĕuēr shĕ bē.
    1   2   3   4   5   6   7

Spenser's Study of English Syllables

The point here is that in the same measure as we must guess at Harvey's scansion, so was he guessing at Spenser's. But the issue toward which all this minute analysis points is larger than the mere inability of friends to produce like scansions of quantitative verse. A final example will reveal the general drift of our whole worm's-eye view of Spenser's syllables.

In letter 3 of the correspondence (in Smith's reprint), Spenser asks for Harvey's opinion of the following tetrasticon in elegiacs. (This, incidentally, is one of those cases where the prosodist's oft-criticized neglect of the "poetry" is a blessing in disguise):

See yĕe thĕ ˡblīndefoūldēd ˡprĕtĭe ˡGōd, thāt ˡfēathĕrĕd|Ārchēr,
Ōf Loŭĕrs Mĭsĕrĭes ˡwhĭch mākĕth ˡhĭs bloŏdĭe ˡGāme?
Wōte yĕ whў ˡhĭs Moŏthēr wĭth ă ˡVēale hāth ˡcoŏuĕrĕd ˡhĭs
   Fāce?
Trūst mē, ˡlēast hĕ mў ˡLoŏue ˡhăppĕlў ˡchaūnce tŏ bĕhōlde.

> (Smith 1.99)

In the next letter of the series, Harvey requites this effort with some verses of his own, but does not omit to give at least a parenthetical criticism of its scansion:[26]

> Now to requite your BLINDFOLDED PRETIE GOD (wherin by the way I woulde gladly learne why *Thĕ* in the first, *Yĕ* in the first and thirde, *Hĕ* and *My* in the last, being shorte, Mē alone should be made longer in the very same). (Smith 1.105)

Harvey's question is a good one. As we might expect, Spenser never answered it, so we have no definitive solution. Yet, it seems clear that *me* in the last line differs in rhetorical emphasis from the other pronouns Harvey mentions. Campion, who in 1591 (as we have seen) tended to refine and codify into rules what Spenser left half-formed and unexplained in 1579, makes the following relevant comments in the course of showing why English iambic pentameters occupy the same amount of time (measured in musical beats) as Latin hexameters:

> The cause why these verses differing in feete yeeld the same length of sound, is by reason of some rests which either the necessity of the numbers or the heauiness of the sillables do beget. For we find in musick that oftentimes the straines of a

song cannot be reduct to true number without some rests pre-
fixt in the beginning and middle, as also at the close if need
requires. Besides, our English monasillables enforce many
breathings which no doubt greatly lengthen a verse, so that it is
no wonder if for these reasons our English verses of fiue feete
hold pace with the *Latines* of sixe.   (Smith 2.334–35)

Of course one of the refinements Campion has made on Spenser (one
that is implicit, too, in the above extract) is to remove the English
dactylic line altogether from consideration as a viable quantitative
form. Some may therefore feel it awkward to apply what he says of
the supposedly equivalent iambic line to Spenser's tetrasticon. But
any awkwardness there might be is insignificant beside the general
bearing Campion's remarks have on the recitation of all English
poetry of whatever stamp. In Spenser's verse, the monosyllables
"Trust me," set off by a comma, certainly enforce what Campion
calls a breathing. And to impart a certain degree of "heauiness" to
these syllables (perhaps by means of stress and long vowel quality
reinforced by a breath) would be most appropriate to whatever slight
impact the poem has, since the phrase "Trust me" is the one plea for
stability that must offset all of the blindfolded pretty god's machinations, productive only of mutability and general woe. But here we
trespass on the critic's job and ruin our blessing in disguise: to say
more would be to mar all. The matter of importance is that, for
Spenser, rhetorical considerations seem, at this small juncture, to
have overridden the consistency of scansion insisted on by Harvey.
Put another way, the rhetorical accent has taken precedence over the
grammatical accent.

    To invoke these Renaissance terms, familiar to us from my intro-
ductory remarks, is quite germane to a situation in which the nature
of pronunciation itself is a key factor—for what have my micro-
scopic analyses urged us to see (and beyond that, to experience) if
not the reigning uncertainty and confusion over this very issue? Is
position related to sound? How does oratorical performance affect
vowel quality—and vice versa? Where should special rhetorical emphasis come into play and how might a poet signal that it has? In
short, what does the scansion of verse have to do with the dark and
secret power of pronunciation (that grand Idea embracing so many
areas of Renaissance lore) which the quantitative experimenters were
striving to make flesh? This is the problem Spenser had in mind
when he penned his well-known remarks about the word *carpenter:*

For the onely or chiefest hardnesse, whych seemeth [in composing English hexameters], is in the Accente; whyche sometime gapeth, and, as it were, yawneth ilfauouredly, comming shorte of that it should, and sometime exceeding the measure of the Number, as in Carpenter the middle sillable, being vsed shorte in speache, when it shall be read long in Verse, seemeth like a lame Gosling that draweth one legge after hir: and Heauen, beeing vsed shorte as one sillable, when it is in Verse stretched out with a *Diastole,* is like a lame Dogge that holdes vp one legge. But it is to be wonne with Custome, and rough words must be subdued with Vse. For why, a Gods name, may not we, as else the Greekes, haue the kingdome of oure owne Language, and measure our Accentes by the sounde, reseruing the Quantitie to the Verse? (Smith 1.98–99)

By *accent* in this passage, Spenser means *rhetorical accent,* the total quality of pronunciation. He is not, as the uninitiated commonly assume, talking only about stress, though the fact of stress, even if unexpressed, is obviously inseparable from Elizabethan (as from all English) pronunciation.[27] Having just read Harvey's assessment of *Iambicum trimetrum,* he is here exclaiming at the difficulty not merely of determining what the rhetorical accent should be, but, even more, of conveying his decisions to another person. If he is to communicate his intentions, he must gather his prosodical thoughts into some sort of formulation that will guide Harvey in reading future productions. It is no surprise that in this very letter he asks Harvey to do the same for him: "I would hartily wish you would either send me the Rules and Precepts of Arte, which you obserue in Quantities, or else followe mine" (Smith 1.99).

Spenser's formulation is, in part, a response to Harvey's problem with words (like *thy*) that need special rhetorical emphasis of some sort to be scanned correctly. The uniform application of ordinary speech patterns to verse leads to error, so Spenser prescribes a separate mode of pronunciation for poetry. As is well known, this idea produced a prime specimen of Harveyan outrage, which we shall examine shortly. Commentators often quote it as a reassuring expression of honest, homely English mother-wit. Indeed, Spenser himself was struck with the awkwardness of his own suggestion, but seemed convinced that gradual habituation would make men see lame dogs and geese as whole ones. Yet, despite all this silliness, the prescription is not nearly so gross a violation of English idiom as most critics, influenced, no doubt, by Harvey's strong language, have believed. Spenser is not saying, as it is commonly assumed he is, that we should shift stress and read cărpénter for cárpĕnter. Nowhere does he call for the deemphasizing of the first syllable. His intent is not to make utter nonsense of ordinary speech, but rather to amalgamate classical prosodic requirements with normal pronunciation in the reading of verse. The rule of position dictates that the middle syllable of *carpenter* be long, just as in the instance discussed above, the rules governing the structure of iambic trimeter demand a long *thy*. Spenser simply asks us to accommodate these factors when reading. The difficulty, of course, is that he does not tell us exactly *how* we are to do this. Presumably, in the case of *thy,* we are to supply the long rather than the short vowel sound (which, in practice, can only be done by stressing *thy* almost equally with *make,* reading máke th[óI] instead of máke th[Ĭ]). For *carpenter,* Spenser probably had in mind some lingering over the *nt* consonant group. In practice, this too would mean giving the middle syllable more weight than was usual in speech: we would read cárpénter, instead of cárpĕnter. Spenser's image of the lame gosling drawing one leg after her is quite suggestive of this slow, labored pronunciation with two stresses. It does not suggest, nor does Spenser recommend, the total distortion, cărpénter: such a gosling could not walk at all.[28]

In the final sentence of the above extract, Spenser, rather unfortunately, garbles the actual statement of his rule. The last phrase in particular ("and measure our Accentes by the sounde, reseruing the Quantitie to the Verse") is poorly worded and therefore very difficult to understand. Not surprisingly, different commentators have put variously unsatisfactory constructions on it. G. L. Hendrickson thinks Spenser's meaning is that we should always pronounce what we read as we do normal speech and consider the rules of quantity only in the construction of verse.[29] Attridge is quick to point out that this interpretation, which is quite a common one, has Spenser nullifying his whole discussion. His own reading is much better, but still falls just short of the mark:

Perhaps Spenser means that we should for ordinary purposes be guided in our pronunciation ('Accentes') by the normal sound, using special 'quantitative' pronunciations only when reading verse.[30]

As I suggested above, the "special 'quantitative' pronunciations" Spenser has in mind are merely to be annexed to normal speech, not contrasted with it. He is telling us, in all probability, that in reading quantitative verse we should stick to the usual pronunciation of English words except in those syllables where classical rules dictate that we supply some form of added rhetorical emphasis in order to indicate and thereby reserve (that is, retain) the proper quantity. The reading of *cárpénter* with double stress is a case in point. We produce, in sum, a slight modification of normal pronunciation, but not a travesty of it. We are never, in short, at a far remove from ordinary conversational English: a slight halting limp does not necessarily imply a cripple.

Campion, as usual, gives us a fuller "realization" of what Spenser had tried to say two decades earlier:

> But aboue all the accent of our words is diligently to be obseru'd, for chiefely by the accent in any language the true value of the sillables is to be measured. Neither can I remember any impediment except position that can alter the accent of any sillable in our English verse. For though we accent the second of *Trumpington* short, yet is it naturally long, and so of necessity must be held of euery composer. Wherefore the first rule that is to be obserued is the nature of the accent, which we must euer follow. The next rule is position. (Smith 2.351–52)

Accent, or ordinary pronunciation, is diligently to be observed, except where modified by the classical rule of position: Campion's formulation bears out our interpretation of Spenser's perfectly. *Trumpington* is clearly reminiscent of *carpenter*, but with one difference: the first syllable, like the second, is unequivocally long by position. Thus, *Trŭmpíngton* is an impossible reading on two counts: (1) it violates normal pronunciation and (2) it does not emphasize a syllable that position requires to be long. The only possible solution is *Trúmpíngton*, and (in retrospect) this suggests strongly that *cárpénter*, not *cărpénter*, is what Spenser wanted us to infer from his remarks on the same subject.

Examples of words like *carpenter* and *Trumpington*, in which the syllable following what we would call the tonic accent is lengthened by position despite the fact that it is swallowed up in ordinary speech, abound in the poems and dicta of the quantitative theorists.

The first two lines alone of Spenser's *Iambicum trimetrum* contain *wĭtnēsse, flŭttrĭng,* and *flȳĭng,* not to mention phrases like *Māke thȳ,* where classical requirements other than position force the lengthening of the post-tonic syllable. (It should be noted that disyllables and trisyllables retained secondary stress in Elizabethan English far more than they do in modern, so that the extent of distortion in pronunciation occasioned by post-tonic lengthening actually seemed less to the Elizabethans than it does to us.)[31] Campion's famed "Rose-cheekt Lawra" (to be examined shortly) has instances of the *Māke thȳ* or *flȳĭng* variety in almost every line. Even Puttenham, for whom stress all but produces length, allows classical rules to bestow vocal weight on syllables that are light in nonpoetic speaking:

> First in *remnant, rem,* bearing the sharpe accent and hauing his consonant abbut vpon another, soundes long. The sillable *nant* being written with two consonants must needs be accompted the same, besides that *nant* by his Latin originall is long, viz. *remanēns.*   (Smith 2.126)

Strange to say, a none-too-extensive search reveals examples of posttonic lengthening in the quantitative verse of Gabriel Harvey himself. In the following hexameter, aside from *Vērtŭē* and *Ăbōundăunce,* note that the second syllable of *blessed* is long by position in its first and second occurrences, though short by nature in its third:

> Ō blēssĕd Vērtŭē, blēssĕd Fāme, ¦blēssĕd Ăbōundăunce.
>   (Smith 1.104)

Surely, a theorist as concerned with pronunciation as Harvey is generally considered to be, does not mean us to gloss over the long syllables, pronouncing *blessed* exactly the same way all three times. The evidence we have been citing suggests that there is more truth than is sometimes thought in R. B. McKerrow's assessment of nearly eighty years ago, that quantitative theorists intended readers to drawl in a way contrary to normal speech when they encountered syllables made long by orthography.[32] And Gabriel Harvey, if his verse is any indication, held to this view, at least with regard to certain words. We must keep this fact in mind as we read his reply to Spenser on the *carpenter* issue, and avoid being seduced into easy misinterpretation by his alarmist rhetoric:

You shal neuer haue my subscription or consent (though you should charge me wyth the authoritie of fiue hundreth Maister DRANTS) to make your *Carpēnter*, our *Carpĕnter*, an inche longer or bigger than God and his Englishe people haue made him. . . . Else neuer heard I any that durst presume so much ouer the Englishe (excepting a fewe suche stammerers as haue not the masterie of their owne Tongues) as to alter the Quantitie of any one sillable, otherwise than oure common speache and generall receyued Custome woulde beare them oute. Woulde not I laughe, thinke you, to heare MESTER IMMERITO come in baldely with his *Maiĕstie, Royáltie, Honēstie, Sciēnces, Faćulties, Exćellent, Tauērnour, Manfŭlly, Faithfŭlly*, and a thousande the like, in steade of *Maiĕstie, Royăltie, Honĕstie*, and so forth. (Smith 1.117–18)

Evidently, from what we have seen, "our common speache and generall receyued Custome" are not sufficiently shaken by the altering of syllables in *blēssēd* and *Vērtūē* to make Harvey class the perpetrator, namely himself, with those "stammerers as haue not the masterie of their owne Tongues." Why, then, is it a greater trespass to lengthen the middle syllable of *carpenter?* The answer (for which, as in so many cases, we must thank the keen intelligence of Attridge)[33] depends on the fact that the *carpenter* debate centers on a conflict between the rule of position and the penultimate rule, by which words of more than two syllables are stressed on the penult if that is long and otherwise on the antepenult. The examples from Harvey's verse belie the ready and easy interpretation that he confounds stress with quantity.[34] Elizabethans were not likely to make this mistake. They read Harvey much the way Attridge does. Thus, Stanyhurst, who actually states the penultimate rule, is quick to cite the very Harveyan passage under discussion by way of corroboration:

Thee infallibelist rule that thee Latins haue for thee quantitye of middle syllables is this. *Penultima acuta producitur, vt virtûtis; penultima grauata corripitur, vt sanŭnis* . . . *Buckler* is long; yeet *swashbuckler* is short. And albeyt that woord bee long by *position*, yeet doubtlesse thee natural dialect of English wyl not allow of that rule in middle syllables, but yt must bee of force with vs excepted, where thee natural pronuntiation wyl so haue yt. For ootherwise wee should bannish a number of good and necessarye wordes from oure verses; as *M. Gabriel Haruye* (yf I mystake not thee gentleman his name) hath verye wel obserued in one of his familiar letters: where hee layeth downe diuerse wordes straying from thee Latin preceptes, as *Maiestye, Royaltye, Honestie,* &c.   (Smith 1.142–43)

For Stanyhurst, as for Harvey, the penultimate rule sorts better with English pronunciation—involves less drawlings or double emphases—than does the rule of position. Every word that Harvey lists involves a conflict between these two rules that can be most easily resolved if we simply pronounce as usual. Of course, the penultimate rule applies only to words of more than two syllables: for disyllables, Harvey and Stanyhurst are stuck, like everyone else, with the rule of position. Stanyhurst's *bŭckler* versus *swashbŭckler* demonstrates the kind of inconsistency that theorists like Spenser and Campion presumably intended to avoid by applying position to all words, regardless of the number of syllables. The *carpenter* issue, then, concerns preference for one or another of two classical rules in cases where they conflict. The argument is not over whether "accent" (that is, pronunciation) should be tampered with at all, but rather over the *extent* to which one needs to tamper with it. In words of more than two syllables, at least—so says Harvey—no alterations are necessary.

The penultimate rule is important because in it stress (the most audible feature of what Elizabethans called "accent") intersects with quantity. Armed with this rule, theorists could legitimately import accent (and not vowel quality or consonant clusters, but what they most naturally *sensed* as accent) into prosodic discussions of quantitative verse. Once again, with the issue of pronunciation so decisively introduced, we circle back to the old problem: what, in English, is the dynamic between rhetorical and musical, and grammatical accents? Do we let the grammatical accent influence the rhetorical, as Spenser does in the last line of the "Blindefoulded Pretie God" bauble discussed above? Or do we insist, as Harvey does, that whenever possible, the rhetorical accent conform to the usual configurations of conversational speech, and that it determine, more or less, the grammatical?

From what we have seen of their theoretical statements and examples, it would appear that Stanyhurst and Harvey are more devoted to English "accent" than Spenser and Campion are. Anyone, though, who has read and compared the quantitative verse of Stanyhurst and Campion knows how false this assessment is. Thus far, we have examined the relationship between accent and quantity only on the tiny scale of the syllable. From this perspective (and even then only with reference to three- and four-syllabled words where the penultimate rule holds sway) the above statement about Harvey and Stanyhurst is true. But accent and quantity also interact on the much grander scale of the whole verse: from this vantage, we observe the total pattern of the rhetorical or musical accent in relation to the total pattern of the grammatical. One cannot, of course, divorce these larger motions from what is happening at the syllabic level. And yet, as a brief examination of some actual specimens of verse will show, it does *not* follow that English accent observed syllable by syllable produces a poem in which the rhetorical accent is typically English.

III. Samples of Quantitative Verse

(a) Stanyhurst

The theoretical remarks that Richard Stanyhurst prefaced to his translation *Thee First Fovre Bookes of Virgil his Æneis* (1582) suggest a mixed bag of criteria for determining quantities: position, penultimate rule, rules of Latin terminations, diphthong, vowel quality, and consonant clusters all, variously, come into play. Orthography is clearly of great importance in this gallimaufry, but at least in theory, Stanyhurst's quantities are generally connected with some facet of pronunciation (i.e., "accent"), either native English or (in the manner of Spenser) modified native English.[35] In practice, the relation of the grammatical accent to any tangible aspect of English speech often seems remote. Still, no one can account for Stanyhurst's fantastic spellings on the basis of Latin rules alone; sound, evidently, must play a role, though one hopes that even an Irishman who had removed to the Low Countries via Oxford, London, and conversion to Catholicism could not actually have *heard* anything quite like what the orthography indicates. With the diction and syntax as corroborative evidence, it is tempting to conclude that Stanyhurst was slightly mad. But all such speculation aside, one *can* produce a correct quantitative scansion of his verse using his own rules, by and large, and fudging only a little. There is, therefore, a grammatical accent, or pronunciation, not consistently maintained, perhaps, but meant to be audible (at least in some way known to Stanyhurst and now partially irrecoverable). The scansion is not merely visual.

Whatever the audible features of Stanyhurst's grammatical accent were, they did not include stress. He deliberately kept this aspect of accent quite apart from any considerations of quantity. And he was sensitive to the fact that English stress did not behave exactly like its Latin counterpart. Of course, he never uses the term *stress,* but he demonstrates his awareness of the thing itself as a vital aspect of English accent, separate from other aspects that have to do with quantities, by commenting pointedly on the inapplicability of Cícero's rule of Latin word-accentuation. "But to rip vp further thee peculiar propretye of oure English," he writes, "let vs listen too *Tullye* his iudgement." He goes on to quote the rule, then says:

> In this saying Tullye obserueth three poinctes. First, that by course of *Nature* euerye woord hath an *accent:* next, one only: lastlye, that thee sayde *accent* must be on thee last syllable, as *propè,* or on thee last saluing one, as *Virtûtis,* or, at thee furthest, on thee therd syllable, as *Omnîpotens.* Yeet this rule taketh no such infallible effect with vs . . . As, *Peremtorie* is a woord of foure syllables, and yeet thee *accent* is on thee first. So *Sêcundarie, ôrdinarie, Mâtrimonie, Pâtrimonie, Plânetarie, împeratiue, Côsmographie, ôrtography,* with many lyke. For althogh thee ignorant pronounce *Impêratiue, Cosmôgraphie, Ortôgraphy,* geeuing the *accent* too thee therd syllable, yeet that is not thee true English pronuntiation.   (Smith 1.143–44)

Evidently, we moderns pronounce as the Elizabethan ignorant did.[36] Be that as it may, Stanyhurst is sensitive to stress as a key factor in English pronunciation, following the dictates of the English language, and not at all bound by the Latin. Only in the penultimate rule, as we saw above, does stress merge with quantity. Otherwise, it is an independent phenomenon. Stanyhurst kept all these things in mind throughout the composition of his poem. Indeed, the most remarkable prosodic fact about the *Aeneis* is not that Stanyhurst reproduced classical quantitative structures, but rather that he copied ancient stress patterns as well.[37] That is, after the manner of Vergil himself, there is only random coincidence of stress and ictus in the first four feet of each verse, but near-perfect coincidence in the last two.

Stanyhurst's object, then, was to use the elements of English phonology to produce a poem in which the interaction of the grammatical and rhetorical accents would be strictly Latinate: *in theory,* we are supposed to *hear* separate and distinct quantitative and stress patterns at the same time. But stress, in Latin as in English, effaces the perception of quantity. And in Stanyhurst's case, the problem is compounded because he is inconsistent in applying the various techniques for producing audible English quantities: he sometimes heeds and sometimes ignores vowel quality and diphthong; occasionally violates the penultimate rule, even though he sets so much store by it in theory; and is unclear about his attitude toward "special pronunciations" in the many cases where he uses the rule of position. The net result, in practice, is that we hear the rhetorical accent almost exclusively, with, perhaps, a few post-tonic drawlings thrown in to remind us of the grammatical.

On balance, with all its inconsistencies between theory and practice, Stanyhurst's translation is a painstaking, scholarly, and remarkably detailed piece of classical reconstruction. Its prosodic sophistication is truly impressive. Yet, as indicated above, its poetry is impressive in a different way. In the introduction to his edition of the text, van der Haar defends Stanyhurst as a master of onomatopoeia.[38] No one could deny Stanyhurst the laurel in the use of this device—but there are limits of decency in all things. From Nashe on, the *Aeneis* has provided matter for many a brave satirical sally. The loftier the vein, the closer the poem approaches to *Jabberwocky*. Saintsbury's description of it cannot be bested:

> It is . . . very difficult to realise how any one, *not* a lunatic, can have ever put to paper first, and then committed to print, stuff which looks like the utterances of a schoolboy, to whom some benevolent but injudicious uncle had given too much champagne, and who should have been simultaneously furnished with a glossary of the most out-of-the-way words in the English language, and permission to spell them as he (and the champagne) pleased.[39]

In the following extracts, I have supplied both a quantitative and a stress scansion, so that the grammatical and rhetorical/musical accents can be more easily followed. A great deal of practice would, of course, be required to give a virtuoso performance approaching the ideals of the quantitative movement. Grammatical and rhetorical pronunciations must take place simultaneously. Thus, the reader must take care to elongate consonant clusters, caress final *ing* endings, supply tense vowels and diphthongs where needed, and also follow the stress markings. The poem's other qualities will, for better or worse, speak for themselves.

(1) These lines, describing the serpents' killing of Laocoon and his two sons, represent Stanyhurst at a more or less average degree of absurdity:

> Thēy chárg ⎟Lāócŏon, būt ⎟fírst thēy ⎟ráght tŏ thĕ ⎟
> súcklīngs,
> Hīs twŏ̀ ⎟yŏ̀ng chíldrēn wĭth ⎟círclē ⎟póysŏnĕd ⎟hóokīng.
> Thḗym thĕy dŏe̊ ⎟chéw, réntĭng thēyre ⎟mémbērs ⎟téndĕr
> ă ⎟súndĕr.
> Īn váyne ⎟Lāócŏon the͞-assáult ly̆ke ă ⎟stícklĕr ắpéasīng
> Īs tŏ̀ sŏne ⎟ēmbáyĕd wĭth ⎟wráppīng ⎟gírdlĕ y̆cóompāst,
> Hīs mídĭl ⎟ēmbrácĭng wĭth ⎟wíg wág ⎟círcŭlĕd ⎟hóopīng,
> Hīs néck ⎟ĕke cháynĭng wīth ⎟táyls, hy̆m ĭn ⎟quāntĭtyĕ ⎟
> tóppīng,
> Hḗe wĭth hĭs ⎟hánds lábŏrĕd thĕyre ⎟knóts tōo ⎟squíse, bŭt
> ăl ⎟hóaplĕs
> Hḗe stríues: ⎟hĭs témplēs wĭth ⎟bláck swárt ⎟póysŏn
> ăr ⎟óynctĕd.   (2.226–33)

(2) In addition to *Aeneid* 1–4, Stanyhurst rendered out of Book 8 Vergil's description of the mighty cyclopes forging implements of war in the fiery caves of Lipare. Here, according to Stanyhurst, "thee Poet played, as yt weare, his price, by aduauncing at ful thee loftines of his veyne."[40] So did Stanyhurst:

> Tw'ārd *Sícĭl* ⎟īs séatĕd, tŏe thĕ ⎟wélkēn ⎟lóftĕlyĕ ⎟péakīng,
> Ā sóyl, y̆cléapt Lĭpárēn; frŏm ⎟whènce, wĭth ⎟flównce
> fùryĕ ⎟flíngīng,
> Stŏáns, ānd ⎟búrlyĕ búlĕts, ly̆ke ⎟támpōnds, ⎟máynelyĕ
> bĕ ⎟tówrĭng.
> V́ndĕr ĭs ⎟ā kénhĕl, wheàre ⎟Chýmnēys ⎟fýryĕ bĕ
> ⎟scórchīng
> Ōf Cy̆clópăn tóstērs, wĭth ⎟rént rócks ⎟chámfĕryĕ ⎟
> shárdēd,
> Lówd dŭb ă ⎟dùb tábĕrĭng wĭth ⎟fráppīng ⎟ríp răp
> ŏf ⎟*Ǣtnă*.

> . . . .

Nów dŏe thĕy ˈráyse gàˌstlȳ lȳghˌtnīngs, nów ˈgrìslȳe
rĕboúndĭngs
Ōf rúffe ˈráffe roáriˌng, mèns ˈhérts wìthˈtérrŏr ăˌgrȳsĭng.
Wĭth péale ˈméale rámpĭng, wìthˈthwíck thwáck ˈ
stúrdĕlyĕ ˈthúndrĭng.　　　　(Fragment of 8.1–6; 20–23)

The latter passage, as van der Haar notes,[41] is doubtless the inspira-
tion for Nashe's famous parody in the preface to Greene's *Menaphon:*

Thén dĭd hĕ ˈmáke heáuens ˈvaúlt tŏ rĕboúnde, wìthˈroúnce
róbblĕ ˈhóbblĕ
Ōf rúffe ˈráffe roáriˌng, wìthˈthwíck thwáck ˈ
thúrlĕrȳ ˈboúncīng.　　　　　　　(Smith 1.315)

Van der Haar says Nashe is not being fair. That is perhaps true as
regards prosodic intricacy, for Nashe botches the coincidence of rhetorical and grammatical accents in the fifth foot of his first line. Still,
the couplet scans much as the *Aeneis* does. And in other respects, the
lines are hardly even a parody.

(b) Spenser and Harvey

With regard to the gross accentual structure of their quantitative
verse, Harvey and Spenser are closer to each other than either is to
Stanyhurst, and this despite the anti-Spenserian coalition on the issue
of the penultimate rule. Attridge[42] sees in the experiments of Spenser
and Harvey no clear decision on the role of stress—in other words,
no definite conception guiding the interaction of the rhetorical with
the grammatical accent. Certainly, this seems true for Spenser's
"Blindefoulded Pretie God" (scanned above). Two out of the four
lines show poor coincidence of stress with length in the fifth and
sixth feet, so there is no attempt, as there *is* in Stanyhurst's *Aeneis,* to
reproduce the total metrical and rhythmical structure of Latin verse.
Likewise, since length and stress are even more combative in the first
four feet of each line than they are in the last two, it is hard to see
how Spenser could possibly be trying to establish a native *English*
relationship between rhetorical and grammatical accents. And yet,
while coincidence is surely the best index of an "English relationship" between the accents, the issue of their interaction is more
complex than that. How could it be otherwise, given the fact that the
grammatical accent alone depends on phonological traits other than

stress, and even with these taken into account, is problematic as regards pronunciation? The ingrained habit of scanning with the eye, we recall, is perpetually at war with the very idea that there *is* a grammatical accent, or mode of pronunciation, that (to repeat a phrase from Zarlino) "follows the long and short times in the quantity of the syllables." So it is in Stanyhurst's vast enterprise, and so it is in this tiny piece of Spenser's. A reader can easily drawl the last two syllables of *blīndefōuldēd*, or supply appropriately "short" vowel qualities to *yee, why, he,* and so on; but what is he to do with *măkĕth* or *blŏodĭe,* where stress and vowel quality alike suggest length, and only the lack of a double consonant allows for shortness? There is no answer; the grammatical accent, as an actual accent, simply ceases to exist for a moment. Nevertheless, there are other moments such as those occupied by the phrase *Trust me,* where grammatical requirements dictate syllabic length *and* influence the rhetorical accent, and where the rhetorical accent (which, after all, is the embodiment of the poem's meaning, that is, its *rhythmos*) wants to be so influenced. Meter and rhythm, stress and vowel quality all converge to create the right English oratorical emphasis. Here, for one important instant in a rather trivial poem, the grammatical and rhetorical accents conspire in a way that naturalizes the first and classicizes the second. It is a perfectly English blend.

Other experimental poems by Spenser and Harvey show frequent enough coincidence of stress with length to confirm that an "English blend" was indeed their goal. Still, the problems with "Blindefoulded Pretie God" suggest a certain lack of success in carrying out the plan consistently, and this sloppiness tends to support Attridge's remarks. But if Spenser and Harvey were never as systematic as Stanyhurst was in carrying out his Latinate solution to the problem of how stress should function in quantitative verse, they nevertheless must be seen as groping toward an English solution to that common problem. In the following extract from Harvey's "Encomium Lauri" (Smith 1.106), there is almost complete coincidence of stress with ictus, but none of that confounding of stress with quantity for which Harvey is so often blamed: the frequent post-tonic lengthening belies it:

> Whát mĭght Ĭ ˈcǎll thĭs ˈTrée? Ǎ ˈLáurèll? ˈÓ bŏnnў ˈ
> Láurēll:
> Néedes tŏ thў ˈbówes wĭll Ĭ ˈbǒw thĭs ˈknée, ànd ˈváyle
> mў bŏnĕttŏ.

Whó, būt thŏu, thĕ rĕnówne ōf Prínce ānd Príncelў
Pŏĕtă?
Th'óne fōr Crówne, fōr Gárlānd th'óthēr thánkĕth
Ăpóllŏ.

The piece is longer than Spenser's "Blindefoulded Pretie God," but
hardly more significant as poetry. As a piece of wit, it is nothing.
Prosodically, Harvey, in the main, gets little rhetorical mileage from
the post-tonic lengthening: giving special emphasis to *fŏr* or to the
second syllable of *th'ōthēr* in the last line, for instance, seems quite
pointless. But the confluence of rhetorical and grammatical accents at
this Tree in the first line is a point of minor interest. The performer
must emphasize *this* more than usual, and in so doing, he influences
the meaning (*this* tree, as opposed to any other tree). The "classical"
caesura in the middle of the third foot serves to punctuate the first
question. The long *Ā* after the caesura aids the voice in picking up
the next question, and the stretched second syllable of *Lāurēll* lends
itself to a slightly elongated interrogatory inflection. In short, the
grammatical and rhetorical accents embody a meaningful oratorical
shape for this line—a small rhythmic effect, to be sure, but an example of the "English blend" just the same.

In "A New Yeeres Gift" (Smith 1.104), the poem about Virtue,
Fame, and Abundance from which I quoted a line to demonstrate
post-tonic lengthening, Attridge[43] finds considerably less stress–ictus
agreement (especially after the first four verses) than in "Encomium
Lauri." The type of correspondence we do find, though, is, in fact,
more indicative than stress–ictus coincidence of an English settle-
ment between rhetorical and grammatical accents. Primary stress
almost never falls on short syllables (a pattern that *is* typical in
Stanyhurst's *Aeneis*), so it follows that stressed syllables are generally long ones, though not necessarily in ictus position. The ictus
syllables are usually those stretched in post-tonic lengthening, so
they receive some sort of heightened emphasis, perhaps a secondary
stress or a drawl. The net result is a pronunciation that moves like
English prose (allowing for Harvey's stilted syntax and boring diction), but has its oratorical phrasing influenced by the quantitative
structures. The rhetorical accent cuts across the classical feet, but
the lengthened ictus syllables and other grammatical features, still
manage to touch the rhetorical accent. I give the first nine lines and
supply a scansion:

SETH WEINER

Vértuē sénděth ă man tŏ Rĕnówne; Fáme léndĕth
  Ăbóundaūnce;
Fáme wĭth Ăbóundaūnce mákĕth ă man thrìse bléssĕd
  ănd háppĭe;
Sō thĕ Rĕwárde ōf Fámoūs Vértuē mákes mănў
  wéalthў,
Ānd thĕ Rĕgárd ōf Wéalthīe Vértuē mákes mănў
  bléssĕd:
Ō bléssēd Vértuē, bléssēd Fáme, bléssĕd Ăbóundaūnce,
Ō thăt Ĭ hăd yŏu thrée, wĭth thĕ lósse ōf thírtĭe
  Cŏméncemēntes.
Nōwe fárewĕll Místrēsse, whōm látelў Ĭ lóuēd ăbóue
  àll.
Thése bĕ mў thrée bŏnnў lássēs, thése bĕ mў thrée
  bŏnnў Ládyēs;
Nót thĕ lĭke Trínĭtie̯ agáine, sàue ónelў thĕ
  Trínĭtie̯ abóue àll.

These lines contain some minor felicities (and major infelicities) in
the way the rhetorical and grammatical accents work to produce a
total oratorical performance. None is worth its space in commentary. The trouble with Harvey's verse generally is that he manages
the "English blend" to no telling effect and that his syntax ruins
everything by being un-English, and indeed un-Latin and un-any-
thing else, except, perhaps, ugly. Spenser, *in practice,* never offends
so much even if, *in theory,* he offends more. Of all the experiments in
the *Letters on Reformed Versifying,* his *Iambicum trimetrum* fares best as
a classical form made native, perhaps because it is easier to manage a
convincing role for stress in lines basically iambic rather than dactylic. Coincidence of length with stress is the norm, and the extra
long syllables that must be drawled usually enforce a pleasing asso-
nance, even if they do not always shape the poem's oratorical movement and meaning. But "not always" does not mean "never," and
often enough, the special quantitative pronunciation—the grammatical accent—functions vitally with the stress pattern, or rhetorical
accent. The required extra emphasis at the end of line II, for instance,
while it does not increase the speed of pronunciation to mirror *fast
flying, does* keep the voice from dipping and makes the verse's

flŭttrĭng wīngs fly directly into the word *Thōught* at the beginning of line III. Harvey complains of the excess of spondees in the poem at large (Smith 1.95), yet the cheerless monotone these spondees enforce in lines IV, V, and VI, is quite appropriate as an oratorical performance. The monotone breaks at the trisyllables, *hēauēnlĭe Vīrgĭnāls,* which demand an uneven speeding-up of the voice combined with an odd stress pattern caused by the clashes of rhetorical and grammatical accent in *Virginals.* The jerky irregularity and distortion embody in pronunciation the reckless attempt to force good cheer with music. As Spenser says later in the poem, "lamenting Loue marreth the Musicall." Harvey, as we saw, laments the marring of disyllabic *Heāunlĭ* and *vĭrgnāls,* but Spenser's modified pronunciations produce a living interaction of grammatical with rhetorical accent and are integrated more into the English fabric of this poem than Harvey's shortened versions could be, even though these last conform more closely to ordinary Elizabethan speech. I give the entire *Iambicum trimetrum,* with scansion supplied for the first six lines. It is the only piece in the Spenser-Harvey correspondence worth anything as poetry:

> Vnhăppĭe Vérse,|thĕ wītnēsse ōf|mў vnhăppĭe státe,
> Máke thў sĕlfe flŭttrĭng wīngs ōf thў|fást flýĭng
> Thóught, ānd flý fórth|vntŏ mў Lóue, whĕrĕsŏĕuēr shĕ
> bē:
> Whéthēr lýĭng|réastlĕsse ĭn héauў bédde, ŏr ĕlse
> Síttĭng sŏ chéerelĕsse ăt thĕ chéerfŭll bóorde, ŏr ĕlse
> Pláyĭng ălóne|cárelĕsse ŏn hĭr héauēnlĭe Vīrgĭnàls.
> If in Bed, tell hir that my eyes can take no reste;
> If at Boorde, tell hir that my mouth can eate no meate;
> If at her Virginals, tel hir I can heare no mirth.
> Asked why? say, Waking Loue suffereth no sleepe;
> Say that raging Loue dothe appall the weake stomacke;
> Say that lamenting Loue marreth the Musicall.
> Tell hir that hir pleasures were wonte to lull me asleepe;
> Tell hir that hir beautie was wonte to feede mine eyes;
> Tell hir that hir sweete Tongue was wonte to make me
> mirth.
> Nowe doe I nightly waste, wanting my kindely reste;

Nowe do I dayly starue, wanting my liuely foode;
Nowe do I alwayes dye, wanting thy timely mirth.
And if I waste, who will bewaile my heauy chaunce?
And if I starue, who will record my cursed end?
And if I dye, who will saye, *this was Immerito?*

IV. Campion's "Rose-cheekt Lawra" as Culmination of the Quantitative Movement

It was left to Thomas Campion, here as elsewhere, to perfect and complete Spenser's attempt. In Campion's best quantitative poems, like "Rose-cheekt Lawra," grammatical and rhetorical accents move as a single pronunciation embodying the ideal union that Zarlino had found only in the inspired utterances of the ancient Hebrews: in holy writ, he tells us, "they produce the grammatical accent coincidentally with the musical [or rhetorical]: that is, one could not find the musical accent at any place in the ditty without also finding there the grammatical."[44] Campion was among the last Elizabethans to write a treatise on quantitative versification, and quite naturally he sought to avoid the failures and confusions of his predecessors in the field. In examining Stanyhurst and Harvey, we experienced something of the awkwardness to which dactylic verses all too often succumbed, whether the blend of accents being attempted were Latinate or English. Campion, intent on an English blend, simply eliminated dactylic verse at the very outset (Smith 2.333). In the iambic and trochaic forms that remained, he tried to base his quantities squarely on the totality of English phonology. This means that he did not isolate stress from vowel quality and then, in the manner of Stanyhurst or Harvey or Spenser, try to decide on the way stress should interact with the quantitative pattern. But neither did he make a complete analogy between stress and length in the manner of Puttenham. Rather, as his rules demonstrate, stress, vowel quality, and even the pronunciation of consonants all conspire to produce the long and short syllables. The rules distinguish four different major "accents," or features of pronunciation: the "rising," the "falling," the "grave," and the "sharp" or "lively." In his eagerness for accurate phonological description, Campion plays havoc with traditional terminology, but not with traditional ideas. "Rising" and "falling" translate the usual "acute" and "grave": they denote stressed and unstressed syllables, respectively, and, like the old words, recall the musical prove-

Spenser's Study of English Syllables

nance of the whole concept of *accent*, or *prosody*. "Grave," as At-tridge shows by examining Campion's application of the term in his examples, refers to syllables that are stretched out by tense (i.e., long) vowel sounds.[45] "Sharp" or "lively" syllables are just the op-posite. Campion combines these terms in almost every conceivable permutation. We quote a few instances (Smith 2.353–55), conflating related parts of the rather desultory exposition:

(1) Rising and falling accents (i.e., stress) influence quantity:

> In words of two sillables, if the last haue a full and rising accent that sticks long vpon the voyce, the first sillable is always short, vnlesse position, or the diphthong, doth make it long, as *dĕsīre, prĕsērue, dĕfine, prŏphāne, rĕgārd, mănūre*, and such like.

> Words of two sillables ending with a rising accent in *y* or *ye*, as *denye, descrye*, or in *ue*, as *ensue*, or in *ee*, as *foresee*, or in *oe*, as *forgoe*, are long in their last sillables.

> Words of two sillables that in their last sillable mayntayne a flat or falling accent, ought to hold their first sillable long, as *n̄gŏr, glōrie, spīrĭt, fūrie, lābŏur*, and the like.

> All words of two or more sillables ending with a falling accent in *y* or *ye*, as *fāirlĭe, dĕmurelĭe, beawtĭe, pīttĭe*, or in *ue*, as *vertŭe, rēscŭe*, or in *ow*, as *fŏllŏw, hŏllŏw*, or in *e*, as *parlĕ, Daphnĕ*, or in *a*, as *Mannă*, are naturally short in their last sillables.

(2) The sound of a consonant modifies this last rule:

> The last sillable of all words in the plurall number that haue two or more vowels before *s* are long, as *vertūes, dutīes, miserīes, fellōwes*.

(3) A grave accent (tense or long vowel) determines syllabic length:

> All monasillables that end in a graue accent are euer long, as *wrāth, hāth* [see Dobson, II, 453 for evidence of tense pronun-ciations here], *thēse, thōse, tōoth, sōoth, thrōugh, dāy, plāy, fēate, spēede, strīfe, flōw, grōw, shēw*.

SETH WEINER

(4) A sharp, lively accent (lax or short vowel) followed by a consonant results in a crisp pronunciation that influences syllabic quantity:

> All Monasillables or Polysillables that end in single consonants,
> either written or sounded with single consonants [e.g., ck = k]
> hauing a sharp liuely accent and standing without position of
> the word following, are short in their last sillable, as *scăb, flĕd,
> pārtĕd, Gŏd, ŏf, ĭf, bāndŏg, ānguĭsh, sĭck, quĭck,* etc.[46]

To emphasize once again the fact that Campion does not confuse
stress with length, we adduce the following extract, in which the
perception of stress and that of duration are kept quite separate—
much as in Spenser's use of the word *Vírgĭnāls* in line VI of *Iambicum
trimetrum:*

> The first of these trisillables is short, as the first of *bĕnĕfit,
> gĕnĕrall, hĭdĕous, mĕmŏrie, nŭmĕrous, pĕnĕtrate, sĕpărat, tĭmĕrous,
> vărĭant, vărĭous;* and so may we esteeme of all that yeeld the like
> quicknes of sound. (Smith 2.353)

Following is "Rose-cheekt Lawra," scanned, as nearly as possible,
according to Campion's rules, and punctuated as in the 1602 imprint.
Smith (2.348) supplies modern punctuation. Since rhetorical divi-
sions according to breaths are of great importance, I should note here
that the colon at the end of stanza 3 did not necessarily imply a pause
in the sixteenth century:[47]

> Rōse-cheēkt | *Lāwră* | cōme
> Sīng thoū | smoōthlў | wīth thў | beāwtīes
> Sīlēnt | mūsĭck, | eīthĕr | ōthĕr
>   Sweētelў | grācīng.
>
> Loūelў | fōrmes dŏ | flōwe
> Frōm cōncēnt dĕŭīnelў | frāmĕd,
> Heāu'n īs | mūsĭck, | ānd thў | beāwtīes
>   Bīrth īs | heāuenlў.
>
> Thēse dūll | nōtes wĕ | sīng
> Dīscōrds | neēde fŏr | hēlps tŏ | grāce thĕm,
> Ōnlў | beāwtў | pūrelў | loūīng
>   Knōwes nŏ | dīscōrd:

Būt stĭll mōoues delĭght
Līke clēare springs rĕnū'd bў flōwīng,
Ēuĕr pērfĕt, euĕr īn thēm-
sēlues ĕtērnāll.

One can easily understand why so many commentators see Campion as basing quantity on stress.[48] To a very large extent, of course, he did, because in being so careful about English phonology he had to give stress pride of place. But we can see other rules in operation too: *thōu* in the second line is long and hence emphasized in pronunciation because of the "grave accent" (i.e., vowel tenseness) rule; and the second syllable of *beawtīes* is long and receives a special vocal caress because "the last sillable of all words in plurall number that haue two or more vowels before *s* are long." Many syllables are stretched in a manner foreign to ordinary speech because of the rule of position, which, we recall, Campion observes with the same scrupulosity as does Spenser. In all, it is not really correct to say that the quantities are based on stress; rather, stress is one among a number of factors (albeit the most important one) determining what Campion hears as actual syllabic durations, some of them natural to English speech and others special to English verse. Daniel's famous remark that Campion's quantitative structures turn out to be nothing more than native English forms "apparelled in forraine Titles" (Smith 2.377) is thus not quite fair as a description, though its ring of authority has been loud enough to sway almost all who have written on this subject. And yet, to quote only this well-known and sounding phrase is not quite fair to Daniel, who most assuredly recognized the practice of post-tonic lengthening in pronunciation, even though he hated and rejected it. Indeed, his commentary on a few of Campion's experiments in the *Observations* (notably those that Campion called the "English March" and the "English Elegiac") constitutes valuable evidence that quantitative versifiers really did intend their productions to be read in a special way:

it had beene much better for the true English reading and pronouncing thereof, without violating the accent [pronunciation], which now our Aduersarie hath heerein most vnkindely doone: for, being as wee are to sound it, according to our English March, we must make a rest, and raise the last sillable, which falles out very vnnaturall in *Desolāte, Funerāll, Elizabēth,*

Prodigāll, and in all the rest, sauing the Monosillables. . . .
Next comes the *Elegiacke* . . . and that likewise is no other then
our old accustomed measure of fiue feet: if there be any difference, it must be made in the reading, and therein wee must
stand bound to stay where often we would not, and sometimes
either breake the accent or the due course of the word.

(Smith 2.377, scansion marks added)

Daniel does more here than attest to the fact of post-tonic lengthening: he confirms for us that the feat was indeed accomplished by
drawling and stressing the syllables in question ("We must make a
rest, and raise the last sillable"). The result is a reading noticeably
slower and more deliberate than usual ("We must stand bound to
stay where often we would not"). If, Daniel notwithstanding, we
actually pronounce "Rose-cheekt Lawra" in the special way Campion intended, it will speak to us perfectly through its oratorical
shaping. The voice, for instance, should not be allowed to dip as the
third stanza spills over into the fourth, nor as the penultimate line
runs into the last one. Only then will pronunciation come to embody
the ever quickening currents of clear springs renewed by flowing, a
motion inherent in the poem's stanzaic structuring and in its punctuation. But the flowing of Campion's springs, like the stationary
blasts of Wordsworth's waterfalls in *The Prelude,* or like the "poem
of the universe" in St. Augustine's *De musica,* is the kind of continuous motion that, viewed in the aggregate, appears as a giant stasis,
and is generally taken as an image of Eternity. Here, too, the correct
pronunciation of "Rose-cheekt Lawra" is essential. The poem is built
out of trochaic clusters (up to six trochees can occur in one cluster,
but the usual number is two or three) separated from each other by
two, three, or four long syllables. By reading the long syllables with
the appropriate stressing and drawling, and by speeding up slightly
at the trochees, we effect a fairly regular alternation of contraction
with expansion, a continual ebb and flow of sound that holds the
smaller syntactical eddies and currents in an eternal stillness.[49]

The oratorical surface of "Rose-cheekt Lawra," then, is a perfect
blend of rhetorical and grammatical accents, based squarely on the
components of English phonology and bodying forth the poem's
meaning. That meaning in turn is founded on Pythagorean aesthetic
ideas; the question naturally arises whether there is a connection
between the ideas and the surface. While evidence on this point is not
quite conclusive, there is certainly enough to suggest some sort of

numerological scheme reflecting Pythagorean cosmological mathematics and (what is more interesting) having its life in a correct pronunciation carried out according to grammatical and rhetorical principles. Campion lays the theoretical groundwork for this in the introductory chapter to the *Observations,* where he distinguishes between arithmetic and music—that is, between numbers as *discreta quantitas* (which he translates as "the disseruer'd [*sic*] quantity") and number as ratio, or "proportion":

> When we speake of a Poeme written in number, we consider not only the distinct number of the sillables, but also their value, which is contained in the length or shortnes of their sound. As in Musick we do not say a straine of so many notes, but of so many sem'briefes [that is, whole notes, commonly used as a *tactus* or beat to measure time] . . . so in a verse the numeration of the sillables is not so much to be obserued as their waite and due proportion. (Smith 2.328–29)

In the Renaissance, as in antiquity, the concept of proportion was integral to the idea of musical speech. How fortuitous is it, then, that in listing a few scholars who sought to recapture the ancient awareness of *proportion* in prose and verse, Campion should choose Erasmus and More, the would-be reformers of Latin *pronunciation?*[50] And is it not equally, perhaps even more, significant that the middle figure on the list, the mediating term, so to speak, is Johannes Reuchlin who, besides his importance as a figure in the German reformation, was one of the chief Renaissance Hebraists, his *De rudimentis Hebraicis* having appeared in 1506? Indeed, Campion's remarks, in conjunction with his list, seem to be telling us that proportion, pronunciation, and the language of Moses are all related—are all integrated into that strange mix of speculative music, phonological fact and fiction, and religious fervor called Renaissance poetics.

Campion's quantitative verse, like anyone's else, can exhibit "due proportion" only if we allow the convention that each long syllable is equal in duration to two short ones, and that each short syllable defines the basal unit of quantity commonly called a "time." Campion used exactly this system in his musical setting of "Come, let us sound with melody," a poem in experimental Sapphics that appeared as number 21, part 1 of *A Booke of Ayres* (1601).[51] There is every reason to believe he intended the same convention to apply to the verse in the *Observations,* and especially to the various Sapphic forms,

SETH WEINER

which, he tells us, are particularly apt for musical setting (Smith, 2.346). Given this rule of one long equals two shorts, we may compute the number of "times" in Campion's poem and perform the relevant Pythagorean operations therewith.[52]

"Rose-cheekt Lawra" is the second of three variations Campion invented on the so-called pure Sapphic form, which Sidney had adapted for English use in *Old Arcadia,* 12, a poem beginning:

> Īf mĭne ēyes căn spēake tŏ dŏo hārtў ērrānde,
> Ōr mĭne ēyes' lāngŭage shĕ dŏo hāp tŏ jūdge ŏf,
> Sō thăt ēyes' mēssāge bĕ ŏf hēr rĕcēaved,
> Hōpe wĕ dŏ līve yēt.[53]

The "second kinde" of Sapphic is Campion's fabrication: he, and not classical authority, controlled the total number of times. In its most regular version, each stanza in this form would consist of (1) a *dimeter,* which commonly has 8 or 9 times ($\smile\smile|\smile\smile|\smile$ or $\smile\smile|\smile\smile|\smile$: it can have 7 times, but this is not the most regular case—see Smith 2.338–39); (2) two trochaic lines of 12 times each ($\smile\smile|\smile\smile|\smile\smile|\smile\smile$), though in theory an irregular 13 is possible, and in practice 14 is frequent; and (3) a line of 6 times ($\smile\smile|\smile\smile$), though the irregularity of the common last syllable quite often means, in practice, a line of 7 times. An ideal stanza, then—one that was perfectly regular—could be diagrammed either as 9 12 12 6 or as 8 12 12 6. In either case, we can generate all of the perfect Pythagorean consonances: $12/12 = 1 =$ unison; $12/6 = 2/1 = $ *diapason,* or the octave; $9/6 = 12/8 = 3/2 = $ *diapente,* or the fifth; and $12/9 = 8/6 = 4/3 = $ *diatesseron,* or the fourth. In fact, none of the stanzas of "Rose-cheekt Lawra" is ideal, and appropriately so, for

> These dull notes we sing
> Discords neede for helps to grace them.

The actual breakdown of times is:

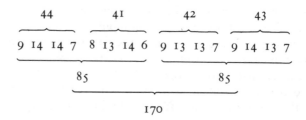

Not surprisingly, these discords really do grace the dull notes we sing and produce a few concords. If we simply bisect the poem and compare the halves, we get 85/85 = unison. Either half compared with the whole gives 170/85 = 2/1 = the *diapason*. Starting with stanza II, the time totals for each stanza are arranged consecutively— 41, 42, 43. If we carry out the implications of the poem itself and renew the flowing by returning to stanza I, we get an endless and eternal circle:

$$41 \rightarrow 42 \rightarrow 43 \rightarrow 44 \rightarrow 41 \rightarrow 42 \rightarrow 43 \rightarrow 44 \rightarrow 41 \rightarrow 42 \rightarrow 43, \text{ etc.}$$
$$\overline{\text{II} \rightarrow \text{III} \rightarrow \text{IV} \rightarrow \text{ I } \rightarrow \text{ II } \rightarrow \text{III} \rightarrow \text{IV} \rightarrow \text{ I } \rightarrow \text{ II } \rightarrow \text{III} \rightarrow \text{IV, etc.}}$$

Within this circle is the less perfect linear progression starting with the first stanza and moving through the last, for 44, the number of times in the first stanza, is a so-called deficient number: its factors (or aliquot parts, as Renaissance arithmeticians would say) add up to something less than itself.[54] In this case, they add up to 40: 1 + 2 + 4 + 11 + 22 = 40. Hence 44 gives rise to 40 by means of a Pythagorean mathematical function, and we get the linear progression:

$$\frac{\text{Stanza I} \rightarrow \text{II} \rightarrow \text{III} \rightarrow \text{IV}}{40 \rightarrow 41 \rightarrow 42 \rightarrow 43},$$

where 41, 42, and 43 are the actual number of times in stanzas II, III, and IV, respectively, and 40 is the sum of the aliquot parts of the number of times in stanza I.

If instead of splitting the poem into stanzas, we subdivide according to oratorical units marked off by punctuation and reinforced by short syllables or by post-tonic lengthening, we produce the following pattern:

$$9\ 14\ 14\ 7 \overset{\cdot\cdot}{} 8\ 13 \overset{\cdot}{} 14\ 6 \overset{\cdot\cdot}{} 9\ 13 \overset{\cdot}{} 13\ 7 \overset{\cdot\cdot}{} 9\ 14 \overset{\cdot}{} 13\ 7$$

$$\underbrace{}_{44}\ \underbrace{}_{21}\ \underbrace{}_{20}\ \underbrace{}_{22}\ \underbrace{}_{63}$$

Most of these numbers carry symbolic meanings related to the poem's contents. Twenty-one, as the numerological mage Pietro Bongo is quick to remind us before cataloging its biblical occurrences,[55] is the triangular number of 6: that is, if we construct an equilateral triangle with 6 dots on each side, the total number of dots will be 21:

Triangular numbers are important, generally, in Pythagorean cosmology because 10, the limit of the divine tetractys, is in this class.
In particular, the number 6, which we have obtained from 21, is
itself a triangular number (of 3), and is also the first of the perfect
numbers, those where the sum of the factors, or aliquot parts, is
equal to the number itself: $1 + 2 + 3 = 1 \times 2 \times 3 = 6$. Six was
frequently associated with the days of creation,[56] which is a subject
quite appropriate to a poem that tells us—

> Louely formes do flowe
> From concent deuinely framed.

And that divine *concent* informing the creation is also inherent in the
number 6: as Zarlino reminds us,[57] this number can generate all the
musical consonances. He adduces the following diagram (fig. 1)
which also brings out the circular perfection of the number:[58]

FIGURE I

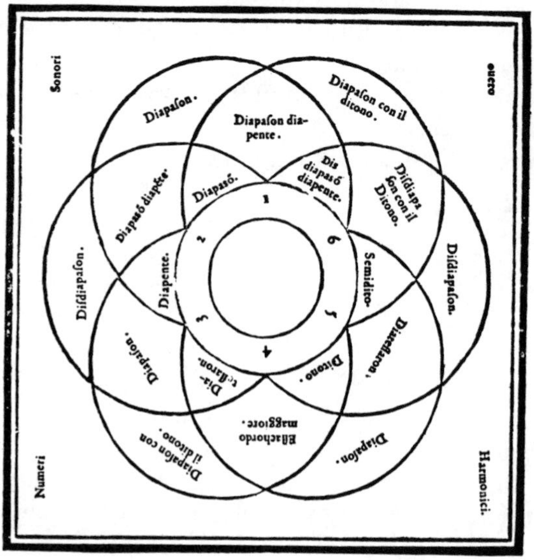

The number 22, the sum of times in the fourth rhetorical division, signifies temperance and chastity,[59] and this is of obvious relevance to a poem that speaks of celestial love and heavenly beauty. Twenty-two is also the number of letters in the Hebrew alphabet, a fact that links "Rose-cheekt Lawra" with the reference to Reuchlin noted above, and hence to the inspired rhythmic pronunciation of ancient prophets and divines and to the kabbalistic lore of rabbis conjured up by the name of that *magus*. Maren-Sofie Røstvig points out that the Bible was traditionally divided into 22 groups or parts; this was held to reflect the circular nature of God, who had declared (in the twenty-second and last chapter of Revelation) "I am Alpha and Omega"—which, according to some commentators was St. John's translation into Greek of "I am Aleph and Thau," the first and last letters of the Hebrew alphabet of 22.[60] But aside from chastity, temperance, and the circular nature of God and his providential word, 22 has a Pythagorean association that fits perfectly with "Rose-cheekt Lawra": the number is linked with a version of the divine tetractys described in Plato's *Timaeus* and passed on to Europeans by Chalcidius, Macrobius, and others. In the Pythagorean cosmic system, the tetracyts, to borrow S. K. Heninger's word, was a mathematical "ideogram" for the creation. A single point, called the monad, gives rise, with a little leap of faith, to another point. These two points define a line. Three points define a plane, and four points, a solid: the three-dimensional universe thus proceeds from the monad, through the series 1, 2, 3, 4. This series is the simplest form of the tetractys. The four steps of the series in the Timean version require some explanation.

Early commentators on Plato, like Proclus and Theon of Smyrna, had arranged the series of numbers around which the master structured his account of creation as two tetractyes along the sides of the Greek letter lambda:

The monad (1) gives rise to 2 and 3, the first even and the first odd numbers. These in turn are squared and cubed to produce first two and then three dimensions. The numbers in the even series are divisible, hence "feminine"; those in the odd series, indivisible and "masculine." For Plato, the birth of the universe, like any normal birth, requires the interaction of male and female.

First Plato fills in each tetractys with the harmonic and arithmetical means between successive terms:[61]

[1] $\frac{4}{3}$ $\frac{3}{2}$ [2] $\frac{8}{3}$ 3   [4] $\frac{16}{3}$ 6   [8]

     ↓   ↓   ↓   ↓   ↓   ↓

     harm. arith.   harm. arith.   harm. arith.

and

[1] $\frac{3}{2}$ 2   [3] $\frac{9}{2}$ 6   [9] $\frac{27}{2}$ 18   [27]

     ↓   ↓   ↓   ↓   ↓   ↓

     harm. arith.   harm. arith.   harm. arith.

Conflating both series, eliminating repeated numbers, and arranging those that remain in ascending order, produces the following progression:

$$1, \tfrac{4}{3}, \tfrac{3}{2}, 2, \tfrac{8}{3}, 3, 4, \tfrac{9}{2}, \tfrac{16}{3}, 6, 8, 9, \tfrac{27}{2}, 18, 27.$$

The operation of taking arithmetical and harmonic means yields (a) the ratios $\frac{4}{3}$ and $\frac{3}{2}$, defining the *diatesseron* and *diapente,* or the harmonic intervals of the fourth and fifth, and (b) various multiples of these ratios. In Pythagorean terms, then, the progression Plato generates is a musical scale. The fourth and fifth are a single tone apart, and if we take the ratio of the one with respect to the other, we get $\frac{3}{2} : \frac{4}{3} = \frac{9}{8}$. Plato divides his scale into a succession of tetrachords, or *diatesserons,* and fills each in with two tones in ratio $\frac{9}{8}$. This leaves a small remaining interval, the semitone, defined by the ratio

$$\frac{\frac{4}{3} \text{ (the } \textit{diatesseron})}{\left(\frac{9}{8}\right)\left(\frac{9}{8}\right) \text{ (the two tones)}} = \frac{256}{243}.$$

F. M. Cornford, for purposes of illustration represents the intervals in Plato's series as notes on a C-major scale extending for four octaves and a major sixth (to avoid overcrowding, only the first octave is completely filled in):[62]

We observe that just as the primitive tetractys 1, 2, 3, 4, can be used to generate all the Pythagorean ratios, so can either of the more complex geometrical tetractyes—1, 2, 4, 8 *or* 1, 3, 9, 27—be used to generate them *by itself.* This fact brings us back to the number 22 and to "Rose-cheekt Lawra." The female series alone produces a scale of three octaves, which, with all tones and semitones filled in, consists of 22 notes (count all lines and spaces between 1 and 8 on the above diagram). Twenty-two, therefore, is the number of terms in a series that is born exclusively of the female tetractys 1, 2, 4, 8, and that functions as a complete mathematical description of a three-dimensional universe tuned according to the standard Pythagorean consonances.[63] But what are we to make of this strange parthenogenetic situation? In the context of "Rose-cheekt Lawra," one would like to link it with the virgin birth, for that would enforce a neat parallel between the holy mathematics of Plato and the pristine love of Christ that brings the dull notes and discords of fallen humanity back to the perfect harmony that graces all creation.

Pietro Bongo, that numerological magician par excellence, tells a strange tale that makes just this link. The Levite priests always maintained their number at 22. When one died, another was immediately elected and had to inscribe his name and the names of his parents in a special ledger. At some point before his ministry, Jesus was elected to become the twenty-second Levite in place of a priest who had just died, and Mary is summoned for the inscribing ceremony. As we might expect, difficulties arise over the father. The doubting Levites make a big fuss about the virgin birth, calling in midwives to make an examination and a whole bevy of women who knew Mary when Jesus was in his infancy. Convinced at last, they take out the ledger and enter the name "Jesus, son of the living God and of the virgin, Mary." Thus, as Jesus becomes the twenty-second Levite, the old Levitical law is symbolically fulfilled in the New Dispensation. The name of Jesus, the virgin birth, and the bringing in of the New Law are all linked with the number 22.[64]

Campion tells us (Smith 2.348), that "the number" of "Rose-cheekt Lawra," by which he means its total accentual structure, or pronunciation, "is voluble, and fit to expresse any amorous conceit." As we see, the numbers that are hidden in that number, that lurk in the patterns of pronunciation, confirm what one might well expect from a poem that starts off by invoking the Petrarchan figure *Lawra,* namely, that Campion is writing about different kinds of *amor,* just as he is writing about different kinds of harmony, about heard melodies and about beauty's silent music.[65]

In the oratorical division of "Rose-cheekt Lawra," the middle term in the series bracketed by 21 and 22 is 20. Bongo opens his chapter on this number by noting that, as a multiple of 2, it derives its essential nature from duality or duplicity, and that we should not expect to see it favorably disposed in holy writ.[66] Two was often associated with the material world, as opposed to the invisible beauty and inaudible music conjured up by numbers like 21 and 22.[67] The "physical" number, then, mediates between the two "spiritual" numbers, just as the discords mediate between the dull notes we hear and the mathematical harmonies we understand, between the rose-cheekt Lawra we see and the Idea of beauty she represents, between the motion of the clear springs and their eternal stillness. The whole poem might well be thought of as a crisis of the physical and the spiritual, of the body and the soul. At any rate, it hardly seems fortuitous that the series 21, 20, 22 sums to 63, the famous climacteric number, symbolizing this very crisis, because it is the product of 7 and 9, the number of the body and the number of the soul. And, as if to drive the point home, the last oratorical division of the poem has 63 times.

It is as yet unclear to me exactly why the first oratorical division has 44 times. Nevertheless, we do get interesting results by considering these 44 times in relation to the 170 that make up the whole poem, for 44 falls one short of being the triangular number of 9, just as 170 is one shy of the triangular number of 18. That is, if the first division had 45 times and the whole poem had 171, there would be an implicit octave: $\frac{18}{9} = \frac{2}{1}$. But the facts just miss coming up to this perfection, and once again the central crisis of the poem has a secret life in its numbers.[68] In the same vein, the process of triangulation reveals at least one more striking instance of Campion's numerical virtuosity. If we take the triangular numbers of the times in each line, we get the following array:[69]

$$45 \;\; 105 \;\; 105 \;\; 28 \, \| \, 36 \;\; 91 \;\; 105 \;\; 21 \, \| \, 45 \;\; 91 \;\; 91 \;\; 28 \, \| \, 45 \;\; 105 \;\; 91 \;\; 28.$$

$$283 \qquad\qquad 253 \qquad\qquad 255 \qquad\qquad 269$$

$$1060$$

The interesting figure is the sum total, 1060. Biographies of Pythagoras popular in the Renaissance had it that his initiates were required to vow silence for three years, or 3 × 365 days. 3 × 365, or 1095, was considered to be the "number of silence."[70] This would be quite appropriate to a poem about "silent music," but we have 1060, and not 1095: there is a difference of 35. Yet that difference is in itself significant, for 35 was commonly known as the "number of harmony": it is the sum of 12, 9, 8, and 6, the numbers used more frequently than any others in generating the Pythagorean consonances.[71] So the sum of the triangular numbers in "Rose-cheekt Lawra" differs from the "number of silence" by the "number of harmony"—quite a lovely discord to grace these dull notes we sing.

No matter how far the machinations of mathematical reasoning take us from Campion's poem, the results always carry us back to it, and more importantly, back to its pronunciation, or *accent;* for just as the oratorical surface of "Rose-cheekt Lawra" bodies forth its meaning, so the mystic numbers in which that meaning has its secret life inhere in the poem's syllables and in their grouping between breaths. Campion's enterprise is a late and certainly the most decisive act in the Elizabethan quantitative movement. He eliminates the hexameter with an air of finality. He transforms Spenser's early and uncertain gropings about English syllables into a list of hard phonological rules. And, finally, he forces the syllables he has mastered into a complex numerological scheme so that, by an act of will, he makes them embody the holy mathematical lore that informs Renaissance prosodic theory. "Rose-cheekt Lawra" is at once a distillation of ten years of squabbling over single syllables and an echo of the Word of God. Perhaps it is odd to think of the squabbling and the Word as being related, or of such a fragile lyric carrying so much weight. Yet, it is just the possibility of such an oddity's being true that charges the study of Renaissance prosodic thought with urgency, that has us always hovering somewhere between the minute details of the structure of a single syllable in some flippant verse by someone like Gabriel Harvey on the one hand, and the stately procession of the poem of the universe on the other.

University of California, Los Angeles

Notes

1. The best book on the quantitative movement is Derek Attridge, *Well-Weighed Syllables: Elizabethan Verse in Classical Metres* (Cambridge: Cambridge University Press, 1974). Attridge is illuminating on Elizabethan prosodic thinking in general as well as being indispensable on the experiments in classical meters.

2. *Three Proper and wittie familiar Letters; Two other very commendable Letters.* Both sets were printed in 1580. All portions relevant to the quantitative movement are reprinted in G. Gregory Smith, ed., *Elizabethan Critical Essays*, 2 vols. (London: Oxford University Press, 1904), vol. 1, pp. 87–122. This set contains most of the Elizabethan prosodic tracts we shall consider. References to volume and page will be given hereafter in the text.

3. For a detailed exposition of what is summarized in the next two paragraphs, with full citations from continental and English writers on the subject, see my "Renaissance Prosodic Thought as a Branch of *Musica Speculativa*" (Ph.D. diss., Princeton University, 1981).

4. The actual ratios are 2:1 for the *diapason,* or octave; 3:2 for the *diapente,* or fifth, and 4:3 for the *diatesseron,* or fourth. Campion, as we shall see, makes much use of these ratios in the numerological structures of "Rose-cheekt Lawra." For a clear explanation of how these ratios are generated on a single string, or monochord, see S. K. Heninger, Jr., *Touches of Sweet Harmony: Pythagorean Cosmology and Renaissance Poetics* (San Marino, Calif.: Huntington Library, 1974), pp. 95–100.

5. Gioseffo Zarlino, *Sopplimenti musicali* (Venice, 1588; rpt. Ridgewood, N. J.: Gregg Press, 1966). A translation of book 8, cap. 13, with a running commentary can be found in Weiner, "Renaissance Prosodic Thought as a Branch of *Musica Speculativa,*" pp. 50–98.

6. Was the Areopagus a joke, a somewhat loose version of an academic society like those in Italy or France, or a spy ring? Attridge gives a short bibliography on the subject (*Well-Weighed Syllables,* p. 130, n. 2). The last alternative (I have a hunch) has not been sufficiently explored. Leslie Hotson, *The Death of Christopher Marlowe* (Cambridge, Mass.: Harvard University Press, 1925) is, of course, quite suggestive here. And Mark Eccles, *Christopher Marlowe in London* (Cambridge, Mass.: Harvard University Press, 1934), demonstrates Marlowe's close association with the sonneteer Thomas Watson, who is in turn traced to the circle gathered around Sir Francis Walsingham in France in the late 1570s. Walsingham was instrumental, as we know, in founding the secret service. What, one wonders, was Watson doing amongst the Catholics at the College of Douai in 1577? There are many titillating details along these lines, all suggesting that a literary circle was also a secret coterie of Protestant spies.

7. Sidney's version of Drant's rules, found in the best *Old Arcadia* manuscript, St. John's College, Cambridge 308, was first printed by William Ringler in "Master Drant's Rules," *Philological Quarterly* 29 (1950), 74. Ringler reprinted these and supplied a convenient numbering of them in *The Poems of Sir Philip Sidney* (Oxford: Oxford University Press, 1962), p. 391. I have used the latter reprint. I designate the various rules according to Ringler's numbering.

8. The patterns as stated here are correct, but somewhat oversimplified. To preserve equality of time, the longs and shorts in the spondees, anapests, and dactyls must be *irrational* with respect to those in the iambs, so that the feet of three times are equal to those of four. For a full exposition see Joseph H. Allen and James B. Greenough, *New Latin Grammar* (1888; rpt. Boston: Ginn and Co., 1931), arts. 618, 609e.

9. John Hollander, *Vision and Resonance* (New York: Oxford University Press, 1975), p. 87 and chs. 3 and 4, passim.

10. Gladys Willcock, "Passing Pitefull Hexameters," *Modern Language Review* 29 (1934), 5.

11. Attridge, *Well-Weighed Syllables*, pt. 1. Scanning and reading did come together now and then under pressure of the penultimate rule, discussed below.

12. T. S. Omond, *English Metrists* (Oxford: Clarendon Press, 1921), p. 3.

13. In these brief remarks on Puttenham, I condense material in Smith 2.118–24.

14. I use *stress* here somewhat reductively because I am only referring to Puttenham's ideas in passing. Of course, Puttenham uses the word *accent* with all the weighty baggage of lore that word carried.

15. E. J. Dobson, *English Pronunciation, 1550–1700*, 2 vols., 2nd ed. (Oxford: Clarendon Press, 1968), vol. 1, p. vii. In my discussion of vowel quality, I have relied on Dobson's general phonology and have not made a detailed study of the regional affiliation and dialect of each theorist I mention. Professor Alastair Fowler tells me the rocky course is really the only one. I agree, and am conscious that I have opted for rough rather than refined accuracy in the few examples I scrutinize. Dobson, of course, takes dialects into account in making his phonology. I cannot, however, afford to overburden this study with even *more* detail. In my own partial defense, I adduce the following extract from Puttenham (Smith 2.149–50) on what dialect a poet should use:

> This part in our maker or Poet must be heedyly looked vnto, that it be naturall, pure, and the most vsuall of all his countrey. . . . Ye shall therefore take the vsuall speach of the Court, and that of London and the shires lying about London within lx. myles, and not much aboue.

I assume that learned affiliates of the court worked within something like these limits. Of course, even within London and within the court there was remarkable variety of pronunciation, and the extent to which there was an artificially set "standard English" to judge all variants by was not as great as it is today: see Helge Kökeritz, *Shakespeare's Pronunciation* (New Haven, Conn.: Yale University Press, 1953), p. 7. The differences that existed within the limits set by Puttenham were doubtless sufficient to account for the problems I shall discuss.

16. Omond, *English Metrists*, p. 5.

17. This diphthong will be totally unfamiliar to most readers. One may get some sense of it if one tries to pronounce *u* as in *cut* and *i* and in *city* at exactly the same time. Kökeritz discusses it cogently on p. 216. I have usually indicated sound equivalents of phonetic symbols with an equals sign (=) and have taken them either from

Kökeritz's table (*Shakespeare's Pronunciation*, p. xi) or from Dobson's (*English Pronunciation* 1.xx–xxi). My criterion in choosing was to give the clearest "lay person's" idea of the sound under discussion. [əI] required further explanation.

18. Dobson, *English Pronunciation* 2.843.

19. Some examples: (1) Spenser's *Iambicum trimetrum*, III, 13 (*shĕ*). The *he, she, the, we* group of words had a weak form [I] as well as the usual strong one, pronounced as today (Dobson, *English Pronunciation* 2.456). Spenser follows Drant, rule 10, which makes these words short. Stanyhurst is concerned with these same words. He makes them common, reflecting both pronunciations, and decides to spell them with *ee* to indicate [i:] and with *e* to indicate [I] (Smith 1.146). The author of an anonymous poem in hexameters called *The First Booke of the Preservation of King Henry the VII* (1599) writes an introduction that includes *A Briefe Rule or prosodie*. He says he reverences Stanyhurst, and when he comes to deal with the *me, the, he, she* group, he (not surprisingly) makes them common. (In J. Payne Collier, ed., *Illustrations of Old English Literature* [London, 1866], vol. 2, no. 3, p. 12.) Campion (Smith 2.355) makes these words short; he usually fulfills Spenser's lead.

(2) Spenser's *Iambicum trimetrum*, III, 1 (*thŏught*). Dobson (*English Pronunciation* 2.667, 985 and elsewhere) records the survival of the voiced Middle English *gh* into the Renaissance, when it was commonly unvoiced. Thus, Drant holds (rule 9): "Some wordes, as they have divers pronounciacons, to be written dyversly (as some saye 'thŏugh', some pronounce it 'thŏ')" (in Ringler, *Poems of Sir Philip Sidney*, p. 391). Puttenham follows this up (Smith 2.120), writing of variant *delite* and *delight, hye*, and *high*. The short forms may be used to make meter "more slipper."

(3) The problem of what to do with the overabundant monosyllables in English is treated variously by Ascham (Smith 1.30), who holds that they are usually long and thus preclude smooth dactyls; by Puttenham (Smith 2.119–20), who says they are usually long, but allows for variation according as their placement in a sentence affects the stress placed on them; by Campion (Smith 2.333), who agrees with Ascham's pronouncement of twenty years before; and by Webbe (Smith 1.280–81) who agrees that they are mostly long, but complains that he nevertheless had to make many of them short in his verses "to supply the want of many short wordes."

Examples could be multiplied, but the point is by now clear: the quantitative theorists concerned themselves with similar specific problems involved in transferring classical meters into English. The degree of agreement on solutions varied: sometimes (the *she, he, we* group) no set way of doing things was established, but several reasonable alternatives emerged; sometimes agreement was reached; sometimes (as with the monosyllable question) complete agreement on the nature of the problem produced no specific rules that anyone could follow.

20. Quoted in Ringler, *The Poems of Sir Philip Sidney*, p. 392.

21. Dobson, *English Pronunciation* 2.455, 460, records variant pronunciations of *my* and *thy*, respectively. On p. 515, he catalogues a short form of *fly*, unexpected by linguistical lights, but there nevertheless.

22. Another result would be that the first syllable of *flying* would be long, the diphthong sound overriding the rule that states vowel before vowel always short (Drant, rule 3, in Ringler, *Poems of Sir Philip Sidney*, p. 391). Such a scansion makes line 2 a perfect catalectic verse in iambic trimeter (⏓–⏑–|⏓–⏑–|⏓––), and bears out Spenser's claim that the verses are all correct. This is preferable to Attridge's scansion (*Well-Weighed Syllables*, p. 190), which freely inserts an extra syllable, reads *flўīng*, and scans *thy* once long, and once short:

Spenser's Study of English Syllables

Māke thȳ⎜sēlfe flŭtt⎜ĕ]rĭng⎜wīngs ōf⎜thȳ fāst⎜flȳĭng.

This works, but takes too many liberties. Hollander (*Vision and Resonance*, pp. 85–86) goes along with the editors of the variorum edition of Spenser in considering *Thought* in line 3 to be properly the last word of line 2:

Māke thȳ sēlfe flŭttrĭng wīngs ŏf thȳ⎜fāst flȳĭng [Thŏught].

This emendation was first made by Francis Davison when he printed *Iambicum trimetrum* in *A Poetical Rhapsody* (1602), and is thus further evidence of Renaissance confusion over Spenser's poem. The meter does *not* demand this emendation, as Davison, the variorum editors and Hollander claim it does. Considering line 2 to be catalectic precludes tampering with the text in any way.

23. That Harvey tended to hear *my* as a "short" sound is suggested by the occasional spelling *mi* that occurs throughout a letter he wrote to Sir Thomas Smith (Smith 1.374). The definition of "occasional spelling" is given and its use as evidence discussed by Kökeritz, *Shakespeare's Pronunciation*, pp. 19–25.

24. Harvey also finds line 6 too long because the words *Virginals* and *Heauenli* are tri- rather than disyllabic (*Virgnals, Heaunli*). The latter way, apparently, was the more natural Elizabethan pronunciation. Spenser himself acknowledges this (Smith 1.99) but opts for the less natural version anyway. Indeed, the whole issue is more related to Spenser's insistence on a special pronunciation for poetry (see below) than it is to the discussion at hand. Here, we are concerned with those problems where *our* need to grope and guess mirrors a similar need on the part of the Elizabethans who produced this quantitative stuff. The problem of trisyllabic *Heauenli* or *Virginals* vs. the disyllabic versions is less a matter of real uncertainty than of personal choice based on *clearly defined* alternatives.

25. Dobson, *English Pronunciation* (2.848) records both a "long" and a "short" pronunciation of the *o* in—*soeuer*.

26. All scansions, unless the context indicates otherwise, are (of course) mine. In the case at hand, though, there is not much room for doubt about the scansion: the elegiac meter is much more tightly governed than the licentiate iambic trimeter. Such required scansions as *mākĕth* and *blŏodĭe* are troublesome because they show a disregard for vowel quality. It seems almost as if Spenser did not bother to worry about this highly uncertain factor when tight rules of scansion made it unnecessary for him to do so. Yet, as my discussion will show, the elements of pronunciation were not entirely absent from his mind in constructing this tetrasticon. Impossible are the ways of the quantitative versifiers.

27. Unawareness that *accent* is a much broader concept than stress is responsible for much misinterpretation of treatises on quantitative verse. Thus, in her generally excellent "Passing Pitefull Hexameters," Willcock notices that many theorists had an almost unconscious sense of stress, and gave it names like "inclination, affectation, proportion, propriety, or natural force, of the word—in short everything but accent" (p. 4). As we have just seen, they *did* use the word *accent* to mean considerably more than stress. The word never lost its association with pitch, and hence with harmonic ratios and with the whole concept of melic utterance. "To import accent into prosodic discussion," says Willcock (p. 4), "was to join that which Priscian had divided." But the word *was* imported into prosodic discussion: that which Priscian had divided, prosodic theory had most emphatically conjoined.

SETH WEINER

28. We omit discussion of disyllabic versus monosyllabic *heaven*, because that instance is much more clear-cut and simple than what Spenser is saying about *carpenter*. See note 24 for fuller remarks about why the *heaven-heav'n* issue is not so interesting or complex as some others.

29. Attridge, *Well-Weighed Syllables*, p. 147.

30. G. L. Hendrickson, "Elizabethan Quantitative Hexameters," *PQ* 28 (1949), 251.

31. See Dobson, *English Pronunciation* 2.445.

32. R. B. McKerrow, "The Use of So-called Classical Metres in Elizabethan Verse," *MLQ* 4 (1901), 177. McKerrow's continuation of this article is in *MLQ* 5 (1902), 6–13. See also R. B. McKerrow, "A Note on So-called Classical Metres in Elizabethan Verse," *MLQ* 5 (1902), 148–49, dealing with an interesting short poem in elegiacs by one James Sandford, published in 1576 in Greek, Latin, Italian, French and English. The verse type is, of course, maintained in all, that being the chief point of the exercise.

33. See Attridge, *Well-Weighed Syllables*, pp. 147–49 on Harvey, and pp. 143–52 on the place of the penultimate rule in the English quantitative movement, generally.

34. E.g., Omond, *English Metrists*, pp. 10–11, and Willcock, "Passing Pitefull Hexameters," pp. 5–6, who says that scansions like *hŏnĕstĭe* give us "an *accentual imitation* of a classical foot."

35. Stanyhurst is often impossible to pin down: for instance, he announces that he makes *sēason* long in *Aeneid*, 1.1, presumably because the vowel quality is long. Then he laments that by his own status as elected poet, he is forbidden to use *sēason* short elsewhere—as if he would violate the long sound if only the preelection rule were not in the way (see Smith 1.139). Elsewhere, he writes that "*passage* is short, but yf you make yt long, *passadge* with D would be written"—seemingly a clear statement in favor of orthography. But he qualifies it immediately: "Albeyt, as I sayd right now, thee eare, not ortographie, must decyde thee quantitye"—so perhaps he means that *passadge* should sound different from *passage,* that we should drawl the last syllable more in the one than in the other (see Smith 1.146).

36. Dobson, *English Pronunciation* 2.448: "In words of more than three syllables the stress is as a rule marked on the first syllable, if not a prefix, in the sixteenth and seventeenth centuries." Shakespeare, not one of the Elizabethan ignorant, would have agreed with Stanyhurst on the placement of stress in *Péremtorie* (at least according to the lists of Shakespearean accentuations in Kökeritz, *Shakespeare's Pronunciation,* pp. 392–98).

37. See Attridge, *Well-Weighed Syllables*, pp. 166–67, and, indeed, his whole chapter on Stanyhurst, pp. 165–72. McKerrow, "The Use of So-called Classical Metres," pp. 6–7, recognized the remarkable coincidence of stress with ictus in the last two feet of each line in Stanyhurst's translation. He surveyed the first 500 lines and found only nine irregular endings.

38. *Richard Stanyhurst's Aeneis*, ed. Dirk van der Haar (Amsterdam: H. J. Paris, 1933). See introduction, pp. 10–24. All extracts from the poem are taken from this (textually, the best) edition. Edward Arber, in his older edition, *The First Foure Bookes of Virgil his Aeneis* (London, 1880) quotes many if not all Renaissance reactions to Stanyhurst. Some are quite amusing.

39. George Saintsbury, *A History of English Prosody*, vol. 2 (London: Macmillan, 1908), pp. 175–76.

40. Van der Haar, ed., *Richard Stanyhurst's Aeneis*, p. 136.

41. Ibid., p. 9.
42. Attridge, *Well-Weighed Syllables*, p. 189.
43. Ibid.
44. Zarlino, *Sopplimenti musicali*, p. 323.
45. Attridge, *Well-Weighed Syllables*, p. 221.
46. Ibid., pp. 219–27, gives a brilliant account of Campion's rules. He reduces the interplay of stress, vowel tenseness, and consonants to a neat and convenient table (p. 222):

Examples:	devine tooth	denie grow	follow thee	parted of	fortune those	scab	Manna a
Stress:	+	+	−	−	−	+	−
Tenseness:	+	+	+	−	+	−	−
Final consonant:	+	−	−	+	+	+	−
Quantity:	long	long	short	short	long	short	short

47. See, for example, Richard Mulcaster, *The First Part of the Elementarie*, (London: 1582), p. 148.

48. E.g., Omond, *English Metrists*, p. 21; McKerrow, "The Use of So-called Classical Metres," (1902), p. 12; Willcock, "Passing Pitefull Hexameters," p. 16 (who thinks that stress always had to coincide with position or vowel quality and that this stricture limited Campion's vocabulary); and Walter R. Davis in the headnote to his edition of the treatise in *The Works of Thomas Campion* (London: Faber and Faber, 1969), p. 289. Willcock and Davis, following Willcock, mention the fact that position thwarts stress patterns now and again, but they brush this fact aside. In general, the "stress = long syllable" idea dominates in all these commentaries.

49. Attridge, *Well-Weighed Syllables*, p. 226 says something very akin to this, but feels the effect is due to "the gently expanding and contracting accentual [i.e., stress] rhythm." If we read the poem as normal English verse, though, the sense of ebb and flow is not nearly so noticeable as it is when we give it the proper "quantitative" reading. Catherine Ing (*Elizabethan Lyrics* [London: Chatto & Windus, 1951], p. 162) gives a phonological analysis of the poem that corroborates the quantitative structure perfectly (as well it might where vowel quality, consonant clusters and stress are all elements of quantity). She finds that the number of consonantal sounds builds from stanza to stanza, until *s, d, t, l, m* and *n* all pool (so to speak) in the last. The number of vowel sounds increases to the third stanza and then falls off in the last one—a flow followed by an ebb. Ing, of course, does not take Elizabethan vowel sounds into account, but this does not markedly weaken her sensitive reading.

50. For a good discussion of Erasmus's views, see Attridge, *Well-Weighed Syllables*, pp. 24, 58, 78–80. More comes in chiefly by way of his association with Erasmus.

51. The poem is printed with the music (lute tablature being transcribed for piano) in *The Works of Thomas Campion*, ed. Davis, pp. 48–49. ♩ = short; ♩ = long, as in the *musique mesurée* of Baïf's French academy; the setting is almost as homophonic as the Baïf experiments.

52. This is not to say that the mere "numeration" of syllables (as Campion would say) is uninteresting: a Renaissance poet does not write a poem of exactly 100 syllables for no particular reason. 100 is, of course, related proportionally to the decad, 10, the limit of the divine tetractys. (For a lucid explanation of the tetractys—the numbers 1, 2,

3, 4 that define the time-space continuum of created nature starting from a point and proceeding to a line, a plane and a solid—see Heninger, *Touches of Sweet Harmony*, pp. 78–86. The decad, 10, is the sum of the series: $1 + 2 + 3 + 4 = 10$.) 100 is also the sum of the cubes of the tetractys: $1^3 + 2^3 + 3^3 + 4^3 = 100$. Some (e.g., Kircher in *Musurgia universalis sive ars magna consoni et dissoni in x. libros digesta*, Rome, 1650) considered this fact to represent an extension of the decad (divine intelligence) into the dimensions of the human soul (see Alastair Fowler, *Spenser and the Numbers of Time* [New York: Barnes & Noble, 1964], p. 276). Others (e.g., Kenelm Digby in his commentary on *FQ* II.ix.22), drawing on the fact that centenaries are composed of denaries (i.e., $10 + 20 + 30 + 40 = 100$), saw 100 as an extension of simple and perfect intelligence into the dimension of physical bodies. (Digby's remarks are reprinted in *The Works of Edmund Spenser: A Variorum Edition*, ed. Edwin Greenlaw et al., 11 vols. [Baltimore: The Johns Hopkins Press, 1932–57], vol. 2, pp. 472–78, esp. p. 475.)

53. *The Poems of Sir Philip Sidney*, ed. Ringler, p. 30.

54. Christopher Butler, "Numerological Thought," in *Silent Poetry: Essays in Numerological Analysis*, ed. Alastair Fowler (London: Routledge & Kegan Paul, 1970), p. 3. The numerological information in the text is mostly Pythagorean/neoplatonic commonplace and can be found in the article above; in Butler's *Number Symbolism* (London: Routledge & Kegan Paul, 1970); in Heninger's *Touches of Sweet Harmony;* in Vincent Foster Hopper, *Medieval Number Symbolism* (New York, 1938); in Alastair Fowler, *Triumphal Forms* (Cambridge, 1970); in Fowler's *Spenser and the Numbers of Time;* and in any number of articles by Maren-Sofie Røstvig. For a few details I have had recourse to Renaissance and ancient sources; these are duly cited.

55. Pietro Bongo, or Petrus Bongus, *Mysticae numerorum significationis liber* (Bergamo, 1585), pt. 1, p. 48.

56. Fowler, *Triumphal Forms*, pp. 136–38, gives a plethora of examples.

57. Gioseffo Zarlino, *Le Istitutioni Harmoniche* (Venice, 1562), p. 25. The diagram is reproduced from the copy in the music library at UCLA.

58. Note that 6:5, the semiditone or third, is represented here. (I omit from consideration the complications of the "greater" and "lesser," that is, major and minor, third.) This so-called imperfect consonance is also treated by Campion at some length in his *A New Way of Making Fowre Parts in Counter-point (circa* 1613/14). Campion's main source is not Zarlino, but rather Zethus Calvisius' *MELOPOEIA sive melodiae condendae ratio* (1592). Yet there are indications that Campion knew Zarlino's rules of counterpoint presented in *Istitutioni Harmoniche*, pt. 3. For more particulars on all of these issues, see Davis's edition of the treatise as well as his headnote and commentary (*Works of Campion*, pp. 320–56).

59. Fowler, *Triumphal Forms*, pp. 177, 182.

60. See Maren-Sofie Røstvig, "Structure as Prophecy: the Influence of Biblical Exegesis upon Theories of Literary Structure," in *Silent Poetry*, ed. Fowler, pp. 51–52. Also, Bongo, *Mysticae numerorum*, pt. 2, p. 52.

61. In the series a, b, c, where b is the arithmetical mean between a and c, $c - b = b - a$. In the series, x, y, z, where y is the harmonic mean between x and z, $z/x = z - y/y - x$.

62. See Frances MacDonald Cornford, *Plato's Cosmology: The Timaeus of Plato* (1937; rpt. New York: Bobbs-Merrill, 1975), pp. 66–72. Cornford writes (p. 69, n. 1): "The fact that the ancient intervals differed slightly from ours is not objection to the use of a notation which is anyhow, in practice, differently interpreted by a violinist and a pianist. Nor does it matter that, strictly, the notes should be written in descending order."

Spenser's Study of English Syllables

63. In fact, as Cornford points out (ibid., p. 69, n. 2), the pseudo-Platonic dialogue called the *Epinomis does* generate the entire three-dimensional universe from 1, 2, 4, 8 alone (see 991a–b). The relevant statements are part of the so-called "mathematical Passage" of the *Epinomis* (900c5–991b4), which has long posed problems of interpretation. The best rendition, with a detailed justification, is probably that of A. R. Lacey, "The Mathematical Passage in the *Epinomis,*" *Phronesis,* 1 (1956), 81–104. The most up-to-date information on this strange dialogue, which reads like a somewhat degenerate rehash of parts of the *Laws* and the *Timaeus,* can be found in the introduction and commentary to Leonardo Tarán, ed., *Academica: Plato, Philip of Opus, and the Pseudo-Platonic Epinomis* (Philadelphia: American Philosophical Society, 1975). This edition includes a full bibliography of scholarship, earlier editions, and translations. The *Epinomis,* of course, appeared in the Renaissance with the works of Plato in Ficino's massive Latin translation (Basle, 1546).

In connection with the subject of musical scales, one wonders whether the number of lines in "Rose-cheekt Lawra" was meant to mirror the so-called Greater Perfect System of 15 notes. If we consider the last two lines ("Euer perfet, euer in them-/ selues eternall") to be *one* line (which is certainly justified by the run-on word) we get the requisite 15 lines, as well as an exact picture of the conjunct and disjunct tetrachords. For a discussion and diagram of the Greater Perfect System, see Gustave Reese, *Music in the Middle Ages* (1940; rpt. New York: W. W. Norton, 1968), p. 22. Renaissance writers commonly arranged the elements and planets on this 15-note scale. See the many reproductions of Renaissance diagrams in Heninger, *Touches of Sweet Harmony,* pt. 2, chap. 2. Note, in the following diagram, that the conjunct and the disjunct tetrachords are exactly matched by the rhetorical breathing in Campion's lyric:

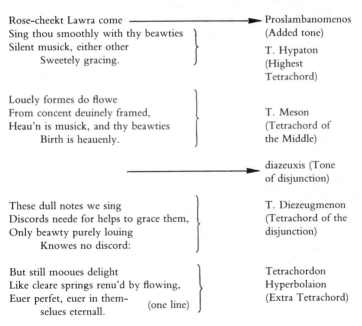

Rose-cheekt Lawra come ⟶ Proslambanomenos (Added tone)

Sing thou smoothly with thy beawties
Silent musick, either other
    Sweetely gracing. } T. Hypaton (Highest Tetrachord)

Louely formes do flowe
From concent deuinely framed,
Heau'n is musick, and thy beawties
    Birth is heauenly. } T. Meson (Tetrachord of the Middle)

⟶ diazeuxis (Tone of disjunction)

These dull notes we sing
Discords neede for helps to grace them,
Only beawty purely louing
    Knowes no discord: } T. Diezeugmenon (Tetrachord of the disjunction)

But still mooues delight
Like cleare springs renu'd by flowing,
Euer perfet, euer in them-
    selues eternall. (one line) } Tetrachordon Hyperbolaion (Extra Tetrachord)

64. Bongo, *Mysticae numerorum* pt. 2, pp. 50–51; Bongo says he got this legend from the entry under *IESU* in a Greek lexicon by Suidas, who probably flourished in the late ninth and early tenth centuries. At any rate, his lexicon was fairly popular during the Renaissance, and was published at Basle in 1565 in a Latin translation by Jerome Wolfe entitled *Historica, caeteraque omnia que ulla ex parte ad cognitionem rerum spectant*. This was reissued with corrections in 1581. I have seen a copy of 1581, which does, indeed, contain the tale that Bongo condenses for his treatise on numbers.

65. Indeed, as Thomas P. Roche, Jr., has shown, Petrarch had embodied a far more complex version of the same message also in a numerological scheme involving the birth of Christ. See "The Calendrical Structure of Petrarch's *Canzoniere*," *SP* 71, no. 2 (April 1974), 152–72. Roche numbers each poem in Petrarch's *Canzoniere* with a day of the year, beginning with 6 April, among other days, the Good Friday in 1327 on which Petrarch first saw Laura. Poem 264, the poem that begins Part II of the sequence (poems written *In morte di Laura*), ends up at December 25, Christmas Day. The death of Christ thus lines up with the birth of Petrarch's earthbound love, and the birth of Christ with the death of that love and the beginning of Petrarch's struggle to love Laura *truly*—that is, for the sake of her virtue. Campion, using a Pythagorean rather than a calendrical structure, celebrates the spiritual end-point toward which Petrarch is striving. "Rose-cheekt Lawra" expresses the beatific bliss of loving Laura for the sake of the heavenly perfection and celestial music mirrored in her earthly beauty and in earthly music.

66. Bongo, *Mysticae Numerorum*, pt. 2, p. 46.

67. See Heninger, *Touches of Sweet Harmony*, pp. 87–89. Heninger's quotation from Plutarch on the contrast between One and Two in the *Morals*, tr. Philemon Holland (London, 1603), is particularly apt: "*Pythagoras* affirmeth, that of the two first principles, Unitie was God, and the soveraigne good; which is the very nature of one, and is Understanding it selfe: but the indefinite binarie, is the divell and evill, about which is the multitude materiall, and the visible world."

68. This business of numerical patterns just falling short of, or just exceeding what they "should" was quite common in the Renaissance. Fowler in *Triumphal Forms* calls the practice "finessing," and gives quite a few examples of it. See the index under "one more or one less."

69. The formula for triangulation is: $\dfrac{(x^2 + x)}{2}$.

70. Butler, "Numerological Thought," p. 16.

71. Ibid., p. 13.

ANDREW V. ETTIN

The Georgics in *The Faerie Queene*

S PENSER KNEW Vergil's poems thoroughly. As the variorum helps us
notice, *The Faerie Queene* is at least loosely laced with lines or phrases that
echo all of Vergil's major works. But these themselves do not show the
Georgics, Vergil's middle poem, to be a major influence on Spenser, a text
at the front of Spenser's mind as he wrote. Even the echoes of the *Georgics*
in this poem, unlike the echoes of the *Eclogues* in *The Shepheardes Calendar*,
generally suggest an encyclopedist's gratitude for a detail or a craftsman's
appreciation of a sound or image. They do not for the most part constitute
a vital and instructive continuing dialogue with Vergil's poem.[1] There are
moments, however, when the dialogue seems to be opened, and these are
moments crucial to the poem's generic and thematic developments.

To understand the significance of the *Georgics* to *The Faerie Queene*, we
need to remember that Vergil's poem is more than what John Philips and
James Thomson made of it. The *Georgics* sets forth a twofold view of life.
Much of the poem does detail the rewards of farming, and how to attain
them; it shows the joyful face of nature, the pleasurableness of sheer pro-
ductivity; it celebrates the satisfaction to be found in facts, both natural
and literary, for the surface of the poem itself shimmers with nature's plen-
itude. This aspect of the poem is the basis for the topographic, instructional
verse that became so popular in eighteenth-century English literature. But
Vergil's poem also has a somber moral dimension that is juxtaposed with
the scenes of delight. Vergil shows the persistent difficulties of life: *labor
omnia vicit* (1.145); work conquered all.[2] Vergil shows that, despite moments of exhilarating freedom, life is a continuing struggle, a challenge set
for us by divine wisdom. Michael C. J. Putnam, objecting to the view of
the *Georgics* "either as a broadside for a revival of agriculture or as a . . .
travelogue among a farmer's treasures," has written that to Vergil,

> outer nature's negative indifference to man's situation can be only
> partially altered by man who, with continuous effort and the con-
> stant imposition of order on her chaos, can expand her rhythms to
> embrace growth as well as decay, creation as well as destruction.[3]

Putnam's view, while extreme, does help us remember that the farmers
of the *Georgics* must often contend with an unpredictable and tyrannical

natural world. Sometimes it is beautiful and invites us to relax our vigilance; sometimes it is intimidatingly hostile and coerces us to give up. Fighting these impulses means mastering ourselves as well as the world around us. In Vergil's poem one fights by remembering and heeding a set of commandments for life and work almost as detailed and emphatic as those in Leviticus and Numbers. The farmers' task asks for physical courage and spiritual determination. These, however, are not demonstrated in the large public sphere; rather, they occur in private encounters with the treacherous or intractable:

> ergo aegre rastis terram rimantur, et ipsis
> unguibus infodiunt fruges, montisque per altos
> contenta cervice trahunt stridentia plaustra.   (3.534–36)

[So they struggle to rip the earth with harrows, and with their own nails plant the corn, and with straining necks haul the creaking wagons up tall mountains.]

The georgic "hero," though struggling with the difficulties of life, is set apart from the outside world and will likely seem indifferent or hostile to the interests, values, and triumphs most commonly rewarded in the culture at large. The lucky farmer, Vergil observes (2.458 ff.), may lack a magnificent home or lavish clothing, but enjoys the rich bounty of generous nature and finds contentment with a way of life different from, and better than, the self-indulgence prized elsewhere. At the end of the *Georgics* comes the ultimate reward for the efforts of the georgic laborer. It comes through a myth or vision of sublime understanding, affirming a divine promise of transformation and rebirth that reconciles the poem's discordant images of life.[4]

The four stanzas comprising the proem to Book I of *The Faerie Queene* (indeed, the proem to the entire poem) place us in a world of epic and romance, as the *horrentia Martis* of Vergil's *Aeneid* joins with Ariosto's *amori* to become Spenser's "Fierce warres and faithful loues." At the same time there is an undertone of unworthiness that seems at first merely part of an opening humility topos appealing for the audience's sympathy. It proves instead to be part of a line of repeated assertions that runs throughout the poem, attesting to the narrator's feelings of inadequacy, laboring, hard-taxed powers of perseverance and articulation. This motif is basic to the whole poem's narrative stance.

The relevance of the *Aeneid* to this proem is clear; but at the end of the *Georgics* is another poetic hinge joining (like Spenser's proem) the author's

past and present works and relating the efforts of the poet to the efforts of
the ruler:

> Haec super arvorum cultu pecorumque canebam
> et super arboribus, Caesar dum magnus ad altum
> fulminat Euphraten bello victorque volentis
> per populos dat iura viamque adfectat Olympo.
> illo Vergilium me tempore dulcis alebat
> Parthenope studiis florentem ignobilis oti,
> carmina qui lusi pastorum audaxque iuventa,
> Tityre, te patulae cecini sub tegmine fagi.   (4.559–66)

[And thus have I sung of the care of fields and flocks and trees, while
glorious Caesar thunders in war by the deep Euphrates, and, victorious, gives laws to willing peoples, making his way on the path to
Olympus. I, Vergil, meanwhile was nourished by sweet Naples, in
the studies of unheroic leisure flourishing, toying with tunes of a
careless shepherd boy, and sang, Tityrus, of you in the shade of the
spreading beech.]

There are clear analogies between Vergil's and Spenser's texts. In both, the
poet defines the work at hand through the opposition between the pro-
tected pastoralism of youth and the responsible public efforts of maturity.
Much as Vergil, acknowledging Caesar's triumphs in war and peace, notes
that he at the time flourished in the studies of unheroic leisure, so Spenser,
once decked "in lowly Shepheards weeds," claims himself "all too meane"
to sing Gloriana's epic. Vergil's pastoral and georgic poems, composed in
careless youth, contrast with Augustus' work, described through the
verbs *fulminat, dat, adfectat.* Spenser, burdened with "my weake wit, . . .
my dull tong, . . . my feeble eyne, mine afflicted stile," must now seek to
match the task at hand, celebrating another living deity, and indeed one
more sublime than Vergil's: not Augustus, making his way on the path to
Olympus, but the "Goddesse heauenly bright," not merely one who gives
laws to willing peoples but "whose light / Like *Phoebus* lampe throughout
the world doth shine." Spenser's proem does not simply recall Vergil's conclusion. It seems at each point to deepen Vergil's contrasts, emphasizing
both the poet's humble preparations and the ruler's magnificence.

Vergil, at the end of the *Georgics,* schematizes the differences between
the arts of poetry and the arts of politics. The verbs *canebam* and *fulminat*
require us to distinguish between singer and thunderer. The difference carries over, of course, into the distinction between cultivating the arts of

nature, which the poet has celebrated in poetry, and imposing the laws of society, which Caesar has celebrated through rulership: "*arvorum* cultu *pecorumque*" ("the *care* of fields and flocks") opposed to "*bello victorque . . . per populos* dat *iura*" (in war victorious *gives* laws to peoples"). At the moment at which Vergil expresses these differences, he is justifying his career by suggesting that life requires both these disparate energies. He is also about to turn to a poem in which he must try to join the one role with the other, to become both the singer and (through his poetic vehicle) the thunderer: "*arma virumque cano*" ("arms and the man I sing"). The end of the *Georgics* shows Vergil to be highly conscious of his thematic, stylistic, and moral responsibilities as an artist and a citizen.

The grammar of the proem to the *Aeneid* suggests that, though his subject will change, Vergil senses a continuity between his earlier poetry and his new work.[5]

> Ille ego, qui quondam gracili modulatus avena
> carmen et egressus silvis vicina coegi
> ut quamvis avido parerent arva colono,
> gratum opus agricolis; at nunc horrentia Martis.

[I am he who on a slender oat once piped my song and, leaving woodlands, compelled the nearby fields to yield to the eager tiller, labor pleasing to farmers; but now, of bristling Mars.]

The verbs *modulatus* and *parerent,* suggesting flexibility, molding, and yielding, serve as the implicit verbs for the concluding phrase, which announces the new subject but does not seem to require a new predicate to describe the poet's work.

Spenser, however, though promising to "*sing* of Knights and Ladies gentle deeds," also announces that he must "for trumpets sterne . . . *chaunge* mine Oaten reeds." He still chooses a musical metaphor, but indicates there is to be a significant difference, not only of matter but of manner, between his earlier and his present work. He does not seem to feel quite so comfortable as Vergil claims to feel about the yoking together of singer and thunderer through a mediating style.

The Faerie Queene begins not only where the *Aeneid* begins; it also begins where the *Georgics* end. This suggests that Spenser, his *Georgics* unwritten, is navigating around the middle passage in his progression through the genres. He will proceed directly from the pastoral to the epic, omitting the poem on cultivating the world's stubborn and plenteous matter. But there are problems here. The narrator of *The Faerie Queene* knows that he is contending with a "labour long" (I.x.7), a "labour huge" (II.x.2). Stylistic adjustments are necessary, special effort is required in addressing a ruler who, as if outdoing Augustus, seems resident already on Olympus. As a piece of literary autobiography Spenser's proem places his career itself against Vergil's; it attempts by rhetorical force to persuade us that the Vergilian pattern has been fulfilled. The one element that has been left out, however, is (suggestively) the one addressed to the pleasures and necessities of constant effort and diligence. It is this aspect of artistic creation that the poet beginning his romance-epic might like to ignore. Spenser was already at work on *The Faerie Queene* when *The Shepheardes Calender* was published, and the fledgling poet (to use E. K.'s metaphor) might well have looked on his masterwork with equivocal emotions. As we have seen, Spenser's proem stresses the poet's inadequacy and the monarch's grandeur, indeed implying that the poem to come will not sound forth with the apparent ease of music but will require rather more strenuous exertions.

Specifically georgic motifs emerge infrequently in Spenser's poem, but at strategically crucial moments: the original end of Book III in the three-book first edition; the proem to Book VI; and the opening of VI.ix. In other words, the metaphors of laboring are most strikingly applied at the poem's two natural stopping-points, and at the dramatic stopping point for the hero of the last book. The passages in question help us understand the relationship of the narrator to the poem, and Calidore's experiences on his mission. At these points Spenser invites us to consider the nature of his undertaking, as well as Calidore's. *The Faerie Queene* is, after all, a poem of cultivation, a poem of growth.

In Spenser's poem the singer and the thunderer are not one. Colin and Calidore remain separate characters; the narrator of Spenser's poem comes to occupy a middle territory between them. For both these other figures represent human effort in different but important and perhaps even related arts, which we (and the Elizabethans) can imagine being yoked together in a courteous civilization. The toiling narrator, though a presence different from the singer and the thunderer, is able to understand both, aiding our judgment and appreciation of these other models of the shaping will and intellect.

The canceled ending of Book III allows us to see the unreconciled differences between the narrator and his characters.

> Thus doe those louers with sweet counteruayle,
>   Each other of loues bitter fruit despoile.
>   But now my teme begins to faint and fayle,

> All woxen weary of their iournall toyle:
> Therefore I will their sweatie yokes assoyle
> At this same furrowes end, till a new day:
> And ye faire Swayns, after your long turmoyle,
> Now cease your worke, and at your pleasure play,
> Now cease your worke; to morrow is an holy day.

The trope may look conventional enough; indeed, Chaucer has used it conventionally in *The Knight's Tale*. But as Kathleen Williams has wisely reminded us, even a common metaphor "can be used for a variety of purposes."[6] Here the narrator, hard at work furrowing the soil, seems to be on a very different natural schedule from the lovers. Furthermore, he seems to distinguish the play that awaits those fair swains from the mere rest that he looks forward to in anticipation of resuming his ploughing.[7] Most striking of all in this passage, though, is the contrast between the lovers locked in their embrace and the narrator contending with the sweaty yoke of his team. These oxen bear little resemblance to Pegasus. The incongruity signifies that whatever the poem may be for its characters and readers, it is gritty work for its author. Or so we should believe.

Throughout Spenser's poem we are reminded of the differences between the narrator's experience of telling the story and the participants' experience of being in it. Here too the narrative stance of the *Georgics* may be relevant. (Not that the *Georgics* would offer the only sources for these narrative stances. Taken together, however, they suggest affinities between these poems deep in their literary techniques.) Vergil's narrator stands apart not only from Caesar but from the actual farmers who are characters in the poem.[8] Like Spenser's narrator (though even more authoritatively), Vergil's speaks about his own task as interpreter, commentator and burdened storyteller or transmitter of facts, often in terms similar to Spenser's:

> Atque equidem, extremo ni iam sub fine laborum
> vela traham et terris festinem aduertere proram,
> forsitan et pinguis hortos quae cura colendi
> ornaret canerem biferique rosaria Paesti   (4.116–19)

[Indeed, were I not now nearing the end of my labors, furling my sails and turning my prow toward shore, I might perhaps sing of the care in cultivating beautiful gardens, of the roses of Paestum that bloom twice a year.]

Vergil's attentive narrator also manages to pretend that his poem is narrowly concerned with agriculture while he is continually drawn to comments on contemporary mores—

> quippe ubi fas versum atque nefas: tot bella per orbem,
> tam multae scelerum facies;   (1.505–06)

[Now, right becomes wrong and wrong right; war sweeps the world, and the many shapes of crime;]

recent political history—

> ille etiam exstincto miseratus Caesare Romam;   (1.466)

[he (the sun) also sorrowed with Rome at the death of Caesar;]

human nature—

> Omne adeo genus in terris hominumque ferarumque
> et genus aequoreum, pecudes pictaeque volucres,
> in furias ignemque ruunt: amor omnibus idem;   (3.242–44)

[So every manner of people and beasts, the hosts of the sea, the flocks, the bright birds fling themselves into the heat of passion; love is the same to all;]

and "the ways of God to men"—

> pater ipsi colendi
> haud facilem esse viam voluit, primusque per artem
> movit agros, curis acuens mortalia corda
> nec torpere gravi passus sua regna veterno;   (1.121–24)

[God himself does not want the ways of farming to be easy, and first made the fields come to life only through skill, not letting his lands grow indolent under heavy sloth.]

Like Spenser's narrator, Vergil's maintains against mounting evidence a determined ingenuousness about the nature of his poem, professing humility and weakness but nonetheless also insisting on his right to speak authoritatively. Like Spenser's narrator, Vergil's makes it clear that he is deciding where to plow the next furrow of verse; unlike Ariosto's, both maintain that they are working on real soil, working on material to which they have some sort of responsibility because it exists independent of their shaping. This aspect of Spenser's narration, perceptively analyzed through contrasts with Ariosto by Robert Durling and Jerome S. Dees, has been eloquently described by Kathleen Williams when she writes that the poet "must choose where to plough" to produce "pleasure and significance. . . . Everything is in some sense already there, as solid and real as the earth, or as Peru or England."9

At the beginning of VI.ix, Spenser directs our attention to his narrator's crucial dedication to worthy results.

> Now turne againe my teme thou iolly swayne,
>   Backe to the furrow which I lately left;
>   I lately left a furrow, one or twayne
>   Vnplough'd, the which my coulter hath not cleft:
>   Yet seem'd the soyle both fayre and frutefull eft,
>   As I it past, that were too great a shame,
>   That so rich frute should be from vs bereft;
>   Besides the great dishonour and defame,
> Which should befall to *Calidores* immortal name.

This passage should be read in the context of the metaphor of nurturing that appears in the proem to this book, in which the narrator tells of "the sacred noursery / Of vertue," hidden from human view

> Since it at first was by the Gods with paine
>   Planted in earth, being deriu'd at furst
>   From heauenly seedes of bounty soueraine,
>   And by them long with carefull labour nurst,
> Till it to ripenesse grew, and forth to honour burst.
>
> (VI.Pr.3)

We are reminded of the effort required in any sort of cultivation. A well-known passage in the *Georgics* affords a useful analogue to this:

> Vidi lecta diu et multo spectate labore
>   degenerare tamen, ni vis humana quotannis
>   maxima quaecque manu legeret.   (1.197–99)

[I have seen seeds, though carefully selected and watched with greatest care, still degenerate, unless every year the choicest ones were chosen by hand.]

Such studious cultivation is necessary if the crop is to be saved, if the species itself is to flourish.[10]

The two Spenser passages are tonally interesting when taken together, because they suggest a hierarchy in which responsibility and enjoyment may be inversely related. The gods who planted and tend the sacred nursery do so with labor and pain. The ploughman also tends his fields, and yet (even when we distinguish him from the jolly swain) his tone seems exuberant as he looks forward to that so rich fruit that will come forth from the fruitful earth. (Further back in the poem's history, of course, is the ploughman who unyokes his oxen while the lovers taste the pleasures of reunion.) These passages, if it is just to consider them together, suggest that the cultivation of the poem is easier, more pleasurable and more immediately gratifying than divine effort (similarly, the delights of love seem more intense than the gratifications of work).

In the immediate context of the last book, these relationships are suggestively ironic. Calidore, loving Pastorella among the shepherds, finds a kind of virtue in the pastoral world, but his life with them does not in itself promote virtue in him. At the end of VI.ix, Calidore also has been farming,

> and in her mynde the seeds
> Of perfect loue did sow, that last forth brought
> The fruit of ioy and blisse, though long time dearly bought.
> (45)

It is one of the specially fine discriminations of Spenser's poem that by this time in the work we are quite prepared to distinguish between the fruit of perfect love and the fruit of perfect virtue, the two perhaps being genetically related but nonetheless different. At the start of the next canto we are reminded that Calidore's suspended quest is really more closely related to the efforts of the gods—perhaps even more closely related to that of the gods than to that of the georgic narrative poet ordering his team turned around: "From henceforth he meanes no more to sew / His former quest, so full of toils and paine" (VI.x.2). Spenser's strategically placed *sew* (here meaning *pursue*) recalls the *sow* three stanzas earlier, as the poet now challenges Calidore's new notion of satisfaction, and brings to mind the "careful labour" and "pain" of the gods in the proem to VI.

However, at the end of VI.ix we have also been asked to consider the plight of Coridon, who

> many gealous thoughts conceiu'd in vaine,
> That this of all his labour and long paine
> Should reap the haruest, ere it ripened were.   (VI.ix.38)

Should we too see Calidore as a sneak-thief who means to cheat the laboring Coridon of what he has worked hard to earn? Such an opinion will not quite do: effort alone is not everything. The metaphor itself is provocative. Is Pastorella merely a ripening tomato waiting to be picked? Is the love of the two suitors really a vegetable love that grows and grows? To what extent is Spenser making some wry observations about the schemes of the two suitors? At the very least he seems to use the georgic motifs of ploughing, planting and harvesting to help us weigh in the scales Calidore's effort and intrinsic merit.

Some readers, like Richard Neuse, see Calidore as a sorry example of the best and brightest, a hollow knight in rapidly tarnishing silver plate.[11] But we should remember that his quarry is in many respects the hardest: the most elusive, the tawdriest. His task indeed is "full of toile and paine," but his labors would call forth from him the qualities of diligence and fortitude that he will need to subdue the Blatant Beast. Superficial though charming graces that comprise the common notion of courtesy ("ciuill conuersation" and "goodly manners," as Spenser calls them in VI.i.1) do not prepare one for this sort of courteous life, in which *noblesse oblige* and "true courtesie" do indeed require a "triall":

> in the triall of true courtesie,
> Its now so farre from that, which then it was,
> That it indeed is nought but forgerie,
> Fashion'd to please the eies of them, that pas,
> Which see not perfect things but in a glas:
> Yet is that glasse so gay, that it can blynd
> The wisest sight.   (VI.Pr.5)

Calidore must learn to cultivate the solider reality of courtesy.

Book VI is not really a book of the pastoral, but is partly about the pastoral. Indeed, the georgic motifs seem to call attention to the distinctions between these two genres, and to separate the narrator's point of view from that of the characters who dwell within pastoral settings. In this structural sense it is similar to the *Georgics,* which at the end of the second and fourth books (the middle and end of the poem) evokes pastoral motifs, reminding us that the pastoral world would be attractive, if it were possible actually to live in it. The dialogue between the two works is more suggestive when we notice that Aristeus, the main figure of the final action of Vergil's poem, is an Arcadian shepherd who also has epical characteristics.[12] It is partly through their movements from one genre to another that these poems teach as well as delight.

The georgic metaphors, thus emphasized by their contexts, remind us that courtesy involves extending oneself for others and for the work itself, perhaps persevering in a task that does not really end and for which the reward lies in seeing what one has accomplished, more than in any immediate gain for oneself. Calidore has listened to Meliboee's apologia for the low life with "greedy eare," and announces his desire to join it by observing that "in each mans self . . . It is, to fashion his owne lyfes estate" (VI. ix.31). When he hopes that he can "in this shore . . . rest [his] barcke," the metaphor covers a temporary, aberrant belief that this spot can be an island paradise for him. He is significantly unlike the nautical narrator at the end of Book I, who also rests his "wearie vessel" on a long voyage, but who at least has passengers to unload and a clear commitment to "fairely finish her intent" (I.xii.42). And he is also unlike the narrator at the beginning of the last canto in Book VI, who also compares himself with a ship.

> Like as a ship, that through the Ocean wyde
> >   Directs her course vnto one certain cost,
> >   Is met of many a counter winde and tyde,
> >   With which her winged speed is let and crost,
> >   And she her selfe in stormie surges tost;
> >   Yet making many a borde, and many a bay,
> >   Still winneth way, ne hath her compasse lost:
> >   Right so it fares with me in this long way,
> > Whose course is often stayd, yet neuer is astray.
> >   (VI.xii.1)

It is one thing to be forced to stay one's course, but quite another to seek (as Calidore does) to change the course for a port that seems more congenial and accessible, and toss the compass aside. And he is unlike Vergil's narrator, making for shore but so conscious of all that remains unfinished that he hastens to include as much as he can from what must remain unsung.

Calidore courting Pastorella is compared with

Phrygian Paris by Plexippus brooke
When he the loue of fayre Oenone sought,
What time the golden apple was unto him brought.

(VI.ix.36)

This allusion, simple enough on its surface, has rich overtones. Phrygian Paris, like Vergil's Arcadian Aristaeus was a shepherd; indeed, his being a shepherd is a fact that George Peele develops for all its potential significance in *The Arraignment of Paris* (published in 1584). And like Aristaeus, who unwittingly sent Eurydice to her death when he pursued her, Paris discovers that one cannot necessarily choose to live a private life, untouched by human or divine plans. Colin Hardie has observed that at the end of the *Georgics* the poet is torn between "timeless Greek mythology *or* contemporary Roman history."[13] Spenser shows Calidore confronting a similar choice, between the timeless pastoral mythos and contemporary history, a choice that the poet too must face as an artist and as a citizen.

So Spenser is able to place that mythos in a context of human values. Though effort is not everything, neither is it irrelevant. The energy of the ploughing, persevering georgic narrator, so determined to get from the soil every bit of potential goodness that it contains, contrasts strikingly with the passivity of the pastoral characters with whom Calidore aligns himself in VI.ix. The pastoral enclave is destroyed while the narrator ploughs on toward his conclusion. Indeed, one could say that the destruction is a consequence of the narrator's concluding his task; it is one of the furrows that gets ploughed as he takes care of unfinished business.[14] The pastoral society lacks staying power. As Meliboee describes it, its virtue is that it prospers without exertion: "The little that I haue, growes dayly more / Withouten my care" (VI.ix.21). Within a little world temporarily exempted from danger, Calidore's error lies in supposing that he can find happiness while claiming for himself that which comes only as a free and temporary gift from divine graciousness. They also prosper who neither stand nor wait.

The ploughing poet in VI.ix is not the poet in his most sublime guise (the seer celebrated by Cuddie in Spenser's October eclogue, for example) but in his most necessary, much as the gardening gods of the proem to VI are not the gods in their most heroic or dramatic but perhaps in their most profound role. Steadfastly cultivating every useful strip of soil, the narrator perseveres. He works with that soil; he works because of it; he works in spite of it. It is not purely of his imagination, nor can it be subdued totally by his imagination. Filled with equivocal emotions, he takes his "weary steps" through "this delightful land" where he is "nigh rauisht with rare thoughts delight" and therefore able to forget his "tedious trauell." For this narrator, though his course may seem astray, the poem "still winneth way." It is always a work in progress, and he may never in fact reach the intended goal; but the perseverance is all.[15] This lesson Calidore must learn, and does after all learn. However, that troublesomely imperfect narrator of *The Faerie Queene* surpasses Calidore by understanding the nature of the task in which he is engaged, and realizing while sometimes ruing what it asks of him. (As Jerome S. Dees has claimed, the narrator reveals an increasing confidence in his understanding and "intellectual grasp of his poetic matter" while at the same time an "increasing desire to be relieved from poetic responsibility in the poem as a whole.")[16] At some point the two genres of georgic and epic make contact, and it is precisely at this issue of exertion and determination, where we see the heroism of the georgic laborer, the endurance of the epic hero.[17]

Spenser has come far, by Book VI, from the diffident but hopeful narrative ambition expressed in the proem to Book I. Perhaps the change constitutes a descent into weariness or even disillusionment; but we can also think of it as constituting a different form of maturity. It is, after all, the matured narrator who, in the *Mutabilitie Cantos,* attempts to synthesize stability with change through an inspired vision, a divine promise of transformation and rebirth. Spenser's pastoral-within-georgic sixth book is the culmination of the poem's movement through genres. As he nears the end of his own labors on the poem, the poet—like the narrator who stands before him—reminds us that for him the work, while at times delightful and refreshing, it not always pastorally recreative, romantically fantastic, or heroically confident.[18] The fashioning of the poem is a model for the fashioning of the virtue courtesy: an ongoing effort of georgic determination, a purposeful devotion to the main task, an affirmation of the value of ploughing on.

William Sessions, also seeing the *Georgics* as a general influence on *The Faerie Queene,* has written that "Spenser's method is not to imitate the actual content of Vergil's poem but its plural structure," which is "a series of cultivating labors with the purpose of redeeming a land and a history from the effects of time's disorders."[19] It is unlikely that there is so detailed a pattern of direct correspondences between the two poems that Spenser's debt to Vergil can be defined neatly. However, there is strong structural and thematic evidence that *The Faerie Queene* was shaped at least in part by Spenser's sympathetic familiarity with the *Georgics.*

Wake Forest University

ANDREW V. ETTIN

NOTES

A shorter version of this essay was presented to the "Spenser at Kalamazoo 1980" proceedings at the Fifteenth International Congress on Medieval Studies, Western Michigan University, May 1980.

1. I would be delighted to learn that there is greater significance to some of the local allusions. I do not claim to have studied them systematically and have no interest in diminishing the importance of Vergil's poem to Spenser's. Many apparent allusions turn out to be analogues, however, not specifically Vergilian references.

2. The Latin text is that of R. A. B. Mynors, *P. Vergili Maronis Opera*, Oxford Classical Texts (Oxford: Clarendon Press, corr. ed. 1972); I have substituted *v* for *u* in consonant positions. Translations are mine. The Spenser quotations follow *The Works of Edmund Spenser, A Variorum Edition*, ed. Edwin Greenlaw et al., 11 vols., (Baltimore: The Johns Hopkins Press, 1932–57).

3. Michael C. J. Putnam, *Virgil's Poems of the Earth* (Princeton, N.J.: Princeton University Press, 1979), p. 7.

4. I have discussed these aspects of the *Georgics* in greater detail in "Milton, T. S. Eliot, and the Virgilian Vision: Some Versions of Georgic," *Genre* 10 (1977), 233–58.

5. The authenticity of this proem is still open to doubt, but in Spenser's day it was widely accepted as Vergil's own. The Latin text is that of *The Aeneid of Virgil*, ed. T. E. Page (London: Macmillan, 1894), 1–4.

6. Kathleen Williams, "Vision and Rhetoric: The Poet's Voice in *The Faerie Queene*," *ELH* 36 (1969), 142.

7. As Williams has observed in "Vision and Rhetoric," p. 141: "The poet instructs us in the art of reading his poem by explaining how he conceives of the art of writing it."

8. As Carol Kaske has pointed out to me, there are some important differences as well. Unlike Spenser, Vergil claims that his theme is lowly, and consequently Vergil's narrator does not take on the guise of a farmer, whereas Spenser's does. My point, however, is that both narrators stand apart from their characters, but praise similar virtues in them.

9. Williams, "Vision and Rhetoric," p. 142. See also Robert N. Durling, *The Figure of the Poet in Renaissance Epic* (Cambridge, Mass.: Harvard University Press, 1965), ch. 7; and Jerome S. Dees, "The Narrator of *The Faerie Queene*: Patterns of Response," *Texas Studies in Literature and Language* 12 (1971), 537–68, esp. 544–49, on the comparison with Ariosto.

10. See Richard Neuse, "Book VI as Conclusion to *The Faerie Queene*," *ELH* 35 (1968), 336, with an interesting citation from Plato's *Republic*.

11. Ibid., pp. 329–53; see also Paul Alpers, "Narration in *The Faerie Queene*," *ELH* 44 (1977), 19–39, for a reading that finds disillusionment in the narrative voice itself in the final books.

12. Colin Hardie, *The "Georgics": A Transitional Poem*, The Third Jackson Knight Memorial Lecture (Abingdon-on-Thames, Berkshire: The Abbey Press, 1971), 21–31, emphasizes the significance of Aristaeus' pastoral associations; P. J. Davis, "Vergil's Georgics and the Pastoral Ideal," *Ramus* 8 (1979), 22–33, sees the poem's highest values as pastoral but stresses the epical characteristics of Aristaeus.

13. Hardie, *The "Georgics": A Transitional Poem*, 29.

14. Humphrey Tonkin, *Spenser's Courteous Pastoral* (Oxford: Clarendon Press, 1972), p. 312, has it that "time moves forward." This, I think, is not adequate to explain Spenser's workings.

15. See Hardie, *The "Georgics": A Transitional Poem,* 27–28, for an interesting discussion of the Aristaeus episode as a commentary on ambition and haste.

16. Dees, "The Narrator of *The Faerie Queene:* Patterns of Response," p. 538.

17. Neuse, in "Book VI as Conclusion to *The Faerie Queene*," 337, writes that "the life of strenuous aspiration" is vulnerable to the undermining of "its energies" and feels that by Book VI the chivalric world no longer has "significant action and aspiration." While disagreeing with his conclusions about the poem, I believe he has framed the issues correctly.

18. Alpers, in "Narration in *The Faerie Queene*," p. 36, says that Spenser's interest in other literary genres late in his career indicates his dissatisfaction with the rhetoric of heroic poetry; it is for this reason that Spenser ends his poem with a lyrical prayer, rather than an epical narration.

19. William A. Sessions, "Spenser's Georgics," *ELR* 10 (1980), 203.

HAROLD L. WEATHERBY

"Pourd out in Loosnesse"

I

*I*N HIS introduction to the Longman's annotated edition of *The Faerie Queene*, A. C. Hamilton makes a strong case for Spenser's delight in words and especially in etymological puns. "Among Renaissance poets he is distinguished by his joy in words"; "he was sustained to write the longest major poem in our language because words released in him enormous creative powers"; "[Spenser's] delight in etymology is one part of his enormous pleasure, which he expects his readers to share, in all kinds of witty word-play."[1] Hamilton shares it to the full, and his commentary opens meanings closed to the verbally insensitive.

One of his best examples of Spenser's etymological wit is to be found in the seventh canto of the first book. Red Crosse has just drunk from a stream (stanza 6) "as cleare as cristall glas" which unbeknownst to him has sprung from the demise of a slothful nymph. Its waters, consonant with its origin, "waxed dull and slow, / And all that drunke thereof, did faint and feeble grow" (stanza 5). The effect upon Red Crosse is immediate: "Eftsoones his manly forces gan to faile, / And mightie strong was turnd to feeble fraile." More specifically, his "chearefull bloud in faintnesse chill did melt"; consequently, at the beginning of stanza 7, we find him "Pourd out in loosnesse."

> Yet goodly court he made still to his Dame,
> Pourd out in loosnesse on the grassy grownd,
> Both carelesse of his health, and of his fame.

At just that moment, "he heard a dreadfull sownd" which proves, of course, to be Orgoglio. Hamilton notes that in the penultimate stanza (51) of the same canto Una describes Red Crosse as "dissolute"; "this term means 'debauched', 'enfeebled', 'relaxed', and 'careless'. Also," Hamilton adds, "it implies 'dissolved' (*OED* I), from the Latin *dissolutus*, loose: the Knight was betrayed when he lay 'Pourd out in loosnesse on the grassy grownd.'" Furthermore, "the Knight is 'dissolute' in the precise sense of being dissolved: by drinking from the fountain, his 'chearefull bloud in

73

faintnesse chill did melt'" (vii.6).[2] To these comments in his introduction, Hamilton adds as a gloss on "pourd out" the "Lat. *effusus*, spread out; hence stretched out. The phrase expresses his dissipation: sexually expended and exhausted, [Red Crosse] is like the water he drank."[3]

Delight in etymology to be sure; but is it original with Spenser? There is a possible source—a work recently published when Spenser was writing Book I of *The Faerie Queene*. I refer to an anonymous English translation of St. John Chrysostom's homilies on Ephesians, published in 1581 by the London printers, Henry Binneman and Ralph Newberie, as *An Exposition Vpon the Epistle of S. Paule the Apostle to the Ephesians*.[4] The title page is dated 24 December, and the entry in the Stationers' Register is 4 January, 1582. Spenser could conceivably have seen the book as early as the winter or spring of that year and could therefore have been influenced by it in his selection of a conceit from Ephesians as a controlling allegorical motif in Book I.[5] In view of the specification of Ephesians in the letter to Raleigh it is surprising that no one (or at least no one to my knowledge) has examined this roughly contemporary commentary. When we do examine it, we find the possibility of influence considerably strengthened by similarity in verbal technique.

The initial point of contact between the two is the motif of the disarmed knight. The prelude to Red Crosse's dissolution is his going unarmed; when we find him prone beside the slothful stream, he is "Disarmed all of yron-coted Plate" (vii.2). Chrysostom employs the same metaphor for a Christian's becoming dissolute: "If then there be a warre . . . if there be spirituall wickednesse: tell me, howe commeth it to passe, that thou liuest deliciously? How art thou *dissolute?* how can we get the victorie, *when we are unarmed?* (p. 309, emphasis added). Here Chrysostom's combining *dissolute* with the circumstances of going without Christian armor and living deliciously is identical with Spenser's; Red Crosse is manifestly living deliciously with Duessa—that is the signature of his dissolution. Moreover, Chrysostom exploits *dissolute* for metaphorical implications very like Spenser's; both writers are aware of the implicit water imagery. Red Crosse, as Hamilton notes, is both *melted* and *poured out;* Chrysostom's disarmed and dissolute soldier "*floweth ouer,* and is dissolute." Red Crosse, besides being poured out, is also *loose*—"Pourd out in loosnesse"—and Chrysostom links *loose* with *dissolute* in much the same fashion: "But such as stand not, can not be straight, but *loose,* and *dissolute*" (p. 317, emphasis added). Finally, Chrysostom's disarmed soldier and Red Crosse are in a similar physical position: according to Chrysostom, "He that is giuen to deliciousnesse, standeth not: he that is letcherous . . . (standeth not) but leaneth" (p. 317). Red Crosse, given to deliciousnesse and lechery, is so far from standing that Spenser places him explicitly "on the grassy grownd," and even that phrase seems to echo Chrysostom: Red Crosse is "Pourd out in loos- nesse *on the grassy grownd*," and Chrysostom's disarmed knight "floweth ouer, and is dissolute in his lusts, and hath all his thoughts trailing *upon the ground*" (p. 317, emphasis added).

Here are the parallel passages in full, with the pertinent phrases emphasized:

> Ere long she [Duessa] fownd, whereas he wearie sate,
> To rest him selfe, foreby a fountaine side,
> *Disarmed all of yron-coted Plate*,
> And by his side his steed the grassy forage ate.   (I.vii.2)

> Eftsoones his manly forces gan to faile,
> And mightie strong was turnd to feeble fraile.
> His chaunged powres at first them selues not felt,
> Till crudled cold his corage gan assaile,
> And chearefull bloud in faintnesse chill *did melt*,
> Which like a feuer fit through all his body swelt.

> Yet goodly court he made still to his Dame,
> *Pourd out* in *loosnesse* on the *grassy grownd*,
> Both carelesse of his health, and of his fame.   (I.vii.6–7)

At the end of the canto Una describes the preceding scene to Arthur:

> At last by subtill sleights she him betraid
> Vnto his foe, a Gyant huge and tall,
> Who him *disarmed, dissolute,* dismaid,
> Vnwares surprised.   (I.vii.51)

The two passages from Chrysostom's commentary read as follows:

If then there be a warre . . . howe commeth it to passe, that thou liuest deliciously? How art thou *dissolute?* how can we get the vic- torie, when we are *unarmed?* Let euerie one say these things vnto himselfe euerie day, when he is ouercome with anger, and with con- cupiscence,[6] when he doth desire to liue suche a *dissolute,* and so vaine a life.   (P. 309)

He that standeth right, standeth, *not dissolutely,* not leaning to any thing. . . . But such as stand not, can not be straight, but *loose,* and *dissolute.* He that is giuen to deliciousnesse, standeth not: he that is letcherous . . . (standeth not) but *leaneth.* . . . He [St. Paul, by his admonitions] bindeth up in a girdle him that *floweth ouer,* and is *dissolute* in his lusts, and hath all his thoughts trailing *upon the ground.*

(P. 317)

II

These similarities may of course be coincidental, but the date of the Chrysostom translation and its pertinence to Spenser's theme suggest influence. So too does a comparison of Spenser's English with Chrysostom's Greek. Let us imagine Spenser, fascinated by the metaphoric implications of *dissolute,* seeking the adjective's source. In three of the sentences we have quoted, Chrysostom wrote διακεχυμένος: "How art thou dissolute?" πῶς διακεχυμένος εἶ; "He that standeth right, standeth, *not dissolutely*" οὐ διακεχυμένος; and, "But such as stand not, can not be straight, *but loose, and dissolute*" ἀλλὰ διαλελυμένοι καὶ διακεχυμένοι.[7] The point of great interest about this participle is that Spenser's "pourd out" renders it more exactly than the anonymous translator's "dissolute." Διακεχυμένος is from διαχέω, to "pour forth" or "disperse," and ultimately from χέω, to "pour." The closest Latin equivalent is *diffusus* (our "diffuse"), but *effusus,* "poured out" (which Hamilton, interestingly, suggests), is a legitimate synonym. It is therefore possible that "pour out in loosnesse" may be less a metaphoric extrapolation from "dissolute" than an exact translation of the Greek source of "dissolute."

Precisely how literal becomes evident when we examine the entry for διακεχυμένος in the standard lexicon of the day. I refer to Henri Estienne's *Thesavrvs Graecae lingvae* (1572)[8] which for διακεχυμένος offers the following: *Ex Chrysost. verò affertur* διακεχυμένοι *etiam pro Effusi, Soluti, Qui molliter educati sunt* (col. 497). (I translate idiomatically: "From Chrysostom, indeed, we get διακεχυμένοι for *Effusi, Soluti,* to describe those who are brought up softly [or 'deliciously'].") For translation of the Latin, Spenser would not, presumably, have required a dictionary; but if he sought help with *Effusi* and *Soluti* it would almost certainly have been in either Sir Thomas Elyot's *Dictionary* of 1538 or in one of Thomas Cooper's augmentations thereof—the *Bibliotheca Eliotae* (1548) or the much expanded *Thesavrvs linguae Romanae et Britannicae* (1565).[9] From any of these Spenser would have learned that *effusus* means "powred out" and *solutus,* "lewsed or louse."

Admittedly, other definitions appear—"payde" for *solutus* and "discomfited, scattered, putte oute" for *effusus.* "Payde," however, is manifestly derivative, and Spenser's certain recognition that *effusus* derives from *effundo* would have directed his attention to "powre out" rather than to the secondary definitions. It is also noteworthy that Thomas Cooper supplements Elyot's original entry with "rennyng abrode, ouerflowyng or rennyng ouer the bankes as ryvers dooe"—a cluster of fluid associations very close to Chrysostom's "him that floweth ouer" and very likely to focus Spenser's attention on "powred out" rather than "putte out." (We should not forget that flowing water is the allegorical cause of Red Crosse's poured-out and loosened condition.) We may then reasonably conjecture that if Spenser read Estienne's entry he would have understood it in some such fashion as the following: "Chrysostom uses the participle διαχεχυμέ-νος to mean 'poured out' and 'loose,' with metaphoric reference to those who live 'deliciously.'" What we have here, complete with Chrysostom's imprimatur, are Latin synonyms of the very adjectives employed for Red Crosse's dissolute condition. Even the order of Estienne's presentation is identical with Spenser's "pourd out in loosnesse."

III

Such a resemblance naturally prompts the question: are there more of the same kind? If Spenser drew once on Chrysostom and Estienne, may he not have done so many times? If the etymological possibilities of *dissolute* were his concern, may he not have explored implications of another Greek word which the English translator renders with the same adjective? I refer to Chrysostom's ὑγρός which appears as *dissolute* in the phrase, "suche a dissolute, and so vaine a life" (p. 309). The difference between ὑγρός and διαχεχυμένος, as Chrysostom employs them, is that while the latter has (as we have seen) largely sexual connotations, the former refers primarily to sloth. Chrysostom ascribes "suche a dissolute (ὑγρόν) . . . life" to "*slouthful* persons"—those who repine and shun spiritual combat, who speak "the words of a cowardlie & *drousie* souldiour" (p. 309, emphasis added). We are reminded, of course, that for Red Crosse sloth precedes and induces lust; and that is Chrysostom's order as well: he speaks first about the ὑγρός soldier and then of the one who is διαχεχυμένος. Great interest therefore attaches to Estienne's account of ὑγρός, for the adjective's etymology suggests the same sequence.

Ὑγρός *est pro lēto, laxo, & non cōtento* (col. 1727), which we may translate, "sluggish, slack and not alert"—literally "not stretched" or "not strained." *Non contentus*, however, presents a possibility for typically Spenserian wordplay and by doing so introduces the notion of sexual dissoluteness. There are two identical Latin participles—the one which Estienne uses, deriving from *contendo* and meaning to "stretch," and the other from *contineo*, to "hold" or to "contain." *Non contentus* can therefore mean not only "slack" (and hence "slouthful" or "drousie") but also "not contained"—as one "Pourd out in loosnesse" is not contained. By virtue, then, of a Latin pun, ὑγρός anticipates διαχεχυμένος (or *effusus*), just as Red Crosse's sloth—his going unarmed, his becoming "a cowardlie & drousie souldiour"—anticipates his being "pourd out" or sexually dissolute. (It is interesting in this regard that the negative of the present participle of *contineo — non continens* — yields the English "incontinent.") The implications, in short, of ὑγρός-non contentus constitute an etymological equivalent of Red Crosse's complex moral (or immoral) state. Nor does the addition of incontinence to the pattern depend altogether from the coincidence of the two Latin participles. Estienne makes clear in another citation (without reference to *contineo)* that ὑγρός can mean "lascivious" as well as "sluggish": ὑγρὸς βίος . . . *voluptariam vitam significat* ("a ὑγρός life signifies a voluptuous life," col. 1727).

That, however, is not the whole story of ὑγρός or even its most interesting chapter. Estienne's etymology could also have provided Spenser with the idea of a stream as the allegorical source of sloth and lust. The adjective's initial, physical meaning is simply "wet" or "fluid"— *humidus, humectus, madidus, liquidus, fluidus.* Its figurative (ethical) significance derives from its fluidity; according to Estienne, that which is liquid is soft and malleable, and soft, malleable characters lack spiritual stamina (col. 1726). The etymology reads like a recipe for an allegory in which physical liquidity, Spenser's "bubbling waue," induces, as that wave does, spiritual malleability and slackness. Moreover, Estienne's synonym *laxus,* besides meaning "slack," carries also the connotation of enfeeblement—another, we recall, of the stream's effects upon Red Crosse. One of the meanings of the verb form, *laxo,* is to "weaken";[10] and no sooner has the knight drunk from the stream than "his manly forces gan to faile, / And mightie strong was turnd to feeble fraile" (I.vii.6).

The possibility of an etymological source for this enfeebling stream draws attention back to Chrysostom's "him that floweth ouer." We have noted already that the phrase bears a close resemblance to "pourd out" and that with διαχεχυμένος (and *effusus*) it could have contributed to Spenser's description. An examination of the Greek not only confirms that suggestion but reveals, as well, a link with the watery implications of ὑγρός. The Elizabethan translator's "floweth ouer" renders Chrysostom's participle διαρρέοντα, which emphasizes even more directly than ὑγρός the etymological connections among water, sloth, and lust. Διαρρέοντα is from διαρρέω, which means, literally, not to flow *over* but to flow *through* (διά), as a stream flows through the land. The latter is Estienne's first definition: *per medium fluo,* "to flow through the midst" of a country as, in his illustration, the Nile flows through Egypt. By that citation Estienne could have provided Spenser with the notion of a stream; and he proceeds to attach to that notion precisely the ethical implications which Spenser attaches. As a synonym for διαρρέοντα Estienne proffers *tabescendum,* "languishing." How can to "flow" mean also to "languish"? Because, says Estienne, *tabescens corpus, velut diffluit*—"a languishing body, as it were, flows apart" (col. 687).

Tabesco would almost certainly have had for Spenser, as it has for us, connotations of weakness, idleness, and also of concupiscence. Elyot defines it as "to languish" and *langueo* as "to be sycke, to be faynt" (the initial effects of the stream upon Red Crosse) as well as "to be idell" (as the nymph has been from whom the stream has sprung). Elyot does not suggest a sexual connotation, but the *OED* indicates that as early as 1300 "languishing" meant not only being faint or idle but also pining in love or lust. Furthermore, though none of the sixteenth-century dictionaries says so, Estienne's *diffluo* can mean not only to "flow apart" but also to abandon oneself to *luxuria.* The new *Oxford Latin Dictionary* indicates classical precedents for that meaning, precedents which Spenser could easily have known.[11] It appears, therefore, that Chrysostom's διαρρέοντα, by way of Estienne's *tabescendum,* provides, as does ὑγρός, etymological justification for a stream which springs from idleness and which in turn induces sloth, faintness, and lust. When we recognize the assimilation of both these words to διαχεχυμένος—fluidity being their common characteristic—we begin to discern a pattern of verbal wit in Chrysostom's text with which Spenser's allegory is remarkably consonant.

IV

"Loose," as we have seen, is the other key word in both Chrysostom's and Spenser's account of dissolution. One of the prose translator's sources for this adjective is the Greek χαῦνος, which appears in a phrase we have not yet quoted but which belongs to the same thematic and rhetorical context: "Howe softe, and *loose* [χαῦνοι] they be" (p. 318, emphasis added). The adjective certainly can mean "loose," and since *loose* responds to *dissolute* one can easily see why the translator chose that synonym. Χαῦνος, however, has a wide range of meanings which Chrysostom clearly intended to exploit. These include, according to Estienne, not only "loose" but also, contradictorily, both "empty" and "inflated." He explains the paradox as follows: "Solent enim ea quae laxa sunt & fungosa, sese extendere & dilatare, nonunquam etiam vento quodam inflari & tumefieri, ita vt aliquando χαῦνος significet etiam Inanis, necnon Inflatus, Tumidus" (Indeed those things which are loose and 'spongy' are wont to extend and dilate themselves, sometimes furthermore to be inflated and blown up by some wind; thus χαῦνος sometimes means empty, sometimes inflated or tumid, col. 403). Since Chrysostom is talking about lechers and, even more explicitly, about lechers' bodies, it seems likely that he expected χαῦνος to convey that whole range of meaning complete with its obvious sexual implications. When the Christian warrior, having laid aside his Pauline armor, is poured out in sexual looseness, he is in the most explicit, physical sense first *tumidus* and then *fungosa*. He is also, of course, by virtue of his sexual pride, vain and empty in the other sense of χαῦνος— "blown up by some wind." "Loose," we therefore see, does scant justice to the implications of Chrysostom's language.

Spenser's allegory, on the other hand, whether coincidentally or deliberately, does that language full justice. No sooner is Red Crosse disarmed and poured out sexually than he is attacked by a vivid personification of (among other vices) tumid, sexual pride. Orgoglio fits perfectly Estienne's account of χαῦνος. The giant is *vento quodam inflari;* Spenser translates almost literally: "puft vp with emptie wind" (I.vii.9). Save for the substitution of "emptie" for the indefinite *quodam,* the English phrase reproduces the Latin exactly; and "emptie," by accentuating the paradoxical quality of Estienne's definition, rather strengthens than weakens the argument that Spenser was working with that definition in mind. There are other similarities as well. Estienne says that χαῦνος can also mean both ὑψηλός, "lofty" or "towering" and ἀσθενής, "without strength" (col. 404). In an extension both of the giant's sexual connotations and of his role as a symbol of worldly pride,[12] Spenser depicts him in precisely those contradictory (or at least alternating) states; when he attacks Red Crosse, who at the moment is χαῦνος in the sexually tumid sense, Orgoglio is ὑψηλός; his "stature did exceed / The hight of three the tallest sonnes of mortall seed" and "his talnesse seemed to threat the skye" (I.vii.8). In the next canto, however, we discover that he is ἀσθενής, and for the very reason implicit in Chrysostom's metaphor and in Estienne's etymology—that that great height is all owing to "emptie wind."

> But soone as breath out of his breast did pas,
> That huge great body, which the Gyaunt bore,
> Was vanisht quite, and of that monstrous mas
> Was nothing left, but like an emptie bladder was.

>   (I.viii.24)

"Pourd out in Loosnesse"

Since Orgoglio is an outward manifestation of Red Crosse's spiritual state, we are not surprised to discover that now Red Crosse too has exchanged an inflated or tumid χαῦνος for its lax and empty opposite. When Arthur finds him in the giant's dungeon, Spenser goes out of his way to insist upon both emptiness *(inanis)* and weakness *(asthenes)*. Red Crosse's voice is "hollow"; his thighs are "feeble," his body (corse) "pined," his eyes "deepe sunck in hollow pits," his cheeks "thin," his sides "empty," and, with a probable allusion to the extended sexual innuendo, "his vitall powres / Decayd, and all his flesh shronk vp like withered flowres" (I.viii.40–41).

V

That Arthur should be responsible for Orgoglio's defeat and Red Crosse's restoration may also be owing to χαῦνος. Estienne in his discussion of the word contrasts false inflation with true greatness of soul, taking as his illustrative citation Aristotle's discourse on the μεγαλόψυχος in the fourth book of the *Ethics*. The passage, as all Spenserians will recognize, is the classic text on magnanimity, a virtue which has been referred to Arthur as frequently as Spenser's own *magnificence*. Though I agree with the critics who believe Spenser knew the difference between the two, the allegory does seem to indicate an assimilation of the latter to the former. Arthur is more frequently magnanimous than magnificent, and even such redoubtable authorities as C. S. Lewis and A. S. P. Woodhouse take the equivalence for granted. Moreover, Arthur is never more explicitly magnanimous (or less obviously magnificent) than in his encounter with Orgoglio, which reads like an exemplum for the distinction between μεγαλόψυχος and χαῦνος. The confrontation has nothing to do with a contrast between liberality and niggardliness but rather with that between a man who is genuinely great of soul and one who, in the lust of the flesh and the pride of life, mistakenly conceives himself to be.

That is precisely the contrast which is set forth in the passage which Estienne quotes from the *Ethics*. First Aristotle describes the ἄνθρωπος χαῦνος as "homo qui inani quam de se concepit opinione inflatur & intumescit, magnum sese existimans, quum tamen nihili sit" (The vain man is "the man who is inflated and puffed up in the empty opinion which he conceives of himself, considering himself great, although in fact he is worthless," col. 403). His opposite is the μεγαλόψυχος, the magnanimous man, "who deems himself worthy of great things, *being worthy*" (*eum qui sese μεγάλων ἀξιοῖ, ἄξιος ὤν*, col. 403). These categories serve very well for descriptions of Orgoglio and Arthur, respectively. Moreover, Aristotle says that the former, the ἄνθρωπος χαῦνος, will be put to the test (ἐξελέγχεται, col. 404) and found wanting—the very sort of reckoning to which Arthur subjects Orgoglio. The consequent exposure of vanity is obvious; Orgoglio's being reduced to an empty bladder proves that he was indeed *magnum sese existimans, quum tamen nihili sit.*

Estienne quotes still another distinction from the fourth chapter of the *Ethics,* which could account for the place of Red Crosse in the allegory of canto eight. Aristotle places the μεγαλόψυχος as the virtuous mean between the χαῦνος and the μικρόψυχος, the small-souled man: the μεγαλόψυχος, he says, *medium constituisset inter* χαῦνον & μικρόψυχον (The megalopsychos constitutes a mean between the vain man and the man of small soul, col. 403). The χαῦνος, of course, is the excess and the μικρόψυχος the deficiency; the fault of the latter is that he deems himself worthy of smaller things than he is in fact worthy of (*qui sese* ἀξιοῖ ἐλαττόνων ἢ ἄξιος). He is excessively humble, lacking in sufficient self-esteem to undertake those at least moderately noble actions of which he is capable. Such is the role which Red Crosse plays in Orgoglio's dungeon: he has been reduced to speaking "piteous plaints and dolours" in a "dreary, murmuring voyce" (I.viii.38). So small of soul indeed has he become that he pleads for death rather than deliverance and life. In such a condition he is the deficiency of the virtue of which Orgoglio until a short while before has been the excess. Arthur as the mean and the realization of magnanimity empties the excess and fills up the deficiency, brings down the one to the earth and raises the other from the pit beneath, literally deflates the one and figuratively at least inspires the other.

VI

Are such suggestions far-fetched? Not necessarily. No link in this chain of associations is impossible or even improbable. We cannot, of course, prove that Spenser read the 1581 translation of the Ephesians commentary, but no improbability attaches to the assumption. He almost certainly knew (or knew of) Chrysostom before 1581, for this perennially popular Church Father was in especially high repute in England in the second half of the sixteenth century. *The Short Title Catalogue* lists thirteen translations or editions between 1542 and 1591, and within a few years of Spenser's death Sir Henry Savile produced the first (and still admired) complete edition (Eton, 1612).[13] A man of Spenser's education and interests would almost certainly have been aware of such a Chrysostom renaissance, especially in view of the fact that Savile's principal editors, Andrew Downes and John Bois, were Spenser's contemporaries at Cambridge. Furthermore, the reason for Chrysostom's English popularity would have attracted Spenser. The golden-tongued Father had been enlisted by such Anglican polemicists as Jewel and Cranmer to defend the Church of England against papal claims.[14] Chrysostom represented the ancient, undivided Church of the East which had consistently resisted Roman usurpation and to which England, by the grace of God and the Tudors, had presumably returned. Spenser's familiarity with that line of ecclesiastical argument is evident from his opposition of eastern Una to western Duessa in Book I of *The Faerie Queene*.[15] That that same book should be indebted for its principal conceit to a new translation of Chrysostom seems not, therefore, implausible.

Whether Spenser read the Greek original of the Ephesians homilies entails a prior question—could Spenser read Greek? The matter is still debated, but more and more critics, and I think correctly so, take it for granted that he did (Hamilton seems to be among them—in his discussion of puns and etymologies).[16] One wonders, indeed, why doubt still attaches to the question, for we know that Richard Mulcaster taught Greek at Merchant Taylors' and that Greek was part of the Cambridge curriculum. It seems unlikely that Spenser could have completed a Master's degree without the capacity at least to construe Greek, even if not to read it fluently. For that matter, there is no serious reason to doubt Lodowick Bryskett's statement that Spenser (by 1581) was "perfect in the Greek tongue."[17] He may indeed have been, and as Bryskett also indicates, well read in ancient philosophy as well. So learned a poet is likely to have been familiar with the Greek Fathers and especially with some of the monumental continental editions produced in the sixteenth century. One of the best known of these was a 1529 Veronese *Opera* of Chrysostom upon which Savile, Bois, and Downes relied and which Spenser could presumably have seen at Cambridge.[18]

If Spenser knew Greek, he almost certainly knew Estienne's *Thesaurus*. To describe that work as "standard" is no exaggeration, and for a Greek student of the late sixteenth century to be ignorant of it would be tantamount to his modern counterpart's not knowing Liddell and Scott. Also Estienne is precisely where we would expect someone with Spenser's "joy in words" to turn for help with etymologies. Furthermore, D. T. Starnes and Ernest Talbert demonstrated long ago that Spenser almost certainly drew mythological references from two other lexicographical productions of the Estienne family—Charles's *Dictionarium Historicum, Geographicum, Poeticum* (1553) and Robert's *Thesaurus linguae Latinae* (1573).[19] Oddly, neither Starnes nor Talbert gives any consideration to the possibility of Spenser's knowing Henri's *Thesaurus,* possibly on the assumption (more widely held a quarter-century ago than now) that Spenser knew no Greek. Given the contrary and more probable assumption, Spenser's use of

Charles's and Robert's dictionaries argues for his use of Henri's as well. There is even reason to believe that Spenser was conversant with the whole field of Renaissance lexicography; at least the array of names in Book VI—Aldus, Calepine, and Mirabella—suggest as much.[20] Someone who knew, or even knew of, so relatively old and obscure a dictionary as Friar Calepino's would almost certainly have known Henri Estienne's far more recent and more comprehensive work.[21]

In view of such considerations and of the subtlety and exactness of the verbal similarities we have examined, Spenser's acquaintance with both Chrysostom and Estienne seems more likely than not. Indeed, it appears that we have either discovered hitherto unrecognized sources of Spenser's language (and allegory) or struck upon an improbably exact set of coincidences.

Vanderbilt University

NOTES

1. A. C. Hamilton, introduction to *The Faerie Queene* (London and New York: Longman, 1977), pp. 14–15.

2. Ibid., p. 17.

3. Ibid., p. 97.

4. (London: Binneman and Newberie, 1581), *STC* 14632, 14632a.

5. We do not, of course, know for certain when work on Book I began, but I suppose all scholars now agree that the part of the poem at which Harvey scoffed in the 1579–80 correspondence was not the "Legende of Holinesse." If, as seems likely, Spenser took his friend's censure to heart, he was probably feeling his way toward a new beginning at just the moment the Chrysostom translation appeared.

6. It is worth noting that Red Crosse is here guilty of precisely these two sins which Chrysostom specifies—anger and concupiscence. The concupiscence is manifest, and we should recall that Red Crosse has got himself into his present compromising position because earlier he fell prey to wrath: as a result of Archimago's deceit, "The eye of reason was with rage yblent" (I.ii.5).

7. For the Greek text of Chrysostom's homilies on Ephesians I have used Sir Henry Savile's complete edition of Chrysostom, Τοῦ ἐν ἁγίοις πατρὸς ἡμῶν Ἰωαννοῦ τοῦ Χρυσοστόμου τὰ εὑρισκόμενα (Eton: John Norton, 1612), *STC* 14629, 14629.5, 14629 a, b, c. For the pertinence of this edition to Spenser, see the final section of this essay.

8. Henri Estienne, *Thesavrvs Graecae lingvae* (Geneva: H. Stephanus, 1572).

9. For a full account of these dictionaries, see DeWitt T. Starnes, *Renaissance Dictionaries: English-Latin and Latin-English* (Austin: University of Texas Press, 1954), p. 45 ff.

10. See entry for *laxo* in Lewis and Short and in the *Oxford Latin Dictionary* (1971).

11. See entry for *diffluo* in the *Oxford Latin Dictionary* (1971). The citations for *luxuria et lasciuia* include Terence, Seneca, Cicero, Apuleius, and Sallust.

12. Estienne (in a citation of Aristotle) attributes the inflation of χαῦνος to *superbia* (*Thesavrvs Graecae lingvae,* vol. 404).

13. In a recently published article on sixteenth-century English patristic scholarship, William P. Haaugaard lists eighty-four editions of patristic works in England, seventy-four of them after 1536. Augustine accounts for thirty-six of these and Chrysostom ranks second. See Haaugaard's "Renaissance Patristic Scholarship and Theology in Sixteenth-Century England," *Sixteenth Century Journal* 10 (1979), 37–60.

14. See, for instance, Archbishop Jewel's *An Apology of the Church of England,* ed. J. E. Booty (Ithaca, N.Y.: Cornell University Press, 1963); and Archbishop Cranmer in *The First Authorized English Bible and the Cranmer Preface,* ed. Harold R. Willoughby (Chicago: University of Chicago Press, 1942).

15. The best exposition of Una as a symbol of "the primitive Eastern Church" is by Frank Kermode "*The Faerie Queene,* I and V," *Bulletin of the John Rylands Library* 47 (1965), 123–50.

16. Hamilton notes, for instance, the "etymological spelling" of giant as "Geant" (I. vii. 8), in reference to Orgoglio, because he is the son of "*Gea,* the earth" (Gr. γῆ). One also recalls what seem to be Greek puns on the name *Acrasia* in Book II; for which see Harry Berger, *The Allegorical Temper* (New Haven, Conn.: Yale University Press, 1957), p. 66.

17. Quoted by Alexander Judson, *The Life of Edmund Spenser,* in *The Works of Edmund Spenser, A Variorum Edition,* ed. Edwin A. Greenlaw et al., 11 vols. (Baltimore: The Johns Hopkins Press, 1932–57) vol. 8, p. 106. Judson concludes that Spenser "was respected for his command of Greek and his knowledge of moral and natural philosophy, and that he had encouraged Bryskett to read Greek and had offered to help him with it" (p. 107).

18. For a full bibliography of Chrysostom editions, see Dom Johannes Chrysostomus Baur, *S. Jean Chrysostome et ses oeuvres dans l'histoire littéraire* (Louvain: Bureaux du recueil, 1907).

19. See DeWitt T. Starnes, "Spenser and the Muses," *University of Texas Studies in English* 22 (1942), 31–58; and DeWitt T. Starnes and Ernest William Talbert, *Classical Myth and Legend in Renaissance Dictionaries* (Chapel Hill: University of North Carolina Press, 1955), p. 61 ff.

20. These names have been noted by several scholars. The fullest discussion is in Humphrey Tonkin, *Spenser's Courteous Pastoral: Book Six of the 'Faerie Queene'* (Oxford: Clarendon Press, 1972), p. 66 ff.

21. Starnes argues for the influence of Calepino in "Spenser and the Muses."

DONALD V. STUMP

Isis Versus Mercilla: The Allegorical Shrines in Spenser's Legend of Justice

CRITICS WHO have tried to work out Spenser's philosophy of justice in Book V of *The Faerie Queene* have had to reckon with two extended passages of conceptual allegory: the episode at the Temple of Isis and that at the Palace of Mercilla. Two of the nagging questions about the book involve the relation between these passages: why did Spenser create two "houses of instruction" for his characters in Book V, and which of them (if either) gives his last word on the virtue of justice? Some critics have tried to solve both problems by arguing that the lesson of each episode is the same, that Mercilla's trial of Duessa is simply an illustration of the principles of equity taught at Isis Church. Thus William Nelson and W. Nicholas Knight both treat equity as the legal equivalent of mercy, and they discuss the Palace of Mercilla as if it were essentially a court of equity.[1] Other critics have taken the position that one episode is clearly subordinate to the other, and with the notable exception of T. K. Dunseath, these scholars have chosen Isis Church as the conceptual heart of the book.[2] Angus Fletcher designates the temple as the primary house of instruction in Book V, and Kathleen Williams calls it "the symbolic shrine of justice itself." In her view, the Palace of Mercilla is only "a lesser companion piece to Isis Church."[3] Thomas Cain quotes with approval Williams's assessment of the two episodes and argues that Spenser intentionally set them in contrast to reveal the "disparity between ideal and action, fiction and history." In his view, Mercilla's treatment of Duessa is so far removed from the ideal of justice embodied in Isis that the trial acts as a subtle criticism of Mercilla's historical counterpart, Queen Elizabeth.[4] Taking a similar position, Michael O'Connell concludes that, in the trial of Duessa, "the Legend of Justice falters." In his view, Mercilla's tears are so ineffectual as an expression of mercy that they "may not be worth making such a fuss about."[5]

I think it is worthwhile, however, to make a small fuss about the tears of Mercilla and about the importance of her court in the allegory of ideal justice. I would argue that Spenser maintained a clear distinction between the virtues of equity and mercy and that he designed the main houses of instruction in Book V to reveal the contrasts between the two.[6] In his view, mercy is a distinctly Christian virtue, and it is as far above equity as revealed religion is above pagan philosophy. However much we may prefer the haunting moonlight visions of Isis Church to the straightforward daylight proceedings at Mercilla's court, canto ix is not simply "a lesser companion piece" to canto vii. The Palace of Mercilla is, in fact, the one true and complete temple of justice in the poem.

What one expects at the allegorical heart of a book about justice is, after all, a great trial, and the only courtroom proceedings in Book V take place, not at Isis Church, but at the Palace of Mercilla. One also expects the primary house of instruction to be of some benefit to the hero of the book, but Sir Artegall learns nothing from the goddess Isis. At the time of the episode at her shrine, he is miles away, spinning yarn for Radigund. The lessons of Isis are for his intended queen, Britomart. His own opportunity to learn comes in the court of Mercilla, where he observes a great and complex trial and takes from the conduct of the judge "royall examples" and "worthie paterns" of mercy (x.5).[7] Finally, one would expect the allegorical shrine of perfect justice to appear after Prince Arthur enters the action. Spenser seems to have designed Book V along the same lines as Books I and II, and there the sequence is as follows: the hero suffers a disastrous fall; he is rescued and joins forces for a time with Prince Arthur; and then he undergoes a thorough reeducation in the virtue that he represents. In Book V, Artegall follows much the same progression: he yields to Radegund and is imprisoned; he is rescued by Britomart and joins Arthur in the struggle against the Souldan and Malengin; and then he goes off to observe the justice of Mercilla. This last episode is the one that best corresponds, in position as well as in function, with the houses of instruction in Books I and II.

The conclusion that Mercilla is Spenser's embodiment of ideal justice is confirmed by the symbolism of the two passages. In nearly every detail, Isis is presented as the inferior of Mercilla. The goddess of canto vii is a pagan idol, an "invention" of the antique world (vii.2–3), and she is fashioned largely of an inferior metal: silver. The poet tells us that she is "framed all of silver fine" and that she and her priests wear garments "hemd all about with fringe of silver twine" (vii.4 and 6). In contrast to this mechanical, silver idol, Spenser sets the living, angelic form of Mercilla, and at her palace, a finer metal dominates the description. Once again, Spenser emphasizes the hem of her garment, perhaps because it is a part traditionally grasped by suppliants. Mercilla's skirts are "bordred with bright sunny beams, / Glistring like gold, amongst the plights enrold" (ix.28). Only "here and there" does silver appear amidst the shimmering gold.

Now, admittedly, the meaning of the gold and silver in the passage is

complex and difficult to sort out. One problem is that the symbols are related to the imagery of sun and moon that runs through Books III–V. The
sun often represents qualities of masculinity and the moon those of femi-
ninity, and critics have quite rightly seen the silver of the moon-goddess
Isis as part of this pattern. As A. Kent Hieatt has shown, much of the
symbolism of Britomart's dream in canto vii looks back to her courtship
with Artegall and ahead to their ideal union as man and wife.[8] But the sun
and the moon also symbolize something greater than their private relationship, namely their public roles as king and queen. Spenser clearly be-
lieves that each should have a part in governing the realm, but not the
same part, not an equal part. In the next episode, that involving the defeat
of Radigund, Spenser reveals his conviction that, except in very unusual
cases, women are not suited to be heads of state. In his words, "wise Nature did them strongly bynd, / T'obay the heasts of mans well ruling
hand" (v.25). Accordingly, the lessons of Isis Church are mainly in one
kind of justice, the kind appropriate to a queen. The moon-goddess exer-
cises "that part of Justice, which is Equity" (vii.3). In contrast, the lessons
of Mercilla's court involve the king's role, and as I shall discuss below,
they encompass all the traditional parts of justice: legal justice and mercy,
as well as equity.[9] The justice of Mercilla is above that of Isis, and Spenser
expresses the distinction in imagery of gold and silver.

A second problem in interpreting the symbolism arises from the presence of a few golden details in the Temple of Isis and a few silver ones in
the Palace of Mercilla. The mixture of metals is most confusing in canto
vii. Although the statue of Isis is silver, it bears a golden crown and stands
beneath a golden vault. If these details carry on the symbolism of masculine and feminine roles, then they are not difficult to interpret. They drive
home the point that the ideal queen is one who takes her direction—and
also her power and her honor—from her king. That is, silver is beneath
gold and is sheltered by it and also crowned in it. But the poet adds yet another twist to the symbolism when he states that Isis "wore a Crowne of
gold, / To shew that she had powre in things divine" (vii.6). This comment might be taken to mean that equity is, for Spenser, the highest sort
of justice. Certainly it shows that he admired the ancient pagans for what
they understood of true justice and that, like others in the Renaissance, he
believed that God sometimes allowed pagan idols and oracles to give men
glimpses of the truth. But it does not show that Isis Church portrays
Spenser's highest ideal of justice. Once again, symbolism reveals the poet's
true position. The Temple of Isis conceals its golden pillars in a dim and secluded shrine, but Mercilla's palace blazes forth its golden light to all the
world. The palace towers are topped with "bright glistering . . . gold, /

That seemed to outshine the dimmed skye, / And with their brightnesse daz'd the straunge beholders eye" (ix.21). The statue of Isis stands almost alone beneath a vault "dispred" with gold, but Mercilla sits upon a golden throne amidst crowds of her loving subjects, and over her head is something almost too marvelous to describe:

> All over her a cloth of state was spred,
> Not of rich tissew, nor of cloth of gold,
> Nor of ought else, that may be richest red,
> But like a cloud, as likest may be told,
> That her brode spreading wings did wyde unfold. (ix.28)

As A. C. Hamilton has pointed out, the image suggests the cloud of glory that surrounds the head of God himself as he sits upon the throne of judgment.[10]

The contrast between Isis and Mercilla is also suggested by the quality of the light in each episode. Britomart arrives at the temple just as night is falling: "The day with dampe was overcast, / And joyous light the house of *Jove* forsooke" (vii.8). The darkness and the fog are ominous, for elsewhere in the poem they are almost invariably associated with ignorance and danger. Whatever light Britomart may receive from her dream, she is still surrounded by the darkness of pagan antiquity. In contrast, Arthur and Artegall arrive at the Palace of Mercilla in broad daylight, and they are continually dazzled. The light is like that of a nimbus, brilliant and unearthly. We have the sense that Mercilla's towers do not so much reflect the natural sunlight as overpower it; as Spenser says, they "outshine the dimmed skye" (ix.21). The hem of Mercilla's skirt also seems to generate its own brilliance, or perhaps we are to imagine it as woven of light itself. It is bordered, not with fabric of gold, but with "bright sunny beams, / Glistring *like* gold" (ix.28, emphasis added).

The inferiority of Isis to Mercilla is further suggested by the figures gathered about their feet. Isis stands with her foot upon a crocodile representing her husband Osyris. The arrangement symbolizes the occasional need for equity to overrule common law and mitigate its harshness. From Britomart's dream, we also learn that the union of Isis and Osyris is to bring forth a lion as offspring, and as Frank Kermode has suggested, the lion is a symbol of "natural law"—that is, the proper balance of common law and equity.[11] Now, a lion appears again in the description of Mercilla, lying chained at her feet, and critics have suggested that this lion symbolizes wrath subdued, the rebellious factions of England under the firm control of Queen Elizabeth, or various other things. But the pattern of parallels between Isis and Mercilla suggests a further meaning to the symbol: it is once again the lion of natural law. Just as equity stands over common law, so mercy stands over them both. Phrased another way, the divine virtue of mercy is superior to the human system of natural law and must control it. Spenser reinforces this point by placing at the feet of Mercilla the classical goddesses known as the Litae, who are ancient symbols of equity.[12] Evidently, pagan equity is a proper servant to Christian mercy, but not its equal. The poet may have had the same point in mind when he mentioned the occasional gleams of silver amidst the golden rays emanating from the hem of Mercilla's skirt. The silver of equity is present, but the gold of mercy dominates.

The final point to be made about the symbolism of the two episodes is that virtually everything associated with Isis is classical, whereas the symbols surrounding Mercilla are both classical and Christian—and the Christian symbols predominate. As A. C. Hamilton, Thomas Cain, and others have pointed out, Mercilla's palace is drawn in the likeness of the holy temple in Jerusalem.[13] Like the temple of the Old Testament, it stands with its gates open day and night; its golden throne resembles the very mercy seat of Jehovah; the angels hovering about Mercilla's head are like the seraphim who surround God, shielding onlookers from the dazzling cloud of his glory; and the "kings and kezers" who lie prostrate at Mercilla's feet recall the Old Testament prophecies that all nations will bow down to the Lord in Zion. The pagan temple of Isis is clearly inferior to this glorious temple—so far inferior, in fact, as to be almost beneath comparison. Whereas Isis admits Britomart as a servant, allows her to sleep at her feet, and inspires her with dim visions of the truth, Mercilla welcomes Arthur and Artegall as friends, seats them as fellow judges upon the very throne of divine justice, and instructs them clearly by her example. Her open friendship with them calls to mind Christ's words at the Last Supper: "Henceforth I call you not servants . . . but I have called you friends; for all things that I have heard of my Father I have made known to you" (John 15.15). One also thinks of Paul's statement in 1 Corinthians 6.2 that "the saints shall judge the world."

Once we recognize that Spenser has systematically subordinated the episode at Isis Church to that at the Palace of Mercilla, we are left to puzzle out his intentions. Why did he create two temples of justice and set them in such sharp contrast? One explanation has to do with the historical allegory. Cantos v through xii of Book V are a more or less chronological account of the lifelong struggle between Queen Elizabeth and the Catholic forces in the British Isles and in Europe. I would suggest that Spenser designed his two allegorical shrines so as to contrast the early years of Elizabeth, when she was weak and vulnerable, with the height of her reign, when she had defeated all her enemies.

When we first see Elizabeth (in the figure of Britomart), she has not yet become a queen. Her coronation and the early years of her reign are portrayed at Isis Church, but only in a prophetic dream. Therefore, it seems fair to suppose that the temple itself represents the conditions in England just before Elizabeth came to the throne, that is, conditions during the reign of Mary Tudor, when the Queen attempted to return the country to the Catholic fold. If we interpret the episode in this way, we can begin to make sense of a number of otherwise baffling details, particularly the suggestions of Catholicism that continually creep into the religion of Isis.

Like Catholic monks, the priests of Isis are bound by vows of chastity, and they lead a hard, cloistered existence to mortify their own "rebellious flesh" (vii.9). Like Duessa in Book I, they wear mitres, which Spenser's audience would have associated with the Catholic priesthood, and when Britomart awakes from her dream, she finds them preparing for morning "Mas" (vii.4, 17).[14] They serve an idol, and this detail recalls the common charge among Protestant polemicists that Catholics are idol-worshippers. Later in Book V, the Souldan and Gerioneo—both figures associated with the Catholic monarch, Philip of Spain—are likewise accused of idolatry (viii.19; xi.19). The altar that appears in Britomart's dream is also suspicious. One of the principal objections that the Protestants raised against the Mass was that it contains a ritual sacrifice of Christ at the altar. The flames and the tempest that arise from the altar of Isis probably represent the domestic disturbances that followed Elizabeth's decision to abolish the Mass. Even the Egyptian setting of the episode may be an allusion to Catholicism, for the reformers of Spenser's day were fond of comparing modern Rome with ancient Egypt. The pope was equated with Pharoah, holding the children of the Lord in bondage in an idolatrous land, and the Protestants were likened to the Israelites who had been led forth out of Egypt.[15] Finally, there are hints of Catholicism in Britomart's behavior during her dream. Just before her coronation, we see her "doing sacrifize / To *Isis,* deckt with Mitre on her hed, / And linnen stole after those Priestes guize" (vii.13). In these lines, Spenser is presenting an accurate picture of Elizabeth's religious position during the reign of Mary. To appease her sister, Elizabeth put on a pretense of Catholic piety. Soon after Mary came to power, Elizabeth began irregular attendance at Mass and even wrote to the Queen asking for chasubles and other Catholic vestments for use in her own private chapel.[16]

Once we perceive the pattern of Catholic details in the passage, it is not difficult to understand Spenser's decision to contrast the darkness and superstition of Isis Church with the sunlight and piety of Mercilla's palace. One represents Elizabeth oppressed and unable to avoid compromising her own Protestant beliefs, and the other presents her victorious and able to defend the reformed church against all the international powers loyal to Rome.

Of course, not every practice in the cult of Isis is a clear reference to Catholicism. Spenser had more than one allegorical intention in the passage, and the complexity of his design makes a few points difficult to interpret. For instance, it is hard to see why Roman Catholic priests should have "long locks comely kemd" (vii.4), unless, perhaps, these are Marian priests who returned to the Catholic form of worship only briefly and did not bother to tonsure their hair. It is also odd that they refuse to partake of flesh, blood, or wine, since the celebrants at Mass are said to eat of bread and wine miraculously transubstantiated into the body and blood of Christ. I would suggest that the priests' hair and dietary laws have to do with a second allegorical pattern that I wish to discuss: the contrast between pagan and Christian.

The concept of equity that is embodied in the goddess Isis is altogether pagan in its origins. As the research of Angus Fletcher, James Nohrnberg, and others reveals, it changed very little from the time of Aristotle to Spenser's own day.[17] However much Spenser may have admired the ideal of equity as an indispensable part of human justice, he clearly had reservations about it as a pattern of divine justice. The priests of Isis are committed to "reasons rule" (vii.12), and their concept of equity was formed without the light of Christian revelation. Their entire cult is of the earth: it originated when men deified an earthly king and queen, and its adherents are but children of the earth, as Spenser suggests by his remark that they choose to sleep "on their mother Earths deare lap" (vii.9). As the story of the origin of wine makes clear, the poet has in mind the Earth who gave birth to the rebellious Titans and bears "inward griefe and malice" toward the celestial gods (vii.10–11). In contrast, Mercilla's strength and authority are from God; she is "Angel-like" (ix.29), and her form of justice originated, not on earth, but in heaven. The poet says of Mercy that "in th'Almighties everlasting seat / She first was bred, and borne of heavenly race; / From thence pour'd down on men, by influence of grace" (x.1). From a Christian point of view, the priests of Isis are lost in their ignorance and superstition, for their religion prevents them from partaking of the body and blood of Christ.

The virtue of equity that they represent is also quite different from Christian mercy. When a judge employs equity, he simply corrects the faults inherent in any human code of law. Since such laws must be brief and must be framed universally, they cannot take into account all the extenuating circumstances that may lessen a defendant's guilt in any particular case. Therefore, judges must be prepared to mitigate judgment by returning to the philosophical principles on which the legal code is based and correcting any deficiencies in the original framing of the laws. But the judge may not soften or eliminate any just punishment; all he may do is insure that the defendant receives precisely what is due.

The difference between this sort of equitable judgment and the Christian pattern of divine justice can be clearly seen in the case of Red Crosse Knight in Book I. In his encounter with Despair, the knight comes to understand that "by righteous sentence of th'Almighties law" he deserves death and damnation. But, as Una explains, God is merciful and does not aim to give those who love him only what is due. Despite the handwriting of God's judgment against her beloved knight, Una seeks to cheer him:

> In heavenly mercies hast thou not a part?
> Why shouldst thou then despeire, that chosen art?
> Where justice growes, there grows eke greater grace,
> The which doth quench the brond of hellish smart,
> And that accurst hand-writing doth deface.   (I.ix.53)

Now, Red Crosse has not been judged too harshly by an imperfect legal code, and Una does not dispute the justice of the death sentence. God is simply willing to cancel a perfectly just sentence for a capital offence. Such mercy would be quite incomprehensible in any system of justice based on the pagan concept of equity.

One reason that critics such as William Nelson and W. Nicholas Knight equate equity with mercy in their interpretations of Book V may be that Renaissance legal authorities made no consistent distinction between the two concepts. Professor Knight informs me that the terms "equity," "clemency," and "mercy" are often used interchangeably in the legal documents of the period. But Spenser is more precise in his usage. In the body of his works, there are more than thirty instances in which the term "mercy" means forgiveness extended to someone who truly deserves to be punished.[18] I have found no instances in which mercy is given because the code of justice is inadequate for the case at hand and must be set aside in order to render what is due. Even on the battlefield, a plea for mercy often presupposes a Christian system of ethics. The conquered knight is supposed to confess that he is in the wrong, repent of his hostile acts, and pledge to give his conqueror faithful service in the future.[19] Of course, Spenser was following the accepted code of chivalry in such cases, but in several passages, he reveals an awareness of the religious origins of such battlefield justice. In Book VI, for example, Sir Calidore makes a clear distinction between what he calls "mercy" and what is justly "due" to a conquered enemy. After defeating the evil knight Crudor, Calidore tells the wretch,

> Who will not mercie unto others shew,
>   How can he mercy ever hope to have?
> To pay each with his owne is right and dew.
> Yet since ye mercie now doe need to crave,
> I will it graunt, your hopelesse life to save.
>   (VI.i.42; see also II.v.12–13)

Behind such acts of beneficence lie the injunctions of Christ: "Love your enemies"; "Be ye . . . merciful, as your Father also is merciful"; "Forgive, and ye shall be forgiven" (Luke 6.35–37).

In contrast to this sort of free forgiveness, Spenser treats equity as a way to "measure out" precisely what is due. At the opening of Book V, the poet explains the lesson in justice and equity that Astraea gave to Artegall. She taught him

> to weigh both right and wrong
> In equall ballance with due recompence,
> And equitie to measure out along,
> According to the line of conscience,
> When so it needs with rigour to dispence.   (V.i.7)

Never, in any of Spenser's poems, is mercy treated in this way as a careful measurement of what is due.

Another reason that critics may have found it difficult to distinguish between the equity of Isis and the mercy of Mercilla is that Mercilla represents Spenser's ideal of justice in all its parts. At her feet is the sword of justice, and in her hand is the royal scepter, which Spenser associates with equity, calling it "the sacred pledge of peace and clemencie" (ix.30). In some cases, such as that of the poet Malfont, she simply hands down the harsh sentence "adjudged . . . by law" (ix.25). In others, she judges according to the classical concept of equity. The trial of Duessa is of this second sort: as the sovereign queen of Scotland, Mary Stuart could not be tried under English common law, and therefore Elizabeth appointed a special commission to act in her case as a court of equity.

But mercy also came into Mary's case. The English queen had two options in the trial: she could accept the equitable judgment of the commission, which was that Mary deserved death for her "vyld treasons" (ix.40), or Elizabeth could invoke Christian mercy and forgive Mary. Now, it was a common notion in the Renaissance that a monarch ought not to extend mercy to defendants in cases involving crimes against persons other than the monarch himself. But if the crimes in question were altogether against the person of the monarch, then the ruler had the option of extending mercy and pardoning the defendant, even if the defendant were guilty and deserved punishment. The sixteenth-century legal authority Jaques Hurault stated the matter succinctly when he wrote, "A prince ought to be merciful, [but] this mercie consisteth in pardonning the offences that concern but the prince himselfe, and the partie that is hurt by them, and not any other mens that are done against the common-weale."[20] Elizabeth was indeed disposed to take advantage of this doctrine of mercy; at the time of the trial, she said explicitly that, if Mary repented of her attempts to overthrow her, Elizabeth would pardon and remit her offense.[21]

Yet Mary would not repent. She refused to acknowledge any guilt for her part in the Babington Plot, the attempt against Elizabeth for which she was tried, and she declined to ask pardon of Elizabeth.[22] In such a case, Elizabeth's hands were tied: not only was she under intense political pressure to execute Mary, but she was also in a moral dilemma. The biblical form of mercy can only be offered in case the offender repents and asks for forgiveness. Elizabeth could rightly set aside the punishment adjudged by the court of equity, but only if Mary humbled herself and approached the mercy seat. And Mary refused. For our purposes, the important point is that Elizabeth was disposed to grant mercy. To express her merciful intention, Spenser portrays Mercilla in tears, and it would be unfair to conclude that she is simply expressing vain pity when she might have acted more effectually. The poet himself gives a clue to the proper interpretation of her weeping when he notes that it expressed "more then needfull naturall remorse" (x.4). These are tears of Christian charity, and they are indeed worth making a fuss about, for they are the only proper expression of mercy possible in this case.

The episodes at Isis Church and Mercilla's palace are part of a larger pattern that runs through the whole of Book V. At the outset, the poet is preoccupied with the greatest problem of justice of them all: what to do with an utterly depraved and fallen world (V.Pr.). Astraea, the Queen of Justice who departed from the world at the end of the Silver Age, has left Artegall to rule over a world fast falling toward the Ages of Brass and Stone. In the course of the book, we work our way back through the Age of Brass, represented by Artegall's early adventures, and in canto vii we come again to the Age of Silver, represented by the silver goddess Isis. The equity of

Britomart is now to subdue the harsh, Brass Age justice of Artegall. But the final stage in the return to the Golden World requires a new dispensation of Christian grace, and this is presented in the allegorical figure of Mercilla. She represents Spenser's ideal of perfect, divine justice.[23] In a fallen world, mere equity will not do, for if God judged men by what is due to them, the sentence would invariably be death. If there is to be a return to the Golden Age of Astraea, then legal justice and equity must be placed at the feet of Christian mercy.

Virginia Polytechnic Institute and State University

NOTES

1. William Nelson, *The Poetry of Edmund Spenser: A Study* (New York: Columbia University Press, 1963), pp. 267–71; W. Nicholas Knight, "The Narrative Unity of Book V of *The Faerie Queene*: 'That Part of Justice Which is Equity,'" *RES* n.s., 21 (1970), 267–94.

2. For an analysis that stresses the importance of Mercilla's court, see T. K. Dunseath, *Spenser's Allegory of Justice in Book Five of "The Faerie Queene"* (Princeton, N.J.: Princeton University Press, 1968), pp. 204–19.

3. See Angus Fletcher, *The Prophetic Moment: An Essay on Spenser* (Chicago: University of Chicago Press, 1971), pp. 259–87; and Kathleen Williams, *Spenser's World of Glass: A Reading of "The Faerie Queene"* (Berkeley and Los Angeles: University of California Press, 1966), pp. 172, 176.

4. Thomas Cain, *Praise in "The Faerie Queene"* (Lincoln: University of Nebraska Press, 1978), pp. 141–46.

5. Michael O'Connell, *Mirror and Veil: The Historical Dimension of Spenser's "Faerie Queene"* (Chapel Hill: University of North Carolina Press, 1977), p. 154.

6. For another interpretation of Spenser's allegory of justice that also emphasizes the distinction between equity and mercy, see J. E. Phillips, "Renaissance Concepts of Justice and the Structure of *The Faerie Queene*, Book V," *HLQ* 34 (1970), 103–20. I have reservations about the definition of mercy that Phillips draws from Lipsius, Elyot, and Hurault, for it is not distinctively Christian and so does not quite match Spenser's usage.

7. I follow the text of *The Faerie Queene*, ed. A. C. Hamilton (New York: Longman, 1977). Archaic spelling inverting *i* and *j*, *u* and *v* has been modernized.

8. A. Kent Hieatt, *Chaucer, Spenser, Milton: Mythopoeic Continuities and Transformations* (Montreal: McGill–Queen's University Press, 1975), pp. 135–45.

9. On the use of this tripartite division of justice in Renaissance legal theory, see Phillips, "Renaissance Concepts of Justice," p. 105. It may seem odd that the king's role should be taught by a queen, but Mercilla represents Elizabeth and hence is one of the unusual cases permitted in Spenser's theory.

10. See Hamilton's edition, ix.28.n.

11. Frank Kermode, *Shakespeare, Spenser, Donne* (London: Routledge and Kegan Paul, 1971), p. 56. As one might expect, lions have an extraordinarily rich set of meanings in Renaissance iconography, but the meaning that Spenser emphasizes most clearly is the union of

justice and equity. For other associations, see Jane Aptekar, *Icons of Justice: Iconography and Thematic Imagery in Book V of "The Faerie Queene"* (New York: Columbia University Press, 1969), pp. 58–69.

12. See Homer's *Iliad* 9.502–12. One of their traditional roles is to carry the prayers of the afflicted to those who have caused the suffering. If the injustice is corrected, the Litae beg Jove for a lighter sentence upon the wrongdoers, but if not, they call for the wrath of the goddess Áté. Spenser emphasizes their role in suing for "pardon and remission" (ix.31–32).

13. See Hamilton's edition, ix.22–29.n., and Cain, *Praise in "The Faerie Queene,"* pp. 138–40.

14. Others have noticed some of the Catholic details, particularly this use of the word "Mas." See D. Douglas Waters, "Spenser and the 'Mas' at the Temple of Isis," *SEL* 19 (1979), 43–53; and Clifford Davidson, "The Idol at Isis Church," *SP* 66 (1969), 72–73. Waters attempts to prove that the word "Mas" and the idol and vestments that appear in the temple would not necessarily have suggested to Spenser's readers the offensive ceremonial practices of the Roman church, but a survey of the Parker Society editions of works from the English Reformation will reveal, I think, a nearly unfailing association of these things with Catholicism. Davidson acknowledges the association but does not attempt to explain its significance. His argument is that the episode teaches Britomart a new dispensation of Christian love with which to correct Artegall's Mosaic legalism.

15. See Edwin Sandys, *Sermons,* ed. Rev. John Ayre (Cambridge: The Parker Society, 1841), p. 180: "As Christ hath delivered all his out of the captivity of Satan and sin, so hath he also us after a more special and peculiar manner out of that den of thieves, out of that prison of Romish servitude. . . . Our God hath used our Moses to deliver us from Egyptiacal servitude, that we may serve him henceforward in freedom of conscience." See also John Jewel, *Works,* ed. Rev. John Ayre, 4 vols. (Cambridge: The Parker Society, 1845–50), vol. 4, p. 880; John Bradford, "A Meditation upon the Ten Commandments," in *Writings,* ed. Aubrey Townsend, 2 vols. (Cambridge: The Parker Society, 1848–53), vol. 1, pp. 149–53; Thomas Becon, *Catechism,* ed. Rev. John Ayre (Cambridge: The Parker Society, 1846), pp. 57–58. Both Bradford and Becon begin a discussion of the Ten Commandments with comments on the flight from Egypt; they then allude to Catholic practices in this context, as if Rome is to be considered a contemporary Egypt.

16. See J. E. Neale, *Queen Elizabeth I: A Biography* (New York: Doubleday, 1957), pp. 33–35.

17. See Fletcher, *The Prophetic Moment,* pp. 280–84; and James Nohrnberg, *The Analogy of "The Faerie Queene"* (Princeton, N.J.: Princeton University Press, 1976), pp. 382–85.

18. See, for example, II.ii.40–41; II.viii.1; III.v.35; V.x.1–5; VI.i.42–43. See also *An Hymne of Heavenly Love,* 204–24. In *An Hymne of Heavenly Beautie,* 134 ff., Spenser pictures the Lord on his mercy seat, and the account is similar in many respects to the description of Mercilla on her throne in V.ix.27–35.

19. See, for example, II.v.12–13.

20. Cited by Phillips, "Renaissance Concepts of Justice," p. 114. See also Sandys, *Sermons,* pp. 147, 229; and Hugh Latimer, *Works,* ed. George Elwes Corrie, 2 vols. (Cambridge: The Parker Society, 1844–45), vol. 1, pp. 484–85.

21. See Neale, *Queen Elizabeth I,* pp. 285–86.

22. See Neale, *Queen Elizabeth I,* pp. 286–87.

23. For details linking Mercilla with Astraea, see Francis A. Yates, "Elizabeth as Astraea," *Journal of the Warburg and Courtauld Institute* 10 (1947), 65–70.

EAMON GRENNAN

Language and Politics:
A Note on Some Metaphors in Spenser's
A View of the Present State of Ireland

*A*S A sonnet sequence like Sidney's *Astrophel and Stella* or as any of Shakespeare's plays will show, the problem of the relationship between language and reality is very much alive in the late sixteenth and early seventeenth centuries. It is "words, words, words," that Hamlet reads; Troilus tears up the letter from Cressida because it is "words, words, mere words, no matter from the heart"; Cordelia is banished because she "cannot heave her heart into her mouth" as her sisters can; and Lear's pilgrimage carries him from the elaborate language of Titans to the simple acknowledgment of "fair daylight," "I feel this pin prick," and "Be your tears wet?"

An especially revealing version of the problem appears in the relationship between political actuality and the language used to talk about it. In *Julius Caesar,* Shakespeare provides a paradigm for this in Brutus's remarkable meditation upon the reasons for killing Caesar (2.1.10–34).[1] Throughout his soliloquy the philosophic assassin again and again abuses logic, not only in the shifting moods of the verbs, but also in the particular use to which certain metaphors are put. "It is the bright day that brings forth the adder," thinks Brutus, "And that craves wary walking." On one level the observation is a cluster of undeniable facts. As Brutus's next words make clear, it also functions as deliberate metaphor: "Crown him that, / And then I grant we put a sting in him." Caesar becomes a venomous serpent, and his assassination logically follows this metamorphosis:

> And therefore think him as a serpent's egg
> Which, hatch'd, would as his kind grow mischievous,
> And kill him in the shell.

Buttressed by metaphor, political theory can enter the world of political fact with profound, logical simplicity: "Therefore . . . kill him."

By means of a biological-zoological figure, Brutus convinces himself of the necessity of a supposedly analogous political act. The metaphor functions implicitly as argument, drawing one unobtrusively between areas that are not in point of fact related. This moment and the dramatic action of *Julius Caesar* as a whole cast ironic shadows on Brutus's character and its decisions, shadows that throw into telling relief the troubled relationship between political action and a certain kind of rhetoric. As literary critics we may easily assess this fact and speak of it in the comfortable idioms of literary judgement and interpretation. A recent reading of Spenser's *View of the Present State of Ireland,* however, was a salutary reminder to me of the existence of this fact in the world beyond the specifically "literary." Reading Spenser's pragmatic account of the political-military campaign and his plan for a successful conclusion to the whole Elizabethan "Irish Question," I was struck by the way his use of some extremely conventional metaphors (conventional in political discourse, that is) did not so much illustrate the situation as compose a justifying "ground" for the political enterprise as a whole. And while no such calculated ironies as those that alert us to the difficulties of Brutus's position can be supposed to operate in Spenser's text, I was further struck by the fact that *these metaphors themselves* exposed inherent difficulties regarding the use to which Spenser wished to put them, difficulties serious enough to suggest that the view of the world out of which they grow (essentially a world view finding its expression in a certain sort of political theory) is not in necessary accord with the world of political fact to which they are applied.

I

The metaphors in question are drawn from two related areas — the agricultural and the medical. They deal with the natural world and the human body, and use both in a conventional way as similitudes for certain aspects of the state. Edward Forset provides a clear statement of the assumptions on which, for the common understanding of the time, such conventional associations rest:

> Seeing that the uttermost extent of mans understanding, can shape no better forms of ordering the affayres of a State, than by marking and matching of the workes of the finger of God, eyther in the larger volume of the universall, or in the abridgement thereof, the body of man: I account these two to be the two great lights for enquiry and meditation concerning this business [of government].[2]

The appearance of such metaphors in a work like the *View,* therefore, is in no way unexpected. Their very conventionality, however, often blinds to what they are actually doing. Such blindness has a particularly serious consequence in a work that is not theoretical but practical, a "view," as the title insists, of the *present state* of Ireland, "by way of conference," as Irenius (Spenser's persona) says, "to declare my simple opinion for redress thereof, and establishing a good course for that government."[3]

Spenser's use of the agricultural metaphor is implicitly justified by his recurrent presentation of the Irish as being in a state of wild nature that needs cultivation to perfect it. Ireland is always "that savage nation" (p. 91), its people "stubborn and untamed" (p. 4), of "savage life" (p. 156) and "brutish behaviour" (p. 156); they exist in a "beastly manner of life and savage condition" (pp. 82–83). Even the Irish moustache (the "glib") bears the marks of a "savage brutishness" (p. 53). It is an easy transition from here to the metaphorical notion of the Irish as uncultivated ground in which a civil state must be planted, a notion appearing incidentally and generally throughout the work. Henry II decided to "plant a peaceable government" among the Irish rather than to "pluck them under" by force (p. 10). There is talk of "planting of laws and plotting of policies" (p. 12), as well as of the fact that "without first cutting off this dangerous custom, it seemeth hard to plant any sound ordinance" (p. 9). The general plan for the establishment of a proper (i.e., English) political system, involves, in the elaborate blueprint for colonization and plantation, a return to literal fact of this particular metaphor.

Apart from its obviously conventional nature, an important if unconscious motive for the use of this metaphor must lie in its essentially benevolent implications. Husbandry is a pacific art, thriving on peace: "Bella execrata colonia — it is most enemy to war and hateth unquietness" (p. 157).[4] In tune with nature, husbandry is also a sufficient sign of the providential moral order as this is reflected in the order of nature. The state is purified to its ideal condition by the implications of this metaphor, as the emblematic (though ironic) garden scene in *Richard II* is enough to demonstrate. It is by husbandry that the brigands of Book VI of *The Faerie Queene* are to be redeemed, just as the thieves, rebels, villains, and "patchocks" among the Irish will be drawn by the "sweetness and happy contentment" of husbandry away from "their wonted lewd life in thiefery and roguery" (p. 157).

Lurking behind the plant metaphor is the unexamined assumption that the relationship between the Irish and the English parallels that between the husbandman and his land. A consequence of this figure is the right assumed by one group of people to establish an ordering and, from their point of view, productive mastery over another group. The extension of the metaphor to the animal world brings this notion of the natural right to rule into even sharper focus.

As with the plant metaphor, practical justification for the animal metaphor may be found in Irenius's description of the Irish. Many of the Irish, says Irenius, are accustomed "to live themselves the most part of the year in Bollies, pasturing upon the mountains and waste wild places . . . to live in herds as they call them" (p. 49). The very houses of the Irish, he asserts elsewhere, "commonly are rather swinesteads than houses," where the Irishman is to be found "lying and living with his beast in one room and in one bed, that is the clean straw, or rather the foul dunghill" (pp. 82–83).

Armed with such facts, the writer can make an easy transition to his figurative treatment of the Irish as animals, the negative connotations of which are clear from the following examples. The presence of the governor among the governed is "a great stay and bridle to them that are ill disposed" (p. 132). The Hibernicised Normans are condemned as "proud hearts" who "do oftentimes like wanton colts kick at their mothers," and who have bitten "off her dug from which they sucked life" (p. 65). A similar critical purpose is clear in the description of the Irish living in the hills, who "think themselves half exempted from law and obedience, and having once tasted freedom do, like a steer that hath been long out of his yoke, grudge and repine ever after to come under rule again" (p. 50).

The assumptions underlying this group of metaphors concern the hierarchical order of natural subordination. Because man is the apex and epitome of creation, it is his natural, God-given right to subdue to his own ends the creatures of the earth. Since the divinely imbued "principall" of the horse, for example, "is a loving and dutifull inclination to the service of man,"[5] it is man's natural and, given this particular world view, moral right to curtail the freedom of such beasts in order to put them to the use for which God intended them. By means of the syllogism implicit in a metaphor which invokes a certain kind of world, the governing power claims a natural right to act upon the freedom of a subordinate (albeit unwilling) people. The metaphor, therefore, is a purposeful rhetorical gesture extending far beyond its merely illustrative function. In this metaphorical language, the political commitment becomes as persuasive, authoritative, and value-laden as the natural truth sanctioned by belief.

A distinguishing feature of this metaphorical language is its adaptability, moving the reader unhindered between natural and moral categories. Morally neutral in the context of horse, both "wanton" and "ill-disposed" take on moral overtones in the human world. In the longer of the above quotations, the moral language of "law and obedience" as used in the human world becomes a physical language of "yoke" as used in the animal world (trailing some allegorical edges that enable it also to function in the moral human world), which in turn becomes the more abstract and explicitly political "rule," a word at home in either world. By means of such plasticity of language, the justice of a specific kind of rule in the political world has been persuasively presented in the colors of a simple truth drawn from the natural world. The ambiguous political enterprise is guaranteed by the unarguable natural facts: metaphor has become moral argument.

Spenser's use of the metaphor of the body politic may be seen in a similar light. In substance the metaphor presents the Irish state and its members as a diseased body, casting the English governors in the role of physicians. In general and incidental usage, the metaphor may be found throughout the *View.* Laws are constantly likened to physic. Their administration is as problematic as the treatment of an illness, which often

> either through ignorance of the disease, or unseasonableness of the time, or other accidents coming between, instead of good it worketh hurt, and out of one evil, throweth the patient into many miseries.
> (P. 3)

A law can be "too violent a medicine" (32); it can be "very evil surgery," and overzealously

> cut off every unsound or sick part of the body, which being by other means due recovered, might afterwards do very good service to the body again, and happily help to save the whole. (P. 81)

The most virulent disease of the body politic is rebellion. During Lord Grey's time, says Irenius, "there was no part free from the contagion" (p. 19). To settle (cure) a state afflicted by such illness, the whole task of government is to prescribe and then apply what amounts to a complete medical regimen:

> the which method we may learn of the wise physicians which require that the malady be known thoroughly and discovered, afterwards do teach how to cure and redress it, and lastly do prescribe a diet with strait rules and orders to be daily observed, for fear of relapse into the former disease or falling into some other more dangerous than it. (Pp. 2–3)

When one governor altered the administrative system of his predecessor, this "manner of government could not be sound and wholesome for the realm" argues Irenius. For it is, he goes on,

> even as two physicians should take one sick body in hand at two sundry times, of which the former would minister all things meet to

purge and keep under the body, the other to pamper and strengthen
it suddenly again.   (P. 109)

Employed politically, this metaphor, like its agricultural counterpart,
tacitly sanctions the colonial enterprise. Both grow out of the assumption
that within the exactitude and economy of God's creation the state is an
organic body analogous in its composition to the natural world and to the
human body. Just as God cured and colonized chaos so as to bring from it
the healthy, orderly body of this universe, and just as the physician brings
the patient's diseased body, that little world, to health, so the wise governor leads the body politic from the chaos of rebellion, the sickness of state,
to the healthy, rational order of *his* political system. Therefore, it is natural, rational, and moral for the governing power to colonize the sick and
savage state. Political colonization, a phenomenon with ethical implications, is obliquely guaranteed by a rhetorical conjunction that ignores the
gap between biological fact and political opinion. As with those drawn
from the agricultural world, this metaphor also functions as a rhetorically
purposeful purification of the adversary relationship between one political
group and another. Metaphor has again become the agent of moral justification, and what is an essentially linguistic reality functions with a clear
conscience as the instrument of actual political oppression.

II

The preceding examples illustrate the ordinary and, as it were, theoretical use of these metaphors in the *View*. It is clear, however, that so used
they ignore some inherent difficulties. A few of these have already been
noted; I now turn to the more serious among them.

Difficulties attending the use of the animal metaphor are of a fairly simple kind. They may be adequately illustrated by the following quotation:
"But what boots it," asks Irenius,

to break a colt and to let him straight run loose at random? So were
this people at first well handled and wisely brought to acknowledge
allegiance to the kings of England, but being straight left unto
themselves and their own inordinate life and manners, they eftsones
forgot what before they were taught, and so soon as they were out
of sight by themselves shook off their bridles and began to colt
anew, more licentiously than before.   (P. 6)

The unspoken purpose of this metaphor is to establish a persuasively negative attitude towards "this people." The introductory rhetorical question

invites easy agreement with an unarguable truth about the natural world. The "so" and the "well handled" translates "this people" into a metaphorical "colt." By doing so, the speaker immediately casts his political opinion into the form of a natural fact, namely, the hierarchical subordination of animal to man. Translated into such a context, the political (and moral) opinions embedded in the adjectives and adverbs ("well," "wisely," "inordinate," "licentiously") become as persuasive as the natural beliefs invoked by the metaphor. In such a context, too, positive value attaches to passive forms of the verb ("handled," "brought," "taught"), while the active forms all possess negative overtones ("run loose at random," "forgot," "shook off," "colt"). While these are acceptable in the assumed hierarchical world of human-animal relationships, in the political world to which we are to apply them they serve as a rhetorical argument in favor of the right of one people to deprive another of its freedom.

In spite of its linguistic energy, however (for example, "colt" used as a verb), this metaphor buckles a bit when applied to the world of political actuality. In words like "inordinate" and "licentiously," for example, the far more usual moral human meaning outweighs to the point of eliminating the simple physical significance attaching to such words in an equestrian context. In addition, while it is easy to say what "handled" and "bridles" mean in this latter context, it is difficult to establish their precise meanings in the world of political action to which they metaphorically refer. And it is this very imprecision which blurs such moral considerations as might attend the exercise of force for political ends.

The problems involved with Spenser's use of the plant metaphors are even more revealing and, it might be said, sinister in their implications. When Eudoxus asks how the necessary task of reformation can be started, Irenius replies:

> Even by the sword, for all those evils must first be cut away with a strong hand before any good can be planted, like as the corrupt branches and the unwholesome boughs are first to be pruned, and the foul moss cleansed or scraped away, before the tree can bring forth any good fruit. (P. 95)

Beginning in the hard world of political fact ("sword"), the statement quickly softens into the metaphorical idiom of political theory. The state is a tree, the military governor a wise husbandman. The plastic language of the metaphor enables the speaker to deal with political actuality in terms of moral abstraction ("evils," "corrupt," "foul," "good") and agricultural concreteness ("branches," "boughs," "moss," "fruit"), both of which draw attention from whatever difficult associations might adhere to "sword."

The sword is metaphorically beaten into a pruning knife and its violent implications disappear into the natural biological benevolence of an act done for the benefit of the tree. The metaphor translates the actual world into a world of theoretical design. That the metaphor encounters difficulty in the world of political actuality, however, is obvious not only at our clarifying distance but also to the other participant in the dialogue. Eudoxus refers to this solution as a violent "medicine." He then resists the preceding benign translation of sword: "Is not the sword the most violent redress that may be used for any evil?" he asks. That Spenser, although his persona is Irenius, includes this interrogation at all suggests that he is at least aware of the critical pressure on this particular use of the metaphor. What follows, therefore, looks like the most obvious attempt on his part to validate one of the important rhetorical components of his text. Forced to justify his means, he turns to the language he has used. "By the sword which I named," he says,

> I do not mean the cutting off of all that nation with the sword, which far be it from me that ever I should think so desperately or wish so uncharitably, but by the sword I mean the royal power of the prince, which ought to stretch itself forth in her chief strength, to the redressing and cutting off of those evils which I before blamed, and not of the people which are evil; for evil people by good ordinance and government may be made good, but the evil that is of itself evil will never become good. (P. 95)

Like Shakespeare's Brutus debating the assassination of Caesar, Irenius is obviously at great pains to make the language mean what he wants it to mean, to have it bend the world to a shape and a meaning corresponding to his desire and need. The speaker's growing difficulty appears in the increasingly theoretical nature of his language. Instead of a theory comfortably embodied in the metaphor of the state as a tree, however, it is expressed with much more difficulty (and less conviction) by the abstract distinctions between "evil people" and "the evil that is of itself evil," or in the equally abstract, almost emblematic identification between the "sword" and the "royal power of the prince." But the struggle implicit here between fact and a certain sort of language remains unresolved by such a strategy. For on Eudoxus' demand for clarification of "that sword which you mean" (which has already been changed into "the royal power of the prince"), the sword is further transformed into "a strong power [company] of men" (p. 95). The passage reveals a rhetorical progression from fact (sword) to metaphor (pruning knife) to abstraction (royal power) back to fact (strong power of men), meaning many swords. In the same circular way, the factual "evils" first mentioned by Irenius (referring to the actual "troubles" of fomenting "rebellion," see p. 94) become in turn the metaphorical "corrupt branches" and "unwholesome boughs," then the abstract "evil that is of itself evil," which in a subsequent passage joins the world of fact again and becomes "all that rebellious rout of loose people which either do now stand out in open arms or in wandering companies do keep the woods spoiling and infesting the good subject" (pp. 95–96).

This sort of linguistic juggling shows that the metaphorical language proper to and acceptable in a rhetoric of theory and belief cannot endure in the more problematic context of political fact. Clearly the discussion at this point centers on the applicability of a certain kind of language to a certain kind of fact. Perhaps the strongest proof that such applicability is in serious doubt is that it is precisely at this stress-point that Irenius abandons the metaphorical rhetoric of belief and resorts to the rhetoric of prescriptive fact. He turns, that is, to the cooler, more convincing medium of numbers, pragmatic tactics, and considerations of an entirely practical kind (see p. 96 ff.). In other words, the benevolent ideal embodied by the original metaphor must bend to the practical necessities of a military campaign, for coping expressively with which the rhetoric of fact is perfectly adequate. The unacknowledged irony, however (an irony dramatically discovered by Shakespeare in Brutus's speech but essentially evaded by the way Spenser conducts his debate), is that the implicit philosophical-ethical guarantor of this political campaign is the failed metaphorical rhetoric itself. It is, as we have seen, the view of the world locked into these metaphors that sanctions and justifies this particular kind of political enterprise. At its deepest level, then, Spenser's struggle here suggests the difficulties and contradictions inherent in any attempt to talk about contemporary political actuality in the idiom of traditional political (and, in a larger sense, cultural) belief.

The medical metaphor provides the final illustration of these difficulties. In traditional political theory the governor's need to rule by punishment is often likened to the doctor's need to hurt the body in order to heal it. "To conclude this point of health," says Edward Forset in a section entitled "We may hurt to heale,"

it is so precious and of so unvaluable a worth, as that when it is not so perfect as wee would have it, or when it is somewhat impaired, we do not stick willingly to do to our selves farther hurt, to the end to heale our infirmities the more soundly. . . . So in our bodie of the Commonweale it is not to be disliked, that (though there be no great fault found, and all things seeme to stand in good order) yet now and then physicall courses be used, by opening some veine, by purging of superfluities, and putting to payne some part thereof, for the more certeintie of the generall good.[6]

Since the "body politic" is a bloodless fiction, such a similitude in theory is perfectly appropriate. Used in the actual context assumed by the *View,* however, the moral propriety as well as the accuracy of the metaphor is open to question.

Because of a change in physician/governors, the body politic that is Ireland has suffered a "most dangerous relapse" and is "now more dangerously sick than ever before" (p. 109). Within the confines of theory the kind of surgical rigour necessary to cure such a condition is easily acceptable. It develops problems, however, in the actual world invoked by Spenser's text. Having described the country as "one sick body" and its governors as "physicians" (p. 109), Irenius goes on to say:

> Therefore, by all means it must be foreseen and assured that after once entering into this course of reformation, there be afterwards no remorse or drawing back, for the sight of any such rueful object as must thereupon follow nor for compassion of their calamities, seeing that by no other means it is possible to recure them and that these are not of will, but of very urgent necessity. (P. 110)

Because of what turns out to be an essential contradiction between the substance and meaning of this metaphor, the passage in general reveals the breakdown in functional capacity of this kind of rhetoric used in an actual political context. First, under the pressure of the actual situation, the speaker alters his earlier medical terminology to the more explicitly political "course of reformation." Then, in place of a diction expressive of the natural distate a doctor feels for the pain he must inflict, he uses a language bespeaking qualms of a rather different kind: "remorse," "drawing back," and "compassion" carry overtones that move beyond the physical and into the ethical area. "Rueful object," and "calamities" remove us even further from the comfortable confines of the exclusively medical metaphor, while the plural "their" and "them" unconsciously translates the "one sick body" politic mentioned earlier into the multiple bodies of those members of the state who must be killed. In the context of such obvious difficulties the return to the pure state of the metaphor in the explicitly medical "recure" (especially with "them" as object) is strikingly (and unintentionally) ironic. For in its mutations the metaphor simply alerts us to the fact that its metaphorical and actual content are contradictory—one signifying restoration to health, the other deprivation of life.

The question remains as to how conscious Spenser was of the kinds of difficulty I'm talking about. Even from the internal evidence of the above passage it seems to me that, while he was not unaware of the problem, he chose (presumably because of the nature of his particular task) to ignore, evade, or (which may amount to the same thing) arbitrarily resolve it. For the passage is riddled with gestures of assertive logicality, from the conclusive "therefore" that initiates it, to the indisputable insistence of "as must thereupon follow" and "seeing that by no other means it is possible." In addition, the speaker also appeals to the transcendent logic of some enforcing fate, allowing "will" (presumably the governor's) to abdicate to "very urgent necessity." It is not the only time in the course of this entire argument that such appeals are made (see, for example, pp. 105, 106, 108). Their frequency, in fact, brings to mind Milton's description of necessity as "the tyrant's plea." As far as the above quotation is concerned, it is also hard not to be reminded again of Shakespeare's Brutus, who begins his examination of the possible reasons for Caesar's murder with the conclusive "It must be by his death," and who proceeds from there to extract justification from some instrumental metaphors.

What happens in the text immediately following the passage I have examined above may be read as confirmation of my argument. For, as with the agricultural metaphors, the hint of the failure or insufficiency of this kind of rhetoric pushes the discussion into pragmatism, into the rhetoric of fact. In this instance the movement is to Eudoxus' straightforward account of the actual problems to be confronted in administering the system. What betrays the strategy as an evasive one is the oddly abrupt way it elbows into the text, without any obvious transition between it ("Thus far then ye have now proceeded to plant your garrisons," p. 110) and the passage I have already quoted which it immediately follows. In addition, the actual problems mentioned by Eudoxus are revealing. These mainly consist of the "corruption of captains," a corruption in no way metaphorical but the simple fact of embezzlement. This leads in turn to a practical account of the duties and responsibilities of the colonel in preventing such corruption, and comes to rest, again, in numbers (see pp. 110–11). Where metaphor falters as the agent of moral justification the text resorts to the indisputable rhetoric of fact uncomplicated by any moral considerations whatsoever.

III

By analyzing one of the rhetorical components of Spenser's text in this way, I have tried to suggest something of the condition and viability at a particular historical moment of certain ways of talking about political experience. This, in turn, is a small but important feature in a larger shift in

EAMON GRENNAN

cultural sensibility concerning the relationship between language and the world, a concern to be found in many explicitly literary texts of the period. Michel Foucault describes this culture shift in part as follows: "The profound kinship of language with the world was thus dissolved. . . . Things and words were to be separated from one another."[7] Dealing as it does with a nonliterary text, my discussion may afford some insight into the reasons for Bacon's impatience with certain schematic modes of thought as these are represented in a rhetoric that obfuscated instead of clarifying the world of things, of nature. For "the human understanding," laments Bacon, is

> prone to suppose the existence of more order and regularity in the world than it finds. And though there be many things in nature which are singular and unmatched, yet it devises for them parallels and conjugates and relatives which do not exist.[8]

That the poet of *The Faerie Queene,* in his capacity as a colonial civil servant, shows himself in *A View of the Present State of Ireland* to be a comparatively uncritical employer of such language may provoke us to consider in an even more thoughtful way rhetorical, aesthetic, historical, and moral assumptions that inform his immeasurably more important poetic text.

Vassar College

NOTES

1. *The Riverside Shakespeare,* ed. G. Blakemore Evans et al. (Boston: Houghton Mifflin, 1974).

2. Edward Forset, "To the Reader," *A Comparative Discourse of the Bodies Natural and Politique* (London, 1606; rpt. New York: Da Capo Press, 1973), p. 2.

3. Edmund Spenser, *A View of the Present State of Ireland,* ed. W. L. Renwick (Oxford: Clarendon Press, 1970) p. 169. Subsequent references will be given in the text.

4. *Colonia* shows how this metaphor stands as justifying agent at the very heart of the colonial enterprise—politics moralized by etymology.

5. Edward Topsell, *The Historie of Foure-Footed Beastes* (London, 1607; rpt. New York: Da Capo Press, 1973), p. 281.

6. Forset, *Comparative Discourse,* p. 70.

7. Michel Foucault, *An Archeology of the Human Sciences* (London: Tavistock, 1966), p. 43.

8. Francis Bacon, *Novum Organum,* book 1, aphorism 45, in *The Works of Francis Bacon,* ed. James Spedding, Robert L. Ellis, and Douglas D. Heath (London: Longmans, 1901), vol. 4, p. 55.

DONALD CHENEY

Tarquin, Juliet, and Other *Romei*

OTH OVERTLY and more cryptically as well, references to the protagonists and incidents of Roman history appear throughout Shakespeare's
works, becoming essential elements of his dramatic vocabulary. This essay
proposes to look at the imagery of two early works, *The Rape of Lucrece*
and *Romeo and Juliet,* in the context of Shakespeare's Roman sources and
his own later Roman plays, and to consider how his vision of Rome may
have figured in the evolution of his language. These earlier works begin to
elaborate the great Shakespearean microcosmic metaphor whereby an individual is seen as besieged city or household, darkly sharing and conspiring
with the enemy forces that seek to ravish and enthrall it. In ways that reason rejects (and the language of the young Shakespeare cannot always accommodate), tyrants and victims alike move from obsession to compulsion, knowing that they are participating in their self-destruction while
remaining powerless to escape what seems the fulfillment of time's promise.

In the case of *Lucrece,* the operation of this microcosmic metaphor is
relatively obvious, for the same reason that modern readers may find it dis-
tasteful: attorneys for the Tarquins of this world have traditionally relied on
more or less blatant forms of it. Thus it is suggested that both Collatine and
his wife share some responsibility for the rape, the former as "publisher /
Of that rich jewel" of his wife's chastity, and the latter as possessor of a
chaste beauty which "itself doth of itself persuade / The eyes of men without an orator." Like Troy itself, Lucrece's mere existence is an invitation to
destruction; she is perhaps unlike Troy in that her destruction is simultaneously the tragedy of her ravisher. On the other hand, although Friar
Laurence's dream of reconciling warring households anticipates a similar
dream on a more heroic and public scale in *Antony and Cleopatra,* readers
have tended to discount much of the portentous and grandiloquent imagery of *Romeo and Juliet* as expressive of the lovers' (or Shakespeare's) youthful exuberance. As a consequence, the degree to which this is a play about
star-crossed lovers and fatal loins has not always been apparent. I want to
suggest that on closer examination the play may be seen to contain some
of those complex, involuted metaphors for self, time, or history which appear as more explicitly Roman motifs in the later works. Rome figures
not only in the first syllable of Romeo's name but also in an implicit

association of Juliet with the *gens Julia,* and in a metaphor of pilgrimage as fatal entry into a holy but forbidden city. Shakespeare's early writings differ from the mode of dramatic "incarnation" generally found in his mature style, and rely more on verbal conceits and a texture of literary allusions which they share with other poets of the 1590s such as Spenser; but they share with the later plays a common set of themes and images.

Thematic discussion of Shakespeare's Rome normally and usefully starts from his Roman plays, especially perhaps those two plays most frequently performed and most immediately concerned with the emergence of Rome's imperial identity. *Julius Caesar* and *Antony* demonstrate a pattern of historical necessity that might be called Vergilian in its sense of the human cost of political stability; it is this pattern, doubtless, that most critics think of when speaking of Shakespeare's myth of Rome. The Rome of these plays is both an invincible political machine and a state of the spirit in which the demands of heroic self-denial have created, or come to symbolize, grave psychic imbalance. One thinks of Portia, the daughter ·of Cato, swallowing fire when Brutus avoids her bed and her counsel; or of the bachelor party on Pompey's galley as contrasted with the coeducational dormitories of Egypt. A similar sense of men without women and women without their womanliness, of a virile society denying its *anima,* is at least as conspicuous in the other Roman plays: in the early Rome of *Coriolanus,* where little Marcius is praised for tearing a butterfly to pieces, and in that legendary but surely late imperial Rome of *The Most Lamentable Romaine Tragedie of Titus Andronicus,* where Roman *devotio* is measured in hewn limbs and the dominant image of family cohesiveness is the tomb of the Andronici. It seems undeniable that one of Shakespeare's principal ideas of Rome was this Vergilian theme of grandeur purchased at great price, a cautionary mirror for Elizabethans in their own most high and palmy state.[1]

I have called this theme Vergilian, since readers today tend to view Augustan Rome largely through Vergil's eyes. But of course Shakespeare obtained his knowledge of Rome from other sources as well, two of which are important not only for the incidents they describe but also for the imaginative context they establish: a context that must have inspired or at least confirmed a major tendency in Shakespeare's poetic. That he was a careful reader of Plutarch is apparent from the adroitness and assiduousness with which he moves among the various lives in adapting episodes and hints of character. What is harder to demonstrate,[2] but no less obvious, is his debt to Plutarch's fundamental method in writing parallel lives. Perhaps the most direct piece of evidence here is a somewhat negative one, Fluellen's parody of Plutarch when he compares the triumphant Hal to Alexander the Pig:

I warrant you sall find, in the comparisons between Macedon and
Monmouth, that the situations, look you, is both alike. There is a
river in Macedon, and there is also moreover a river at Monmouth.
. . . If you mark Alexander's life well, Harry of Monmouth's life is
come after it indifferent well, for there is figures in all things.

(*Henry V* 4.7.24–33)

Although Fluellen may be limited, in his reading of such figures, to noting
that there are salmons in both rivers, the reader of the *Henriad* may observe
other, more instructive parallels. After taking the crown from Richard,
Henry Bolingbroke has scrutinized the behavior of two younger Henrys
for auguries of his own undoing. Though he may dream of exchanging
sons with Northumberland, in order to have one "who is the theme of
honor's tongue," in fact, it is Hotspur who is the usurper and Hal who
will prove himself the loyal and rightful heir to the throne. Plutarch had
compared Alexander to Julius Caesar; Fluellen compares Alexander to a
British king who has imitated Junius Brutus in spending his youth in pre-
tended foolishness, lest he be taken for a later Brutus with regicidal, indeed parricidal tendencies, or for a would-be Caesar with designs on the
center of political power. By the time Fluellen speaks, Hotspur's time has
had an abrupt stop, and the elder Henry's has flowed to its natural end in
the Jerusalem Chamber; Hal is a conquering Caesar with a dream of imperial union with France. Shakespeare's audience will be reminded by the
epilogue that Henry VI will lose all that Henry V gains; and they may feel
in this present passage that Fluellen's attempt to contrast Alexander's
drunken killing of his friend Cleitus with Hal's sober repudiation of Fal-
staff raises some awkward questions about the morality, or psychic integrity, of the new king; but it is clear, at least, that the method of the *Parallel
Lives* is alive and functioning in the history plays.

The other principal source for Shakespeare's complex of Roman myths
is Livy's history "From the Founding of the City," *ab urbe condita*, the first
book of which provides the material for his poem on Lucrece. And since
the fall of Lucrece coincides with the rise of Junius Brutus, Livy's story of
the primitive origins of Rome must have figured in Shakespeare's continuing fascination with this early Roman hero, an archetype of the Hamlets
and Hals and Edgars who survive by means of play-acting. Livy's narrative
stresses a number of elements which are not made explicit in Shakespeare's
Lucrece but help to explain some of that poem's brooding intensity as well
as its anticipations of the imagery of the later plays. One such element is
the omnipresence of Tarquins in this early, claustrophobic Rome. Not
only is Lucrece's rapist a Tarquin, Sextus Tarquinius, son of the usurping
King Tarquin the Proud; but also her husband is Lucius Tarquinius Colla-

tinus, and Junius Brutus himself, savior of Rome when he banishes the Tarquins, is a son of the king's sister Tarquinia. So there is a fine irony to the piece of theatre with which the story of poor Lucrece concludes: "The Romans plausibly did give consent / To Tarquin's everlasting banishment." This moment of Rome's liberation, effected by the eloquent funeral oration of Brutus over the body of Lucrece, may have occasioned applause from Romans then and in times to come; but the idea that this could represent a definitive banishment of Tarquins seems less plausible when one notes that the new consuls of Republican Rome, Brutus and Collatinus, are themselves members of the detested family.

Another element in Livy's story of Lucrece and Brutus seems strikingly pertinent to Shakespeare's evolution of his microcosmic metaphor. When he is exiled from Rome, Sextus Tarquinius unaccountably and suicidally decides to return to a city, Gabii, which he had previously betrayed to his father. There, not surprisingly, he is put to death—like Coriolanus in Corioli, whose story appears in the next book of Livy's history. In these and other respects, Livy's story of civil or interfamilial strife turns out on closer examination to be essentially intrafamilial, even to the extent of being intrapersonal, at times virtually a psychomachia. Shakespeare sets his poem in a period of Roman history when the nation's further evolution seems mired in its leaders' inability to move beyond the first marriage of Trojan and native Italian stock that Vergil had celebrated at the conclusion of his epic. The marriage of reason and passion has collapsed, so to speak, and become a battleground for renewed struggle between patriarchal and matriarchal forces; political ambition and sexual passion are seen turning inwards once again, infesting the royal household and appearing bewilderingly even in the names of people and places. Lucrece herself seems yet another of these curiously subjective pieces of the Roman landscape, for she is wed to a collateral Tarquin whose name, Collatinus, and residence at Collatium, echo the sense of latency, of "lurking to aspire" as Tarquin's lust for her is characterized, that is implicit in the name of Latium itself, the region in which this Rome is located.

Shakespeare's opening stanza, with its abrupt motion and difficult epithets, introduces the reader to this psychological landscape:

> From the besieged Ardea all in post,
> Borne by the trustless wings of false desire,
> Lust-breathed Tarquin leaves the Roman host,
> And to Collatium bears the lightless fire,
> Which in pale embers hid, lurks to aspire,
>   And girdle with embracing flames the waist
>   Of Collatine's fair love, Lucrece the chaste.

Tarquin is turning from the protracted siege of one city to a more active assault on another, Lucrece. The name of the first city, Ardea, with its suggestion of burning, ardor, gives point to the image of bearing "lightless fire" to Collatium; that Tarquin is "lust-breathed" suggests not so much that he breathes out lust as a dragon breathes fire, as that he is inspired by lust, has breathed it in at his earlier view of Lucrece, and also perhaps confuses it with his parallel lust for the city of Ardea.

Driven by "trustless wings of false desire," Tarquin is shown in a self-destructive frenzy which is essentially irreversible once he is admitted to Lucrece's presence, or for that matter once he has left Ardea with his burden (or gift) of fire. The situation is not unlike that of Catullus's Attis, who is driven over deep seas of unfathomed emotion, to make a sacrifice of his manhood to Cybele. Obviously, from Lucrece's viewpoint there is a world of difference between rape and self-mutilation, but Tarquin does not seem to see it. Like Attis, Tarquin is consumed by self-loathing, and as he proceeds to his victim's bedchamber he broods despairingly on his inevitable disgrace: "He doth despise / His naked armour of still slaughter'd lust." Since it is clearly his naked "weapon" or phallus which is the object of his concern, it is noteworthy that Tarquin seems to see it as both the instrument and the *object* of his destructive will.[3] Presumably this embodiment of his lust is characterized as "still slaughter'd" in that it repeatedly "dies" but springs back to new life.

Much of Tarquin's protracted debate with himself elaborates the inherent confusion he seems to feel over the meaning of his act. In his view, the warrior enters the city as the male enters the female, with a desire to possess the other and a fear of being possessed by it in turn:[4]

> I know repentant tears ensue the deed,
> Reproach, disdain and deadly enmity,
> Yet strive I to embrace mine infamy.   (502–04)

This seems much the same image as that of lightless fire at the beginning of the poem, seeking to girdle its victim's waist; the difference is that by now it is clear that Tarquin is concerned less with subverting or corrupting Lucrece than with encompassing his own destruction.

Lucrece, meanwhile, is as vulnerable to envy as the city of Ardea had been — or as Eden. In Shakespeare's companion poem, Adonis succeeds in resisting Venus's attempted rape and is rewarded with a flowery metamorphosis which fulfills his desire "to grow unto himself."[5] But Lucrece lives in the harsh world of Roman history, and is not subsumed into an Ovidian metaphor of fertility at the end of her story. Instead, she finds an infinitely divided image of herself, when she scans a painting of Troy's destruction to find an apt image of her own condition. She can compare Tarquin to Sinon with some ease, and feel that "as Priam him did cherish, / So did I Tarquin—so my Troy did perish" (1546–47). Or she can identify with Hecuba as a grieving matron; but she cannot overlook the fact that the fall of Troy resulted from another kind of rape, that of Helen. She can only grieve with Hecuba by tearing at the beauty of the strumpet who was the object of Paris's lust.

At length she realizes that she cannot exhaust her vengeance on painted images, or on partial reflections of herself; she must let out the pure blood along with the corrupt. Similarly, with both her father and her husband competing in their lamentation at having lost the claim that each had in her, it remains for Brutus to turn their energies away from narcissistic, self-destructive complaint, and toward the less "childish" or effeminate arena of political action. To do so is to reverse the pattern seen at the opening of the story. By publishing Lucrece's virtue, Collatine had diverted energy from war to lust; now it is for Brutus to publish her virtue in such a way as to provoke Tarquin's banishment and his own accession to power in Rome. Such publication makes Brutus a playwright of sorts, a rhetorician who knows how to show Lucrece to best advantage and win the applause of the people; but language is being used in the service of political rather than purely artistic, sentimental goals: history is being written, or revised.

Finally, then, both Sextus Tarquinius and Lucrece are shown to be tragic victims whose stories are of secondary importance compared to the heroic emergence of Junius Brutus. Like Turnus and Dido in the *Aeneid,* they stand in the way of historical process and are destroyed by flames of misdirected energy. I would suggest that the imagery of Shakespeare's poem owes much to Vergil as well as to Livy. Lucrece's painting (or tapestry)[6] of Troy seems borrowed from Dido's similar representation described in book 1, which had shown Aeneas that in Carthage there was sympathy for human suffering; and from the tale of Troy's destruction that Aeneas subsequently relates. The entire story of Dido is framed in fire, from the first stirrings of the old flames which she had denied herself since her husband's death, to the flames of her funeral pyre which prefigure the destruction of Carthage itself in later times. Even Augustine's question of the legitimacy of Lucrece's suicide[7] is anticipated by this Vergilian model: it takes a special act of pity on Juno's part to release Dido's soul for death before her allotted time. But Sextus Tarquinius is no Aeneas, capable of escaping the flames; like Coriolanus and other victims of matriarchal nemesis, he is swallowed up and destroyed by the cities he has subverted, by Gabii if not by Lucrece.

The Rome of such plays as *Julius Caesar* or *Antony* may perhaps be understood more easily, without reference to these darkly subjective, introverted elements in the fundamental myths of its origins; but once one is outside the clearly charted, Augustan purposefulness of those plays, Shakespeare's Roman protagonists take on a hectic compulsiveness that partakes of the demonic quality of Livy's primitive Roman cityscape. This is even more the case with allusions to these Roman myths when they appear in the other tragedies. Hamlet is such another Junius Brutus, feigning madness while trying to survive in a primordial setting of fratricide and incest; but he is also, in his distraction, that other belated Brutus, whose brute part it was to kill the capital calf, Polonius, who had played Caesar in his own student days. In the dark and confused world of Elsinore, with its mirrored chambers where characters are doubled almost endlessly, it is not easy to identify precisely what drama is being enacted, or by whom.

Nor, for that matter, is it altogether easy to do so in the Rome of Shakespeare's Caesar. Plutarch tells us that Caesar was reputed to have been Brutus's natural father. Consequently, hints of parricide lurk not only in Hamlet's wild thrustings in his mother's bedroom but also in the undercurrents of Brutus's honorable musings, alongside the prospect of mere regicide. When Cassius works on Brutus in act 1, he sounds a note that is heard repeatedly in Shakespeare: the frightening but exhilarating, liberating possibility that names need not be definitive, that they may be transferable, negotiable, or perhaps even synonymous at root:[8]

> Brutus, and Caesar. What should be in that Caesar?
> Why should that name be sounded more than yours?
> Write them together, yours is as fair a name.
> Sound them, it doth become the mouth as well.
> Weigh them, it is as heavy. Conjure with 'em,
> Brutus will start a spirit soon as Caesar.   (1.2.142–47)

Cassius's passionate scorn in this speech is like Hamlet's in contrasting his father and uncle as Hyperion and satyr (1.2.140): his overt purpose is clearly to deny Caesar any divine status, though it has seemed strange to some that the evidence of Caesar's human frailty should awaken such powerful resentment. At the same time, however, this speech may be heard as one of temptation. Cassius seems to suggest a yoking of names in accordance with Roman practice. A successful Brutus may become a Brutus Caesar; alternatively, he may already be Caesar's son and/or heir-designate. Yet the glory of Brutus's name is that it denotes a Republican hero, so that the linking of the two names creates an oxymoron, provided that like Brutus we take "Caesar" anachronistically, in its later sense of "emperor." Brutus would excise "the spirit of Caesar," Caesarism, from his friend; but there is no unambiguous evidence that such a thing yet exists. Caesar is not yet a Caesar, any more clearly than Marcus Brutus is a Junius Brutus. Perhaps Brutus is neologizing, by projecting his own unnamed aspirations on someone whose name and history seem to offer opportunities for such metaphorical extension.

A crucial theme of the two plays, *Caesar* and *Antony,* is the process by which the name "Caesar" acquires its modern sense.[9] In this process the killing of Julius Caesar causes the spirit of Caesar to walk abroad, so that the ultimate and true heir of Julius is found neither in the earlier, Republican dream of Brutus, nor in the later and grander imperial dream of a larger harmony of north and south, male and female, power and love, whose time has not yet come but is dimly prefigured by Antony, enthroned with his predecessor's mistress in Egypt and attempting to legitimize Caesarion. Rather, Caesar's spirit passes to Octavius, and to that more limited, first imperial Rome of the *pax Augusta.* Julius, rather anticlimactically, is followed by Augustus as inevitably as August follows July in the normal order of things. One may conjure with the names of Brutus and Caesar; but one cannot expect to turn back from Julius to Junius.

Such a succession seems anticlimactic chiefly because Julius Caesar has seemed so heavily fraught with traits which set him apart either as hero or as victim. He bears the divine gift or curse of epilepsy, the falling sickness, as does Othello. Like Macduff he was ripped untimely from his mother's womb, in that first Caesarian section which prefigured his later impatience, his readiness to cut Gordian knots like the Alexander to whom Plutarch so naturally compares him. Like so many of the tragic kings in Shakespeare's plays and his audience's historic memory, he lacks a legitimate heir and so invites speculation as to just what part of him will survive his passing. He is known and resented, finally, as Plutarch tells us (and as Sigurd Burckhardt brilliantly suggests is expressed through the notorious use of anachronisms in *Julius Caesar*)[10] for his reform of the calendar, perhaps the most profoundly tyrannical act anyone can perform against the received order of things. As Marvell remarks of a later Caesar similarly advancing on his capitol,

> To ruine the great work of Time,
> And cast the kingdome old
> Into another mold

creates a profoundly disturbing readjustment of one's sense of time and place, however necessary such a revolution may sometimes be when the times are sufficiently out of joint. In fact, if August follows July today it does so as a result of man's naming as well as of time's passing.

The disjointedness that Brutus senses at the beginning of the play is at first interpreted reductively, as the threat of a tyrannical coup to be put down in the old manner. But Shakespeare's audience, with its enhanced perspective on Roman history, can see that more than one pattern is involved. Livy is said to have asked whether the birth of Julius Caesar had brought more good or ill to the state;[11] that he remained a favorite of Augustus after asking it suggests that the question was meant to be problematic, not simply rhetorical. Similarly, at the opening of *Julius Caesar,* Rome is being asked to evaluate the combination of attributes that is Caesar—the Caesar syndrome, as it were. In the person of this first Caesar and his private story, we may be seeing a replay of the tragic compulsion to enter the forbidden city and be destroyed thereby, like a Tarquin or a Coriolanus. In the extended meaning of Caesar's name, we are watching the emergence of Roman imperial polity, in its most confident Augustan phase. But finally, as spectators at a much later date, we can sense in the confusing and contradictory metaphors of these Roman plays the impending arrival of a religion of love that will triumph over the first Rome where Antony fails. References to Herod of Jewry, and reminders that the empire embraces the Middle East as well as Africa, hint that a stronger toil of grace than Cleopatra's is yet to come, with its most radical revision yet of the calendar of human time.[12]

Finally, from the perspective of Elizabethan England, there is a further dimension to these complex Roman names. Every Briton is descended from yet a third Brutus, the legendary Trojan refugee and accidental parricide who founded the British race; Julius Caesar casts a similar if later and more historical shadow over England, in the reminders of his conquest and civilizing effect on the island: especially, we may recall, in the ambivalent symbol of the Tower of London which Shakespeare attributes to him more than once.[13] If the British regard these earlier conquests with conflicting emotions, viewing them as alien incursions which are yet now a part of their modern heritage, how much more must this ambivalence be a factor with respect to the final Roman invasion, the coming of Roman Christianity to England? In their own lifetimes, they have seen themselves freed of this latest Roman authority. But as if to underscore the parallels between the time of Caesar and the present time, Pope Gregory had decreed in 1582 his own reformation of the Julian calendar.[14] Protestants who rejected this calendrical reform as a consequence of having asserted their own ecclesiastical reform must have watched the fall of Julius Caesar with an acute sense that one man's step forward is another's refusal to recognize the time of day. And their myth of Rome was complicated now by a sense of it as a forbidden city from which they were excluded even as they might feel drawn toward it as an object of Christian pilgrimage. Even more, Shakespeare's audience might have associated such a mixture of the sacred and the politically menacing with the Christian Italy of *Romeo and Juliet*, and been drawn to such an association by the name of Romeo and his adoption of a pilgrim's identity at Capulet's ball.[15]

I have tried to suggest the extraordinary range of associated meanings which attach themselves to Shakespeare's Roman vocabulary: Brutus, Caesar, Rome; Julius, Augustus. Repeatedly in his plays, Shakespeare accepts Cassius's invitation to conjure with such names; but it is clear from the very different spirits that may be started that such names carry an odd mixture of powers. This is especially clear with *Romeo and Juliet*. Juliet's famous attempt to deny the fatal power of Romeo's name, claiming that a rose's aroma is independent of its name, introduces one of the principal verbal motifs in the play, a concern to pluck out the mystery hidden in names, often syllable by syllable and letter by letter.[16] Whatever may have been "the prettiest sententious" that Juliet is said to have invented concerning Romeo's name, with or without reference to rosemary, the play provides repeated analyses of that name's constituent elements, from the dog's letter that opens it to its syllabic elements of sexuality (roe), self-as-object (me), and lamentation (o).[17] Alongside such wordplay is a parallel obsession with time and decorum. The lovers debate over the time of night and day; the early Romeo is rebuked for trying to live, love, and rhyme according to outmoded styles; the impatient Capulet repeatedly asks the day of the week, and insists on adjusting the date of his daughter's wedding. In a remark which suggests the degree to which relative time is fundamentally unclear, Capulet notes: "It is so very very late / That we may call it early by and by" (3.4.34–35). Indeed, the play as a whole has often seemed a tragedy less of character than of false timing.

In adapting earlier versions of his story, Shakespeare seems determined to diminish the importance of the feud, and to obscure any external forces which may determine the fate of the lovers.[18] Though old Capulet later plays the parental tyrant when Juliet unaccountably resists the marriage which he has proposed as an antidote to her melancholy at Tybalt's death, the earlier impression of his household is one of freedom and tolerance. Capulet has insisted on the primacy of Juliet's choice in marriage: "My will to her consent is but a part" (1.2.17). And he refuses to show discourtesy to the Montagues when they appear at his ball. Indeed, virtually every reference to the enmity of the two families appears in a context which casts doubt on its importance to the action. By moving the action of the play from Easter to mid-July, Shakespeare creates a midsummer urban environment where tempers are short and mischief is abroad. The rough humor of the servants in the opening scene, and Mercutio's fatal movement from casual bawdry to the baiting of Tybalt, both suggest the dominantly casual and even playful tone to much of the hostility. Those who are moved to fight are peripheral to centers of authority in the two households: though old Capulet and Montague arrive in a bit of bluster once the uproar has begun in the first scene, they show little inclination to venture beyond earshot of their wives' skeptical commentary; their masculine bravado is made to seem as weary and half-hearted as that of their servants. Meanwhile Tybalt, the most determined defender of the Capulet name, is nephew to Lady Capulet and a kinsman only through marriage, while his antagonist Mercutio belongs to the Prince's family and has only a friendly relationship to the Montagues. It seems that this blood feud is being maintained by volunteer armies. More importantly, perhaps, Romeo is already in love with Capulet's own niece, Rosaline: her refusal of him seems to have nothing to do with family enmity; nor does Montague's nephew, Benvolio, hint that this might be an issue when he suggests that Romeo attend Capulet's ball in order to measure Rosaline's beauty against the other "admired beauties of Verona."

What does it mean, then, to speak of star-crossed lovers under these circumstances? In proportion as the feud loses importance as a barrier to their love, do not Romeo and Juliet come to seem naively melodramatic in their conviction that they are tragically isolated? What is the basis for their ominous dreams, when they are surrounded by liberal and benevolent parents, priests, and friends? Perhaps the answer to this question must come from the play's metaphors rather than its action, from the universal psychological threats posed by the prospect of loving rather than from specific external threats against this pair of lovers. Essential to the wordplay characteristic of this early Shakespearean work is a sense that love represents a fatal attraction toward a perilous and forbidden enemy. Romeo, of course, is drawn to the Capulet household from the start; since the fair rose Rosaline is disdainful, coolly determined to preserve her apartness (as an allusion to Spenser may suggest),[19] he moves to the more warmly named Juliet who is more threateningly placed at the very center of the household.

In terms of the personal drama of moving away from narcissism and toward the capacity to love another person, the threat is a meaningful one. The woeful story of Juliet and her Romeo is at least potentially analogous to the story of Spenser's Scudamour and Amoret, or to the earlier allegories of love to which it alludes. By minimizing the importance of the external feud, Shakespeare invites the audience to see how lovers can project an internalized feud upon their situation, drawing upon what today would be called the family romance. This romance was available to Shakespeare in

Livy's history. An audience can laugh easily at some of Romeo's posturings as frustrated lover in the play's opening scenes; but it is important, though somewhat more difficult to a modern taste, to appreciate the serious content in what the lovers say. When they first exchange kisses, at the end of their first sonnet as "passionate pilgrims," Romeo concludes, "Thus from my lips by thine my sin is purged." Juliet responds, "Then have my lips the sin that they have took." Although the tone here is playful, the lovers employ a conceit developed far more darkly in the context of Lucrece's story. At the very least, Juliet is taking on some of Romeo's shameless rhetoric, if not his guilt; she exclaims soon after, with the exclamatory antitheses characteristic of the young Montague, "My only love sprung from my only hate! / Too early seen unknown, and known too late!"

Finally, then, although the balance between comic and tragic attitudes in the play is frequently precarious,[20] the star-crossed love may be understood in terms of a pair of reciprocal compulsions, mutually self-destructive. On one side is Romeo the questing pilgrim of love, drawn toward a holy city which he can enter only in disguise or by stealth. On the other is a Juliet who was born not merely in Caesar's natal month but at the very point of it, July 31, Lammas Eve, when the month of Julius meets that of Augustus, and a festival of the Loaf-mass celebrates the ripening of the grain. Like *Antony and Cleopatra* later, the tragedy of these two lovers enacts a dream of reconciliation—between and by means of grace and rude will, as the friar puts it. The later play places such a dream in the context of a public pattern of historical process; the two lovers fail to realize their dream, but at a time when a new religion of love is in fact about to be realized. The earlier play enacts a more private, internalized drama, in the absence of a grand historical backdrop which gives ironic confirmation to the lovers' dream. The marriage bed becomes the charnel house which is our final view of Verona, and the dead lovers can engender no more than a pair of golden icons. Instead of the festival of fertility that should have followed on Juliet's birth- and marriage-days, only a sterile August peace has been established, and Verona is left without an heir apparent, a society of aging leaders talking and waiting in vain.[21]

University of Massachusetts, Amherst

NOTES

1. A useful survey of recent studies on Shakespeare's treatment of Rome is provided by John W. Velz, "The Ancient World in Shakespeare: Authenticity or Anachronism? A Retrospect," *Shakespeare Survey* 31 (1978), 1–12.

2. E. A. J. Honigmann considers the evidence for Shakespeare's use of Plutarch's comparisons in "Shakespeare's Plutarch," *SQ* 10 (1959), 25–33.

3. The metaphor appears in a more obvious form in Gascoigne's "Adventures of Master F.J.," for instance. Although the *OED* cites an obsolete use of *armour* to include offensive as well as defensive gear, its use here to refer only to a single offensive weapon seems unusual, and perhaps a function of Tarquin's confusion of roles.

4. See Leslie A. Fiedler, *The Stranger in Shakespeare* (New York: Stein and Day, 1972), especially the introduction ("The Passionate Pilgrim") and first chapter ("The Woman as Stranger").

5. Observe, however, that this limited triumph of Adonis is dependent on his sexual immaturity and impotence, a cruel if partly comic irony which calls for contrast with Tarquin's tragically adequate armor.

6. S. Clark Hulse, "'A Piece of Skilful Painting' in Shakespeare's 'Lucrece,'" *Shakespeare Survey* 31 (1978), 13–22.

7. *De civitate Dei* 1.23, 22.

8. Myron Taylor ("Shakespeare's Julius Caesar and the Irony of History," *SQ* 24 [1973], 301–08) points out that Cassius, as an Epicurean, "thinks neither name will conjure any spirits"; and that in fact the linking of the two does evoke supernatural actions that comment on the political events of the play.

9. An especially clear instance of this Shakespearean device is seen in the case of Cressida: the presence of cressidas in the audience in effect limits the freedom of the Cressida on stage to act in any way other than that which will give her name its subsequent meaning.

10. Sigurd Burckhardt, "How Not to Murder Caesar," in *Shakespearean Meanings* (Princeton, N.J.: Princeton University Press, 1968), pp. 3–21.

11. Seneca, *Nat. Quaest.* 5.18.4.

12. Perhaps the reference to Caesar's 33 wounds (5.1.53) carries a similar hint of christological significance.

13. Most notably in *Richard III* 3.1.68–88, a passage rich in its mixture of questions of Caesar, history, and internecine menace.

14. Burckhardt, "How Not to Murder Caesar."

15. In his edition of *Romeo* (New Haven, Conn.: Yale University Press, 1954, p. 138), Richard Hosley notes, "In the Middle Ages the word [Romeo] was originally used in Palestine and elsewhere to designate pilgrims from Italy, but it ultimately grew to refer to a pilgrim's destination rather than his place of origin." If Shakespeare was aware of this double meaning to the word, rather than the single later meaning mentioned by Dante (*Vita nuova* 40) and more generally known, it may have contributed to the metaphor of a double quest in the play. In any case, however, Shakespeare needed no such precedent for his romance doubling in this incident.

16. Harry Levin notes in "Form and Formality in *Romeo and Juliet*," *SQ* 11 (1960) the irony that Juliet no sooner completes her argument against the importance of names than she demands the name of her intruder.

17. For earlier attempts to interpret some of this wordplay, see H. H. Furness, ed., *A New Variorum Edition of Shakespeare: Romeo and Juliet* (Philadelphia: Lippincott, 1871), esp. pp. 124, 141–43. Later attempts to deal with the bawdry have variously understood Romeo's being without his "roe"; but it may be worth noting that the "me" at the heart of Romeo's name is surrounded by syllables that signify the object of his quest: on the one side the "roe" and on the other the "open et cetera"—"O, Romeo, that she were, O that she were / An open et cetera, thou a poperin pear!" (2.1.37–38).

18. See Coppélia Kahn, "The Rape in Shakespeare's *Lucrece*," *Shakespeare Studies* 9 (1976), 45–72; and "Coming of Age in Verona," in C. R. S. Lenz et al., eds., *The Women's*

Part (Urbana: University of Illinois Press, 1980), 171–93. I have found these studies of the patriarchal societies of *Lucrece* and *Romeo* helpful and illuminating, although I take issue with Kahn's assumptions about the centrality of the feud in the latter.

19. Such an allusion appears not only in the similarity of Rosaline to the Rosalind of the *Shepheardes Calender,* but also perhaps in a Spenserian tendency to link pairs of lovers by overlapping syllables (Romeo : Rosaline :: Fradubio : Fraelissa). Note, too, that Juliet's identification of Romeo as a rose mediates such a relationship of terms.

20. Shakespeare's choice of the Pyramus and Thisbe myth for purely comic treatment in *Midsummer Night's Dream* provides further evidence of his recognition of the comic potential in such a tale of adolescent love-tragedy.

21. Dante's allusion to the Montecchi and Capelletti *(Purg.* 6) is in the context of his criticism of the emperor for neglecting the brutalization of Italy, with the consequence that a waste land is appearing; *"che'l giardino dello'mperio sia deserto."* Shakespeare's conclusion seems strikingly similar.

DENNIS MOORE

Philisides and Mira:
Autobiographical Allegory in the *Old Arcadia*

*I*T IS easy to see why Bertram Dobell, who rediscovered Sir Philip Sidney's original *Arcadia,* singled out one passage as being "of greater interest than any other in the whole work."[1] In the story of the melancholy lover Philisides, he had brought to light an amusing self-portrait, brief and conventional yet distinguished by Sidney's eloquence, ingenuity, and artful self-display. The detailed parallel between Philip Sidney and Philisides has naturally prompted readers to try to identify his beloved Mira as well, but with little success. Philisides says he first saw her in a dream which doomed his love to despair; after that, when he met and courted her, Mira's hot-and-cold temperament drove him into exile in Arcadia.

> But having spent some part of my youth in following of her, sometimes with some measure of favour, sometimes with unkind interpretations of my most kind thoughts, in the end having attempted all means to establish my blissful estate, and having been not only refused all comfort but new quarrels picked against me, I did resolve by perpetual absence to choke mine own ill fortunes.[2]

We simply don't know of any such frustrating young love in Sidney's life. However, if we turn from his private life (about which we know so little) to his political career, Mira begins to look more familiar. As the woman responsible for the young man's rustication, as she who has dashed his fondest hopes, she greatly resembles Queen Elizabeth.

Sidney probably wrote most of the first *Arcadia* in 1580 while in the country for about eight months, much of that time with his sister Mary, Countess of Pembroke. Late 1579 marked a low point in the fortunes of Sidney's faction at court, the Protestant interest led by the Earl of Leicester (Sidney's uncle) and Sir Francis Walsingham (whose daughter Sidney later married). Queen Elizabeth seemed determined to marry the French king's brother, the Duc d'Alençon, and the task of writing her about Protestant objections to this Catholic match fell to Philip. He may not have expected her to look upon his letter as a standard item of court business, for it begins with a confession of guilt:

> Most feared and beloved, most sweet and gracious Sovereign: to seek out excuses for this my boldness, and to arm the acknowledging of a fault with reasons for it, might better show I knew I did amiss, than any whit diminish the attempt; especially in your judgement, who is able lively to discern into the nature of the thing done. It were folly to hope with laying on better colours to make it more acceptable.[3]

Many biographers suppose she simply banished him for his letter, but no evidence supports that assumption. In fact, a revealing letter to Leicester suggests that he left under his own will, though constrained by royal neglect.

> For my selfe I assure yowr Lordeshippe uppon my trothe, so full of the colde as one can not heere me speake: whiche is the cawse keepes me yet frome the cowrte *since my only service is speeche and that is stopped.* As soone as I have gottne any voice I will waite on yowr Lordeshippe if so it please yow. Althoughe it bee contrary to that I have signified to her Majestie of my wante, I dowt not her Majestie will vouchesafe to aske for me, but so longe as she sees a silk dublett uppon me her Highnes will thinke me in good cace. At my departur I desyred Mr Vichamberlaine he woolde tell her Majestie *necessity did even banishe me frome the place.* And allwaies submitting my selfe to yowr judgement and commandement, I thinke my best, either constantly to waite, or constantly to holde the course of my poverty, for comming and going neither breedes deserte, nor wittnesseth necessity.[4]

Elizabeth preferred to advance those whose first allegiance was to her, not to the militant Protestant cause she had so many doubts about. As Fulke Greville testifies in his *Life of Sidney,* "How mild soever those mixtures of favours, and corrections were in that Princely lady: yet . . . they fell heavy in crossing a young mans ends."[5] Although one biographer says this letter "shows clearly that his long absence was not due to the Queen's wrath at his opposition to the French marriage,"[6] his actions in the tense months of late 1579 (including both the Alençon letter and his quarrel with the Earl of Oxford) must have confirmed her doubts about his usefulness. The remark about service and the quibble on "cace" in his letter to Leicester both hint at the difference between his high aspirations and limited success, revealing his bitterness at her indifference; so does the pointed message he gave Hatton. Apparently she did not banish him outright, but her disfavor drove him away just as surely.

Seen in this biographical perspective, the exile of Philisides corresponds strikingly to Sidney's banishment by necessity. More than forty years ago, Kenneth T. Rowe proposed that Mira figures Elizabeth, as did Michel Poirier a decade later.[7] But since neither critic explained how the hypothesis affects our understanding of the Philisides episode, it has never been taken very seriously. William Ringler does not even mention it when surveying ideas about Mira,[8] and other critics have ignored it as just another arbitrary historical identification. While an $X = Y$ claim is not worth much in itself, we should remember what Ringler says about the autobiographical aspect of *Astrophil and Stella*: "Sidney put it there, and if we ignore it we ignore one of the effects he intended. The legitimate critical procedure is, not to ignore the biography, but to find out what kind of biography it is."[9] A close look at Philisides' dream-vision reveals the value of seeing Mira as Elizabeth.

Through most of the romance, Philisides remains a mysterious stranger in Arcadia. Time and again the natives ask to hear his tale, but he refuses to mar their festivities with such sadness. The Fourth Eclogues changes all that. Since the shepherds gather to lament the death of their prince, several "stranger shepherds" take advantage of the occasion to complain about their loves, and Philisides finally yields to entreaties "that he would impart some part of the sorrow his countenance so well witnessed unto them." His life story of education, martial exercise, travel, and great expectation follows the pattern of Sidney's youth (and Astrophil's) — until his love for Mira "diverted this course of tranquillity" (Robertson, *Arcadia*, pp. 334, 335). This prose story sets out the events leading up to his pastoral retreat and introduces the song which records his prophetic vision of Mira, "Now was our heav'nly vaulte deprived of the light." The parallels between Sidney and Philisides, Elizabeth and Mira, become more abstract and elusive because the poem develops them symbolically, combining several traditional motifs into a myth about angered goddesses. In order to understand the parallels, we must interpret Philisides' allegorical vision.

Like many dream poems, the vision of Philisides has a complex narrative structure, beginning with the frame provided by the prose speech introducing it. The poem itself starts with a long description of night and sleep, subjects which Sidney amplifies through a process of analysis and explication. He builds up a series of contrasts, one pair of ideas after another — daylight and darkness, waking and sleeping, mind and body, and above all, guilty worry and natural rest.[10] Like the alexandrines and prominent figures of verbal repetition, the almost didactic tone of the opening contributes to the high style of the poem. It also acquaints us with the contemplative character of the speaker, who rests easy because he pursues a life of "simple course, and unentangled mind":

> Far from my thoughts was ought, whereto their minds aspire,
> Who under courtly pompes doo hatch a base desire.
> Free all my powers were from those captiving snares,
> Which heav'nly purest gifts defile in muddy cares.   (15–18)

The steady verse, the careful explanations, the speaker's innocence: all indicate the peace of mind we already know Philisides to have lost, the tranquil course diverted by Mira. And as he complains at the end of the vision, he is not even awake when he loses it.

The dream begins with a scene of contemplation, no sooner established than disrupted by the poem's main action. Philisides dreams he is a sylvan philosopher in his native land, which he described earlier by saying, "The name of Samothea is so famous that, telling you that I am of that, I shall not need to extend myself further in telling you what that country is." Nonetheless, modern readers had forgotten that country's fame until Katherine Duncan-Jones revived it: the opening pages of Holinshed's *Chronicle* cover the ancient days when England went by that name, its inhabitants famed for civic harmony and natural philosophy.[11]

> Me thought, nay sure I was, I was in fairest wood
> Of *Samothea* lande; a lande, which whilom stood
> An honour to the world, while Honour was their ende,
> And while their line of yeares they did in vertue spende.
> But there I was, and there my calmie thoughts I fedd
> On Nature's sweet repast, as healthfull senses ledd.
> Her giftes my study was, her beauties were my sporte:
> My worke her workes to know, her dwelling my resorte.
>
>   (35–42)

This simple picture of retirement and contemplation leads to a description of the high knowledge he seeks, and despite his comment about healthy senses and calm thoughts, his course of study strikes an ominous note:

> Those lampes of heav'nly fire to fixed motion bound,
> The ever-turning spheares, the never-moving ground;
> What essence dest'nie hath; if fortune be or no;
> Whence our immortall soules to mortall earth doo flowe:

What life it is, and how that all these lives doo gather,
With outward maker's force, or like an inward father.
Such thoughts, me thought, I thought, and straind my single mind
Then void of neerer cares, the depth of things to find.   (43–50)

Star-knowledge had symbolized the pitfalls of a contemplative life at least
since the days of Thales, and Philisides moves on to still more curious matters. When he asks about the essence of destiny and what life is, we may
agree with Philanax that "reason can not shewe it self more reasonable,
then to leave reasoning in things above reason."[12] Even the repetition in
the next-to-last line diminishes our confidence in his strained ideas, since
they are but supposed thoughts of thoughts.

Philisides' meditations may bring to mind the astronomical inquiries in
book 8 of *Paradise Lost*, which Milton uses to symbolize the pride of
searching into the depth of things to question providence. For instance,
recall Adam's astronomical doubts and his summary statement after Ra-
phael clears them up: useless speculative knowledge "is fume,"

> Or emptiness, or fond impertinence,
> And renders us in things that most concern
> Unpractic'd, unprepar'd, and still to seek.
>   (*PL* 8.195–97)

As if to confirm our doubts about his curiosity, a sudden catastrophe
catches Philisides wholly unprepared and once more involves him in judging matters over his head. With a terrible noise,

> The moone a sunder rent (O godes, o pardon me,
> That forced with grief reveales what greeved eyes dyd see)
> The Moone a sunder rent.   (55–57)

A moment before, he inquired boldly into secret causes. Now he begs forgiveness for revealing what he has seen.

When a chariot guided by doves and sparrows emerges from the moon,
Philisides takes it for a sign of apocalypse, but his astonishment gives way
to disappointment when he sees the patronesses of sundered moon and flying chariot:

> Straunge were the Ladies' weeds; yet more unfit then strange.
> The first with cloth's tuckt up as Nymphes in woods do range;
> Tuckt up even with the knees, with bowe and arrowes prest:

Her right arme naked was, discovered was her breast.
But heavy was her pace, and such a meagre cheere,
As little hunting minde (God knowes) did there appeere.
The other had with arte (more then our women knowe,
As stuffe meant for the sale set out to glaring showe)
A wanton woman's face, and with curld knots had twinde
Her haire, which by the helpe of painter's cunning, shinde.

(65–74)

Mythographic tradition leads us to expect that the chariot belongs to
Venus,[13] and it may seem that the dreamer should recognize her and
Diana. Philisides does rival Chaucer's dreamers in obtuseness, and with
similar comic effect, but in this case there is a good reason for his slowness.
Venus's crass artifice and wantonness are not even attractive by mortal
standards, and Diana, with heavy pace and "meagre cheere," betrays little
mind for her hunt.[14] When he hears their names, Philisides can justly declare that their fame "from truth had greatly jard," for their beauty and
power have faded considerably since the days of Troy.[15]

The dreamer's disparagement of the ridiculous goddesses prefaces his en-
thusiastic praise for Diana's attendant, Mira, whose splendor seems doubly
wonderful by contrast. She is

    a Nymphe that did excell as farr
All things that earst I sawe, as orient pearles exceed,
That which their mother hight, or els their silly seed.
Indeed a perfect hewe, indeed a sweet consent
Of all those Graces' giftes the heavens have ever lent.
And so she was attirde, as one that did not prize
Too much her peerles parts, nor yet could them despise.
But cald, she came apace; a pace wherein did move
The bande of beauties all, the little world of love.   (82–90)

While Philisides has questioned Diana's own devotion to the hunt and its
values, the goddess herself praises Mira as "the pleasure of my minde, / In
whom of all my rules the perfect proofe I finde." The order of things
would seem to require Mira's subordination to the goddess, yet our sense
of her clear worth would elevate her. Philisides announces his own solution to this dilemma at once: "*Mira* I admirde: her shape sank in my brest."

The poem now moves swiftly to its climax. The goddesses are meeting
together to resolve their differences, a circumstance which will surprise
anyone familiar with their traditional rivalry as portrayed in such works as

The Faerie Queene and Lyly's *Gallathea*.[16] According to Diana, their fortunes have declined because of their ancient discord, so she proposes that they consolidate their assets: "Let one the Princesse be, to her the other yeeld,"

> And let her have the giftes that should in both remaine:
> In her let beautie both, and chastnesse fully raigne.
>
> (129, 131–32)

But who will yield? Diana recommends that they submit themselves to the judgment of Philisides, a youth "as yet of spotlesse truth."

> This crowne of amber faire (an amber crowne she held)
> To worthiest let him give, when both he hath beheld.
>
> (141–42)

Smirking Venus, who remembers Paris and forgets her own age, accepts the offer without hesitation. Meanwhile, Philisides warms to the task of meddling in divine affairs:

> I that was first agast, when first I saw their showe:
> Now bolder waxt, waxt prowde, that I such sway might beare:
> For neere acquaintance dooth diminish reverent feare.   (158–60)

This admission of pride reinforces the doubts raised by his arcane studies, and here again, as when the moon split, the event confirms our doubts. After the goddesses swear by Styx to accept his decision, his abrupt decree astounds them:

> How ill both you can rule, well hath your discord taught:
> Ne yet for what I see, your beauties merite ought.
> To yonder Nymphe therefore (to Mira I did point)
> The crowne above you both for ever I appoint.[17]   (163–66)

The goddesses swear immediate revenge upon the "ungodly rebell," though their ill-considered oaths bind them to his judgment, and with cruel decorum they punish him by means of his own decision. He will love the beautiful, chaste princess. Venus assures him he will wish he were blind; Diana promises despair.

Philisides awakens shaking with fear and reflects upon his mishap:

Was it a dreame? O dreame, how hast thou wrought in me,
That I things erst unseene should first in dreaming see?
And thou ô traytour Sleepe, made for to be our rest,
How hast thou framde the paine wherewith I am opprest?
O cowarde *Cupid* thus doost thou thy honour keepe,
Unarmde (alas) unwarn'd to take a man asleepe?   (181–86)

The note of complaint sounds louder as we progress through this climactic
series of apostrophes — to the dream for its visionary power, to sleep for its
traitorous oppression, and to the god of love for his cowardly attack. Like
the goddesses, Cupid plays a low part.

Sidney's variation on the judgment of Paris, the heart of the poem, clari-
fies the nature of Philisides' error. Elizabethan poets enjoyed taking the
golden apple from Venus and awarding it to another, most often to Queen
Elizabeth (five of seven instances between 1566 and 1584 honor her), so
seeing Mira as Elizabeth puts the poet's choice of this device in a new perspective.[18] Of course Sidney deviates significantly from the traditional
story, and as the above account of the poem suggests, some of the most
important changes work together to emphasize the theme of hybris. For
example, the most venerable exposition of the judgment of Paris treats it
as an exemplary case of bad judgment. Thus Fulgentius compares the three
goddesses to the active, contemplative, and voluptuary lives and explains
that "the shepherd Paris, being neither straight as an arrow nor sure as a
spear nor handsome of face nor wise of mind, did a dull and stupid thing
and, as is the way of wild beasts and cattle, turned his snail's eyes toward
lust rather than selected virtue or riches."[19] Yet this moralization obviously has little relevance to the story of Philisides. Even though he judges
according to appearances, it would be hard to escape the conviction that he
chooses the worthiest of the three. The failure in judgment which brings
about his fall resembles that of Tiresias rather than Paris. As Abraham
Fraunce reports,

> *Jupiter* jesting with *Juno,* whether man or woman had more pleasure,
> the matter was referred to *Tiresias,* who had been both woman and
> man: but giving sentence with *Jupiter,* was deprived of his sight by
> *Juno.* It is not good therefore to judge between our betters. *Tiresias*
> was a sage and contemplative man: and such are comonly blinde to
> other matters, for that they scorne those inferior things, as having
> vowed their whole soules to more heavenly cogitations.[20]

Tiresias has excellent grounds for his opinion, but common sense — which
the contemplative man is said to lack — dictates that he keep it to himself.

Similarly, Philisides' mistake would appear to lie not in favoring Mira over the goddesses but in presuming to judge so high a matter at all. The pleasures of his *otium* and his lack of "neerer cares" betray him into the sort of imprudent abstraction Fraunce attributes to Tiresias.

Hybris also explains another innovation, the substitution of an amber crown for the golden apple of Ate. A symbol of regal authority, the crown recalls the poem's repeated references to orderly government, and the appropriateness of a crown to Elizabeth is equally clear. But why a crown of amber? Because the gem's primary poetic and mythological associations link it to a prime classical example of the overreacher. Ovid recounts how the Heliades, Phaeton's sorrowful sisters, turn into trees after months of disconsolate weeping for him:

> inde fluunt lacrimae, stillataque sole rigescunt
> de ramis electra novis, quae lucida amnis
> excipit et nuribus mittit gestanda latinis.

[Still their tears flow on, and these tears, hardened into amber by the sun, drop down from new-made trees. The clear river receives them and bears them onward, one day to be worn by the brides of Rome.][21]

Thanks to Ovid, amber and the Heliades became an almost indispensable part of the Phaeton legend, and a long tradition interprets the moral meaning of that youth as pride of a specific sort. As Erasmus writes in *De copia,* his celebration of commonplaces, "Thus doubtless the fall of Phaeton teaches that one should not undertake the execution of a task beyond his powers."[22] When Diana revealed the amber crown, the dreamer would have done well to remember the origin of amber. The example of Phaeton might have checked his presumption.

It will seem strange to many readers that Sidney presents his political problems in an amorous allegory, but it would not have surprised his contemporaries. Since Philisides suffers for presuming to judge matters too high, it is easy to apply his misfortunes to Sidney's case, whether we think of him leaving court because of the Alençon letter ("this my boldness," as he calls it) or more generally because of the queen's suspicions about his ambitions. The fiction of "Now was our heav'nly vaulte deprived of the light" allows Sidney to praise her by showing how Philisides became devoted to his idol, at the same time that it offers the poet an opportunity to express bewilderment and dismay at his difficult position at court. Elizabethan love poetry often confronts us with just such a confluence of poetic convention, courtly fiction, and political fact. The queen enjoyed being addressed as a Petrarchan *donna,* so courtiers out of favor like Sidney's friend Dyer were quick to see the advantage of adopting a pose of amorous devotion when complaining to her:

> And though I seeme to use the Poets fained stile,
> To figure forth my wofull plight, my fall, and my Exile;
>
> Yet is my greefe not faind, wherein I strive and pine:
> Who feeleth most, shall finde it least, comparinge his with mine.[23]

Melancholy pastoral exiles stricken with love for the queen are perfectly commonplace, as Dorcas reminds Elizabeth in Sidney's *Lady of May* (1578?):

> How many courtiers, think you, I have heard under our field in bushes make their woeful complaints, some of the greatness of their mistress' estate, which dazzled their eyes and yet burned their hearts; some of the extremity of her beauty mixed with extreme cruelty; some of her too much wit, which made all their loving labours folly? O how often have I heard one name sound in many mouths, making our vales witness of their doleful agonies![24]

In a direct address to Elizabeth in a royal entertainment, that one name must be hers.

However much the Philisides episode has in common with works addressed to the queen, we cannot assume that Sidney intended it for her. The slight evidence available suggests he wrote *Arcadia* primarily for his own diversion and that of a limited circle who would see the manuscript (Robertson, *Arcadia,* pp. xxxix–xli, 3). Beyond that, we can only guess what expressive or pragmatic ends Sidney wished his autobiographical allegory to serve, what readers he hoped to reach. Fortunately, we do not need to know whether Sidney thought of Elizabeth as a special member of his audience, or even a likely one. To appreciate the allegory, it is enough to see how wittily he uses the idiom of courtly compliment to complain about his difficulties with the queen.

This posture of devotion to Mira does not seem to have interested Sidney after 1580. The *New Arcadia* gives us a new Philisides, and the two characters exemplify the differences between the works in which they appear. In the revised romance, Philisides is an Iberian gentleman who loves "the Star" and appears in a tournament decked out as a "Shepherd Knight," his entrance announced "with bagpipes in steed of trumpets," his attendants disguised as shepherds, and the knight dressed in wool "so enriched with Jewels artificially placed, that one would have thought it a marriage between the lowest and the highest."[25] Although he retains a pastoral guise, his rustication is metaphorical. In the *Old Arcadia*, it is a literal fact.

University of Iowa

NOTES

1. Bertram Dobell, "New Light Upon Sir Philip Sidney's 'Arcadia,'" *Quarterly Review* 211 (1909), 90.
2. *The Countess of Pembroke's Arcadia (The Old Arcadia)*, ed. Jean Robertson (Oxford: Oxford University Press, 1973), p. 341.
3. *Miscellaneous Prose of Sir Philip Sidney*, ed. Katherine Duncan-Jones and Jan Van Dorsten (Oxford: Oxford University Press, 1973), p. 46.
4. 2 August 1580, *Prose Works of Sir Philip Sidney*, ed. Albert Feuillerat (Cambridge: Cambridge University Press, 1912), vol. 3, p. 129 (emphasis added).
5. Fulke Greville, First Lord Brooke, *The Life of Sir Philip Sidney*, ed. Nowell Smith (Oxford: Oxford University Press, 1907), p. 146. Greville rehearses his own problems to illustrate this point. For Sidney's political and financial disappointments after 1577, see James M. Osborn, *Young Philip Sidney 1572–1577* (New Haven, Conn.: Yale University Press, 1972), pp. 496–516.
6. Mona Wilson, *Sir Philip Sidney* (1931; rpt. London: Hart-Davis, 1950), p. 108. Katherine Duncan-Jones, who presents the fullest argument against connecting Sidney's retirement to the Alençon letter, bases her case in part on a letter from Hubert Languet to Sidney (dated 22 October 1580), but her quotation omits the crucial phrase expressing Languet's dismay over the Alençon letter's possible consequences (Duncan-Jones and Van Dorsten, *Miscellaneous Prose*, pp. 33–34). Compare *The Correspondence of Sir Philip Sidney and Hubert Languet*, ed. Steuart A. Pears (London: Pickering, 1845), p. 187.
7. Kenneth T. Rowe, "The Love of Sir Philip Sidney for the Countess of Pembroke," *Papers of the Michigan Academy of Science, Arts, and Letters* 25 (1939), 579–95; Michel Poirier, *Sir Philip Sidney* (Lille: Université de Lille, 1948), p. 50. John A. Galm briefly expands Rowe's account in an appendix to *Sidney's Arcadian Poems* (Salzburg: Universität Salzburg, 1973), pp. 210–25. However, his assertion that "the marriage negotiations not only continued but became more serious" fits early 1581 better than 1580, for the negotiations lapsed entirely during Sidney's absence. See Conyers Read, *Lord Burghley and Queen Elizabeth* (New York: Knopf, 1960), pp. 221, 226.
8. *The Poems of Sir Philip Sidney*, ed. William A. Ringler, Jr. (Oxford: Oxford University Press, 1962), p. 418.
9. Ibid., p. 440.
10. Erasmus sensibly observes that "the first way to embellish thought is to relate at length and treat in great detail something that could be expressed summarily and in general" (*On Copia of Words and Ideas*, trans. Donald B. King and H. David Rix [Milwaukee, Wis.: Marquette University Press, 1963], p. 43). Note particularly his discussion of *peristasis* and varieties of amplification, e.g., *ratiocinatio* (pp. 57–60).

DENNIS MOORE

11. Katherine Duncan-Jones, "Sidney in Samothea: A Forgotten National Myth," *RES* n.s. 25 (1974), 174–77.

12. Sidney, *Prose Works,* vol. 1, p. 510. Christian writers from Saint Paul and Augustine to Calvin and Sidney's friend de Mornay emphasize the hazards of curious studies, and notable Elizabethan contributions include Greville's *Treatie of Humane Learning* and Sir John Davies's *Nosce Teipsum.* See Howard Schultz, *Milton and Forbidden Knowledge* (New York: Modern Language Association, 1955), chs. 1–2.

13. Abraham Fraunce notes that "Swans and Doves drawe [Venus'] chariot; Doves are wanton, and Swans are white and musicall, both being means to procure love and lust" *(The Third Part of the Countess of Pembrokes Yvychurch: Entituled, Amintas Dale* [1592], p. 45). For the musical swans, Sidney substitutes the notoriously lecherous sparrow—"Venus sone," as Chaucer calls him in *Parlement of Foules.*

14. Ringler parenthetically identifies Diana as Elizabeth (Sidney, *Poems,* p. 418), but Sidney's outrageous portrayal of the goddess makes the identification doubtful at best. Since a manuscript could have found its way to the queen, Ringler's observation presupposes considerable foolhardiness on Sidney's part. The identification might gain some plausibility if it helped us understand the poem, but the only conclusion Ringler draws from it is that Mira might be one of Elizabeth's attendants.

15. Maurice Evans asserts that Philisides' vision "makes the same point about the decline of the gods" as Giordano Bruno's *Spaccio de la bestia trionfante* (1584), and he even declares that to be the theme of the poem, but Sidney gives us no reason to think that his goddesses' imperfections signify their inferiority to Bruno's universal deity, the twin god Truth and Absolute Virtue, and that is the principal conceit of *Lo Spaccio.* The two works have little in common, their similarities limited to such incidental details as some remarks about their abandoned altars, matters hardly central to the English poem. See *Arcadia,* ed. Maurice Evans (Baltimore: Penguin, 1977), p. 861; cp. Giordano Bruno, *The Expulsion of the Triumphant Beast,* trans. Arthur D. Imerti (New Brunswick, N.J.: Rutgers, 1964), esp. pp. 98–103, 106–07.

16. For Spenser and Lyly, see Thomas P. Roche, Jr., *The Kindly Flame* (Princeton, N.J.: Princeton University Press, 1964), pp. 110–14, and Peter Saccio, *The Court Comedies of John Lyly* (Princeton, N.J.: Princeton University Press, 1969), pp. 129–47.

17. Against the argument that Mira cannot be Elizabeth because she waits on Diana, Rowe ("The Love of Sidney," p. 585) points out that the queen "was commonly figured either as Diana or as a nymph or shepherdess devoted to Diana, with the pastoral mode, as in the *Arcadia* and in *Amarillis,* lending itself more readily to the humbler guise." He cites several more instances, most notably George Peele's *Arraignment of Paris* (1584), in which the nymph Eliza/Zabeta gets the golden apple because she surpasses Venus, Diana, Juno, and Minerva by combining all their gifts.

18. John D. Reeves, "The Judgment of Paris as a Device of Tudor Court Flattery," *N&Q* 199 (1954), 7–11. Of twelve instances after 1584, Reeves lists only two concerning the queen. The device seems to have become popular and passed into the standard repertoire of courtly praise.

19. Fulgentius, *Mythographies,* 2. 1, in *Fulgentius the Mythographer,* trans. L. G. Whitbread (Columbus: Ohio State University Press, 1971), p. 65. Emblem books frequently use Paris to illustrate bad judgment. For examples, see Barptolemaeus Anulus, *Picta Poesis* (Lyons, 1552), p. 65, and Joannes Sambucus, *Emblemata* (1566; Antwerp, 1584), p. 143; cp. Geffrey Whitney, *A Choice of Emblemes (1586),* ed. Henry Green (1866; rpt. New York: Benjamin Blom, 1967), p. 83.

20. Fraunce, *Third Part of Yvychurch,* p. 16.

21. Ovid, *Metamorphoses,* 2. 364–66, trans. F. J. Miller, Loeb Classical Library (London: Heinemann, 1916), vol. 2, pp. 84–85.

22. Erasmus, *On Copia,* p. 70. Compare Pierre Bersuire, *Metamorphosis Ovidiana Moraliter* (Paris, 1509), fol. 26; Natalis Comes, *Mythologiae* (1596), p. 556.

23. Edward Dyer, "Hee that his mirth hath loste," in Ralph M. Sargent, *The Life and Lyrics of Sir Edward Dyer* (1935; rpt. Oxford: Oxford University Press, 1968), p. 187. The late Elizabethan poets' debt to Dyer as a pioneer never shows more clearly than in the Philisides story, and Sidney acknowledges his debt in the first Philisides poem by alluding to a well-known Dyer complaint (Sidney, *Poems,* p. 24: "Up, up, Philisides," 61–65). On "The Political Petrarchism of the Virgin Queen," see Leonard Forster, *The Icy Fire* (Cambridge: Cambridge University Press, 1969), pp. 122–47; Patricia Thompson, "The Literature of Patronage, 1580–1630," *EIC* 2 (1952), esp. p. 273; and E. C. Wilson, *England's Eliza* (Cambridge, Mass.: Harvard University Press, 1939).

24. Sidney, *Miscellaneous Prose,* p. 28.

25. Sidney, *Prose Works,* vol. 1, pp. 184–85. See James Holly Hanford and Sarah Ruth Watson, "Personal Allegory in the *Arcadia:* Philisides and Lelius," *MP* 32 (1934), 1–10; D. Coulman, "Spotted To Be Known," *JWCI* 20 (1957), 179–80; Frances A. Yates, "Elizabethan Chivalry: The Romance of the Accession Day Tilts," in *Astraea* (London: Routledge & Kegan Paul, 1975), pp. 88–111; and Sidney, *Poems,* pp. 378, 418, 435, and 493.

THOMAS P. ROCHE, JR.

Astrophil and Stella: A Radical Reading

Angels enjoy the heavens' inward choirs:
Stargazers only multiply desires. —Caelica, 17

I

SIDNEY'S *Astrophil and Stella,* although the third English sequence in order of publication, holds pride of place as the most influential of the English
sequences. Its author was a young nobleman who died a hero's death in
1586; its heroine a beautiful lady of the court. The story of Astrophil's love
for Stella, as told in the poem, was well known through circulated manuscripts before it appeared posthumously in 1591 in a pirated edition by
Thomas Newman and in 1598 in an edition authorized by Sidney's sister,
the countess of Pembroke, which contained 108 sonnets among which
were interspersed eleven songs.[1] The appreciation of Sidney's achievement
over that of his predecessors is clearly announced by his first critic,
Thomas Nashe, in the preface to the 1591 edition:

> *Tempus adest plausus aurea pompa venit,* so endes the Sceane of Idiots,
> and enter *Astrophel* in pompe. Gentlemen that haue seene a thousand
> lines of folly, drawne forth *ex vno puncto impudentiae,* & two famous
> Mountaines to goe to the conception of one Mouse, that haue had
> your eares deafned with the eccho of Fames brazen towres, when
> only they haue been toucht with a leaden pen, that haue seene *Pan*
> sitting in his bower of delights, & a number of *Midasses* to admire his
> miserable horne pipes, let not your surfeted sight, new come frō
> such puppet play, think scorne to turn aside into this Theater of
> pleasure.[2]

Nashe's prediction proved true, for not only did *Astrophil and Stella* become a quarry for pickpockets of others' wits but also its 108 sonnets became a symbol to other poets of Sidney's achievement, through which
they paid him the compliment of using 108 as a structural device in their
own poetry.[3] Spenser's elegy for Sidney, *Astrophel,* to which is added the

Doleful Lay of Clorinda (presumed by some to be the work of the Countess of Pembroke) contains 216 lines (2 × 108) and the *Lay* 108. Mute tribute is also paid by the 108 poems of the anonymous *Alcilia* (1595) and of Alexander Craig's *Amorous Songs, Sonnets, and Elegies* (1606), some of which are addressed to Lady Penelope Rich, Sidney's Stella. The 109 poems of *Caelica* with their numerous borrowings from Sidney may also be an acknowledgment of praise from Fulke Greville, Sidney's closest friend. Of such emulative influence there can be no question; the excellence of Sidney's wit guaranteed that, as Nashe foresaw.

What is surprising is that a story of such moral bleakness should have found such welcome from the moral Elizabethans. Again, Nashe's description is instructive, for his theater of pleasure offers

> a paper stage streud with pearle, an artificial heau'n to ouershadow the faire frame, & christal wals to encounter your curious eyes, whiles the tragicommody of loue is performed by starlight. The chiefe Actor here is *Melpomene,* whose dusky robes dipt in the ynke of teares, as yet seeme to drop when I view them neere. The argument cruell chastitie, the Prologue hope, the Epilogue dispaire, *videte queso et linguis animisque fauete.*

The accuracy of Nashe's description is attested to by the fact that most later critics use it as the starting point of their own critiques of Sidney. Few critics cite the equally instructive dedication by Thomas Newman, who like Nashe appreciates Sidney's achievement in "the famous deuice of *Astrophel and Stella,* which carrying the generall commendation of all men of iudgement, and being reported to be one of the rarest things that euer any Englishman set abroach," but he nevertheless worries that "the Argument perhaps may seeme too light for your graue viewe" (i.e., the view of Frauncis Flower, to whom it is dedicated). Both Newman and Nashe give unqualified praise to the excellence of the poetry, but Newman's concern for the possible lightness of the argument in the grave view of Mr. Flower should alert us to the discrepancy between Sidney's excellence and his argument, a discrepancy implicit in Nashe's description. His "Theater of pleasure" is nothing more or less than a "paper stage . . . , an artificial heau'n to ouershadow the faire frame" in which "the tragicomedy of loue is performed by starlight. . . . The argument cruell chastitie, the Prologue hope, the Epilogue dispaire." Sidney's rival creation is filled with shadows and false lights and ends in the darkness of despair, facts that have not deterred modern critics from finding cause to praise Astrophil's pursuit of desire. But to the Elizabethans who firmly believed that "all the world's a stage," the pleasures of such theaters lay in their just imitation of nature to teach true morality. As Sidney himself writes in the *Defense of Poetry:*

> that imitation whereof *Poetrie* is, hath the most conveniencie to na-
> ture of al other: insomuch that as *Aristotle* saith, those things which
> in themselves are horrible, as cruel battailes, unnatural monsters, are
> made in poeticall imitation delightful. Truly I have knowne men,
> that even with reading *Amadis de gaule* which God knoweth, want-
> eth much of a perfect *Poesie,* have found their hearts moved to the
> exercise of courtesie, liberalitie, and especially courage.[4]

Poetry teaches the lessons of morality, but we must ask then what kind of morality Astrophil's despair teaches. It teaches us about a man pursuing a married woman for whom he has conceived a passion, "Not at first sight," a man who steals a kiss from her while she is asleep, worrying all the while about her anger and later chiding himself for not being more adventurous (Song II), a man who frankly propositions her despite her gentle, "No, no, no, no, my dear, let be" (Song IV), and then churlishly vilifies her because she has not given in (Song V), a man who once more tries rather gawkily to seduce her (Song VIII), is again repulsed and retires into pastoral exile (Song IX), only too soon to be found under her window still refusing to accept her refusal until she sends him packing (Song XI) to the despair of the final sonnets. In a theater this would be viewed as morally reprehensi-ble behavior in spite of the fact that the majority of modern critics feel a necessity to praise Astrophil's actions because he is, after all, driven by love. The poetic success of Astrophil's failure to win Stella has captivated these critics into believing that we should follow his lamentations and praise of Stella with total sympathy for his endeavors. These lenient mod-ern assessments of Astrophil, it seems to me, miss the point of Sidney's poem. I think that Sidney wanted us to be delighted by Astrophil's wit and to be instructed by the image of a man whose reason gives way to his will and whose hopeful desires finally lead him into despair.[5] Astrophil is not a hero, and he is not a hero precisely because he succumbs so whole-heartedly to the pursuit of his desires. He teaches morality by negative ex-ample. The vacancy at the heart of Sidney's poem proclaims in chorus with all the other English sequences: Go, and do not likewise.

The most explicit statement of the virtues of negative example is the ad-vice of the anonymous "gentleman friend" Philaretes to the author of *Alcilia:*

> In perusing your Loving Folly, and your Declining from it; I do be-
> hold Reason conquering Passion. The infirmity of loving argueth

you are a man; the firmness thereof, discovereth a good wit and the best nature: and the falling from it, true virtue. Beauty was always of force to mislead the wisest; and men of greatest perfection have had no power to resist Love. The best are accompanied with vices, to exercise their virtues; whose glory shineth brightest in resisting motives of pleasure, and in subduing affections. . . . Yet herein it appeareth you have made good use of Reason; that being heretofore lost in youthful vanity, have now, by timely discretion, found yourself!

Let me entreat you to suffer these your Passionate Sonnets to be published! which may, peradventure, make others, possessed with the like Humour of Loving, to follow your example, in leaving; and move other *Alcilias* (if there be any) to embrace deserving love, while they may.[6]

Interpreting the sonnets as negative example makes sense of Newman's hesitation about the lightness of Sidney's argument and places Nashe's description in a context that shows that accurate description does not necessarily imply approbation or praise. The "paper stage" betrays the lack of a firmer foundation; the "artificial heau'n" does "ouershadow the faire frame" of God's intended creation; the "tragicomedy of loue is performed by starlight" only for lack of better light. The argument is "*cruell* chastitie" only because that chastity will not respond to Astrophil's desires. Sidney, as I hope to prove, is using Astrophil's journey from hope to despair as a fictional device for the analysis of human desire in Christian terms.

Most commentators on Sidney find an irresistible impulse to draw into *Astrophil and Stella* the final two sonnets of *Certain Sonnets,* "Thou blindman's mark" and "Leave me, O Love, which reachest but to dust."[7] The impulse is entirely understandable not only because those two sonnets analyze the inadequacies of human desire within a context that accounts for the inadequacy but also because the ending of *Astrophil and Stella*, if read as a justification or glorification of Astrophil's actions, is grievously inconclusive and uninstructive. Those two explicitly Christian poems cry out to be included unless one sees that beneath the witty surface of Astrophil's lamentations and selfish demands lies the old battle of the "erected wit" and the "infected will" that as Sidney assures us in the *Defense of Poetry* continues to deprive us of the golden world that was once ours by right. Nevertheless, it would be a great mistake to include those two poems in the sequence. They show a repentance and a knowledge of desire that Astrophil never achieves. The brilliance of Sidney's negative example is that he realized that Astrophil must end in despair because he never learns from his experience. We the readers are meant to supply the Christian context that will make sense of the insufficiencies of Astrophil's insights into his predicament.

The title itself should give us some hint of the disjunction that is Sidney's subject: *Astrophil and Stella.* Most sonnet sequences, if titled, use only the name of the lady, the presumed subject and object of the poetry. Sidney uses a copulative title, one part derived from Greek and one from Latin, announcing even before we start to read a disjunction, minor but perhaps significant. Even disallowing the etymological disjunction, inspection reveals a disunity in the title, a doubleness, a duplicity. Two names are joined by a grammatical copula, which we accept out of hand as a unity, which it will not become. We are so used to accepting the unity of a Romeo and Juliet that we forget that the true coupling is the full title: *The Tragedy of Romeo and Juliet.* Misfortune and not love is their final union, and that is the reason we still read their story. Astrophil and Stella are separate from the moment the title is read, and if we stop to think even for a moment about the title, what possible union is there for a star-lover and a star? Petrarch makes his Laura into a false sun; Scève creates a false moon (Délie), but neither one uses as the major name of his loved one a name from another order of nature. I do not know how common the name Stella was for women in the sixteenth century, but surely Sidney is indicating in his choice of names a being of a different order, distant, unattainable, and reflected, a light that does not illuminate, that leaves us in the dark, a light that is shared and shown by thousands of other Stellas, which goes far to dispute the uniqueness of Astrophil's claims for his Stella.

The ambiguity of the title is carefully demonstrated in the sequence. The tragicomedy of love performed by starlight is inadequately lighted. Stella's eyes, "nature's chiefest work," are black, "that sweete blacke which vailes the heav'nly eye" (sonnet 20). Astrophil's starlit stage is dark and perilous. His theatre is of the mind "that sought fit words to paint the blackest face of woe" (sonnet 1). The face can be none other than his own face, his own rejected desires. Astrophil, in calling for "some fresh and fruitfull showers upon my sunne-burn'd braine" (sonnet 1), is sounding a retreat from the light of common day, a retreat that will engulf him in the blackness of his own mind as figured by the blackness of Stella's eyes. Who ever heard of black stars before the discovery of black holes?[8]

The metaphor of blackness expands under Astrophil's preoccupations. He reaches out to the common sunlit world he has rejected to find the metaphors to describe the blackness he now recognizes as his world:

> I call it praise to suffer Tyrannie:
> And now employ the remnant of my wit,
>   To make my selfe beleeve, that all is well,
>   While with a feeling skill I paint my hell. (Sonnet 2)

His painting of the scenery of his starlit world draws upon the common Christian opposition of heaven and hell, but no lover has ever thought that a denial of what he considers heaven is anything else but a hell. By sonnet 86 he has transferred the responsibility for his fate to Stella:

> Use something else to chast'n me withall,
>   Then those blest eyes, where all my hopes do dwell,
>   No doome should make one's heav'n become his hell.[9]

Astrophil at this point is playing a more skillfully feeling game in drawing in other common words from Christian eschatology. "Doome" carries a heavy overtone of Christian damnation, of judgment against the speaker, but in point of fact, the "doome" is nothing more than Stella's judgment of his love suit, which has turned his heaven into his hell. Astrophil has inverted every image he uses. Black has replaced light. Heaven is Stella's submission to him; Hell is her refusal of her grace. Astrophil exploits every ambiguity of common Christian imagery to paint his own case in the most salutary light, which he calls in sonnet 1 "the blackest face of woe." In every way he uses spiritual meanings for physical ends:

> So while thy beautie drawes the heart to love,
>   As fast thy Vertue bends that love to good:
>   'But ah,' Desire still cries, 'give me some food.'
>
> (Sonnet 71)

These lines are the mid-lines of the entire sequence, a point to which I shall return in the last section of this essay. At this point we need only say that Astrophil is painting most skillfully but only feelingly, that is, selfishly.

This simple technique of inversion is evident even in the light imagery used to describe Stella. The single star that Stella's name implies becomes by sonnet 7 two black stars, her eyes, which Astrophil would have us believe to be Nature's "chiefe worke." By sonnet 68 Stella has become "the onely Planet of my light, / Light of my life, and life of my desire," and by sonnet 76 his star has been metamorphosed into his sun: "But now appeares my day, / The onely light of joy, the onely warmth of *Love*." By the end of the sequence his sun is only memory because of Stella's absence from him (sonnets 88, 89, 91, 96, 97, 98).

> But soone as thought of thee breeds my delight,
>   And my yong soule flutters to thee his nest,
>   Most rude dispaire my daily unbidden guest,[10]
> Clips streight my wings, streight wraps me in his night,
>   And makes me then bow downe my head, and say,
> Ah what doth *Phoebus'* gold that wretch availe,
> Whom iron doores do keepe from use of day?   (Sonnet 108)

The imagery of light associated with Stella's eyes is, to say the least, contradictory: "When Sun is hid, can starres such beames display?" (sonnet 88). The contradiction is intended by Sidney to alert us to the confusion of Astrophil's apprehension, climaxed most explicitly in sonnet 89, the only sonnet in the sequence to employ just two rhymes:

> Now that of absence the most irksome night,
>   With darkest shade doth overcome my day;
>   Since *Stella's* eyes, wont to give me my day,
> Leaving my Hemisphere, leave me in night,
> Each day seemes long, and longs for long-staid night,
>   The night as tedious, wooes th'approch of day;
>   Tired with the dusty toiles of busie day,
> Languisht with horrors of the silent night
> Suffering the evils both of the day and night,
>   While no night is more darke then is my day,
>   Nor no day hath lesse quiet then my night:
> With such bad mixture of my night and day,
>   That living thus in blackest winter night,
>   I feele the flames of hottest sommer day.

Every possible inversion of day and night is wrung out of this infernal litany of the lover's despair. The literary sources of this inversion of day and night is Vergil, *Aeneid*, 4.522–32 and more directly Petrarch's *Canzoniere* 22, but Sidney complicates the issue by having Astrophil confuse both inner and outer day and night. They have become all one to him, and from this point on the sequence is shrouded in darkness both physical and moral.

The permutations of Stella's light-giving qualities in these later sonnets is anticipated in an earlier block of poems (31–40), which also describe the lover's night world. Sonnet 32, the central sonnet of the first unbroken block of sonnets (1–63), about which I shall speak later, is an invocation to Morpheus, which will require some elucidation because of its importance to Astrophil's predicament. Morpheus, the son of Somnus, god of sleep, is most elaborately described in Ovid's story of Ceyx and Alcyon (*Metamorphoses*, 11.591 ff.). He is the god who appears to dreamers in human shape, and it is he who appears to the grieving Ceyx to inform her of her husband's death. Ovid describes him:

> At pater e populo natorum mille suorum
> excitat artificem simulatoremque figurae
> Morphea: non illo quisquam sollertius alter
> exprimit incessus vultumque sonumque loquendi;
> adicit et vestes et consuetissima cuique
> verba. (633–38)

[But the father rouses Morpheus from the throng of his thousand sons, a cunning imitator of the human form. No other is more skilled than he is representing the gait, the features, and the speech of men, the clothing also and the accustomed words of each he represents.][11]

Ovid emphasizes the artifice of the verisimilitude. Sidney undoubtedly knew the Ovidian story because he imitates lines 623–26 in sonnet 39, but he would also have known Chaucer's use of Ovid's story in *The Book of the Duchess* where the ambivalence of this beneficent dissimulator is more apparent. We should also recall that Spenser has Archimago send to the house of Morpheus to fetch him evil spirits to deceive Una and Red Crosse (*FQ* I.ii.36–44). Thus, an invocation to Morpheus should not be read as a simple request for sleep:

> *Morpheus,* the lively sonne of deadly sleepe,
>   Witnesse of life to them that living die:
>   A Prophet oft, and oft an historie,
> A Poet eke, as humours fly or creepe,
> Since thou in me so sure a power doest keepe,
>   That never I with clos'd-up sense do lie,
>   But by thy worke my *Stella* I descrie,
> Teaching blind eyes both how to smile and weepe.

Morpheus' power over Astrophil is that he is the bringer of Stella's image, but it should be observed that even Astrophil is aware of the artifice. I am not so sure that Astrophil is aware of the double edge of those "blind eyes" or of the earlier "Witnesse of life to them that living die." Sidney's invocation of Morpheus introduces a note of the hellish nature of Astrophil's infatuation. He has closed out every consideration of the waking world. In sonnet 30 he enumerates the great political problems of his time and concludes:

> These questions busie wits to me do frame;
> I, cumbred with good maners, answer do,
> But know not how, for still I thinke of you.

In sonnet 31 he projects his wretched plight onto the moon ("With how sad steps, o Moone, thou climb'st the skies") before succumbing to the blandishments of Morpheus in the sonnet under discussion. Astrophil is busy enclosing himself in the night of his own desires under the dubious patronage of Morpheus.

The complex of metaphors I have been describing derives ultimately from a common Christian metaphor, most forcefully stated in Romans 13. 10–14 (Geneva version):

> Loue doeth not euil to his neighbour: therefore is loue ye fulfilling of the law.
> And that considering the season, that it is now time that we shulde arise from slepe: for now is our saluation nerer, then when we beleued it.
> The night is past, & the day is at hand: let vs therefore cast away the workes of darkenes, and let vs put on the armour of light,
> So that we walke honestly, as in the day: not in glotonie, and dronkennes, neither in chambering and wantonnes, nor in strife and enuying.

Paul's injunction to put on the new man of spirituality and to put away the old man of bondage to sin, couched here in metaphors of light and dark, sleep and waking, is picked up again in 1 Thessalonians 5.5–6: "Ye are all the children of light, and the children of the day: we are not of the night neither of darknes. Therefore let vs not slepe as do other, but let vs watch and be sober." The Genevan gloss to these lines is instructive: "Here slepe is taken for contempt of saluation, when men continewe in sinnes, and wil not awake to godlinesse." "Watch" is glossed: "And not be ouercome with the cares of the world." Astrophil's concerns throughout the sequence lock him up in his "sleep of the senses" and prevent his seeing that worship of the idol he himself has created has imprisoned him in his hellish night. Sidney's brilliant inversion of traditional imagery cries out for the Christian context, which finally does give meaning to Astrophil's negative example of what a lover should be.

II

The negative example of Astrophil's wit is not restricted to inversions of explicitly biblical metaphors. The informing spirit of Christian charity extended itself to include even the epic tales of Homer. We have long accepted the fact that the Stella of the sonnets is a fictionalized account of a supposed romance that Sidney had with Penelope Lady Rich.[12] More recently it has been argued that her first name suggested to Sidney a structural device for his sequence, the 108 sonnets representing the 108 suitors of Homer's Penelope, who played a game of trying to hit a stone called the Penelope stone to decide who would win the lady. The structure of *Astrophil and Stella* truncates that game, fruitlessly invoking an absent Penelope. I would like to suggest that there is another submerged Homeric metaphor in the structure of the sequence: the 119 poems are one short of the number of months Ulysses spent returning to Penelope, and thus Astrophil's 119 attempts to win his Stella are doomed by the very form of the sequence.[13] Astrophil is a negative example of the fortitude and fidelity of Ulysses. Roger Ascham, toward the end of the first book of *The Scholemaster,* in his tirade against the Italianate Englishman, proposes Ulysses as an exemplar both of "wisdom and wareness":

Which wisdom and wariness will not serve neither a traveler except Pallas be always at his elbow, that is, God's special grace from heaven, to keep him in God's fear in all his doings, in all his journey. For he [the English traveler] shall not always, in his absence out of England, light upon a gentle Alcinous and walk in his fair gardens full of all harmless pleasures; but he shall sometimes fall either into the hands of some cruel Cyclops or into the lap of some wanton and dallying Dame Calypso, and so suffer the danger of many a deadly den, not so full of perils to destroy the body as full of vain pleasures to poison the mind. Some Siren shall sing him a song, sweet in tune, but sounding in the end to his utter destruction. If Scylla drown him not, Charybdis may fortune swallow him. Some Circe shall make him, of a plain Englishman, a right Italian. And at length to hell, or to some hellish place, is he likely to go, from whence is hard returning, although one Ulysses, and that by Pallas' aid and good counsel of Tiresias, once escaped that horrible den of deadly darkness.[14]

Ascham concludes that the effects of such ungodly journeying are four:

> The first, forgetfulness of all good things learned before; the second, dullness to receive either learning or honesty ever after; the third, a mind embracing lightly the worse opinion and barren of discretion to make true difference betwixt good and ill, betwixt truth and vanity; the fourth, a proud disdainfulness of other good men in all honest matters.[15]

Ascham's terms, borrowed from Plato, may be used as a gloss on the actions and speeches of Astrophil throughout the sequence. We need not repine at the moral strictures of Ascham's judgments. The man chosen to be tutor to Queen Elizabeth, we may be sure, would represent those values and commonly held moral opinions esteemed by the court for the education of their future ruler. His allegorization of Ulysses as exemplar rests firmly on an allegiance to virtue and wisdom, the right use of the reason to control temptations, and a firm belief that the fear of God is the beginning of wisdom. Ascham's terms are the insights of a learned and pious Christian humanist. His often quoted comments on the "open manslaughter and bold bawdry" as the "whole pleasure" of the *Morte d'Arthur* of Malory is often used to dispose of him as a simplistic moralizing critic, but his comments should at least be given the grace of their context, the Horatian *utile et dulce:* "This is good stuff for wise men to laugh at or honest men to take pleasure at."[16] Wise men, one assumes, would laugh at the follies that destroyed Arthur's kingdom: honest men would take pleasure in the negative example that Malory's Arthurian world presents. Ascham knew what he was about, and his analysis of the effects of the unheroic inversion of Ulysses' voyage back to his wife can act as a gloss to the upstart, surrogate Ulysses that Sidney is postulating to make obvious Astrophil's absurdities of wit in that most Italianate poetic form, the sonnet sequence.

That he has forgotten what he and every other schoolboy in the Renaissance has learned needs no further investigation than sonnet 1, in which he completely inverts the sequence of the laws of rhetorical composition: *inventio, dispositio, elocutio.* As Ringler notes: "Astrophil began in the wrong order with an inadequate method. He first sought words (*elocutio*) rather than matter, and tried to find words through imitation of others rather than by the proper processes of invention." Sidney, as the first major theoretical literary critic of the English Renaissance, could not have been un-mindful that his Astrophil was breaking one of the primary rules of composition, and it is not, in spite of Kalstone's eloquent defense,[17] Sidney's attempt to discover the new eloquence of love poetry. Sincerity and dramatic energy are hardly the point to be considered when reading the final tercet:

> Thus great with child to speake, and helplesse in my throwes,
>   Biting my trewand pen, beating my selfe for spite,
>   'Foole,' said my Muse to me, 'looke in thy heart and write.'

There is as much wit and probably more sincerity in Sidney's rendition of Psalms 7.14:

> Lo he that first conceiv'd a wretched thought,
>   And great with child of mischeif travail'd long,
>   Now brought abed, hath brought nought forth, but nought.

The Genevan version of this same verse provides an interesting comparison: "Beholde, he shal trauaile with wickednes: for he hathe conceiued mischief, but he shal bring forthe a lye." The similarity of Sidney's imagery in both sonnet 1 and Psalm 7 suggests that we pay attention to the matter rather than the manner of his utterance. Renaissance commentators on the heart suggest that it is not the most reliable or discriminating of the natural organs. Thomas Wright in his *The Passions of the Minde* cites the heart as the "place where passions lodge" and concludes:

> Yet supposing the Passions principally reside in the heart, as we per-ceiue by the concourse of humours thereunto . . . the humours con-curre to help, dispose and enable the heart to worke such operations: for as we proue by experience, if a man sleepe with open eyes, al-though his sight be maruelous excellent, yet he seeth nothing, be-cause in sleepe, the purer spirits are recalled into the inner parts of the body, leauing the eyes destitute of spirits, and abandoned of force, which presently in waking returne againe: euen so I conceiue the heart, prepared by nature to digest the blood sent from the liuer yet for diuers respects, not to haue the temperature which all pas-sions require; for loue will haue heat, and sadnesse cold, feare con-stringeth & pleasure dilateth; the heart therefore which was to be

subiect to such diuersities of Passions, by Nature was depriued of al such contrary dispositions.[18]

Wright was a respectable medical authority, and his verdict on the capacity of the heart invites us to ask two further questions of the final lines of sonnet 1. What muse would direct a poet to such an inadequate touchstone? What muse would call her poet a fool? Considering Astrophil's other references to muses and his apparent total self-sufficiency poetically, I think we cannot take the muse's command in sonnet 1 as a beneficent beginning for this sequence or even as the beginning of the romantic movement.

Astrophil's forgetfulness of all he has learned appears again in sonnet 3: "Let daintie wits crie on the Sisters nine, / That brauely maskt, their fancies may be told." If he has learned anything from his Muse in sonnet 1, it is that he must rely on the passions of his heart, yet here he rejects as mere artifice the attempts of other love poets, and in sonnet 6 he has already put aside the whole pretense of Muses: "Some Lovers speake *when they their Muses entertaine* / Of hopes begot by feare, of wot not what desires." But we need not restrict our catalogue of Astrophil's forgetfulness to the lessons of the Muses. He has forgotten the precepts of Virtue (sonnet 4), of Christian morality (sonnet 5), of Reason (sonnet 10), of Truth (sonnet 11), of friends (sonnets 14, 21), and of literary convention (sonnet 15). One should not require a full catalogue of the poems in which Astrophil's desires blind him to the dictates of the outside world, which he has learned but put aside as impediments to his desires. Seneca, Plato, Socrates, all that he has learned has been superseded by his love for Stella.

His forgetfulness of what he has learned is climaxed in sonnet 63 when he addresses that most basic of learning tools: *O grammer rules* and triumphantly concludes:

> But Grammer's force with sweet successe confirme,
> For Grammer sayes (o this deare *Stella* weighe,)
> For Grammer sayes (to Grammer who sayes nay)
> That in one speech two Negatives affirme.

His conclusion of the sonnet is based on the simple fact that Stella "twise said, No, No." As Ringler rightly notes: "Astrophil's argument is doubly sophistical: (a) in the sixteenth century the double negative was a common and accepted English usage, so that his 'grammer rules' apply only to Latin and not to English; and (b) grammatically 'no, no' is a repetition for emphasis and not a double negative at all."[19] One might also point out that the first line of sonnet 64 is: "No more, my deare, no more these counsels trie," an argument that Astrophil should have foreseen, one that Stella might have taken up, had she been so foolish or given the opportunity.

Astrophil's inability to learn anything new can be illustrated by the juxtaposition of sonnet 72 and Song II:

> Desire, though thou my old companion art,
>   And oft so clings to my pure Love, that I
>   One from the other scarcely can descrie,
> While each doth blow the fier of my hart. . . .
> But thou Desire, because thou wouldst have all,
> Now banisht art, but yet alas how shall?

This apparent repentance on Astrophil's part is immediately countered by his discovery of Stella asleep: "Have I caught my heav'nly jewell?" The irony of that "heav'nly" cannot be unintentional on Sidney's part. One is reminded of Lady Wishfort's "What's integrity to an opportunity?" But Astrophil, the slow learner, his integrity lost, cannot seize the opportunity and blames himself in the last stanza for not overachieving:

> Oh sweet kisse, but ah she is waking,
> Lowring beautie chastens me:
> Now will I away hence flee:
> Foole, more foole, for no more taking.

His callousness is enough to stagger the mind. The intellectual decision of sonnet 72, clearly difficult to implement as the pathetic "but yet alas how shall" of the last line shows, is followed immediately by a course of action that negates the decision. An intellectual decision followed by a totally contradictory action fits well Ascham's third effect: "a mind embracing lightly the worse opinion and barren of discretion to make true distinction betwixt good and ill, betwixt truth and vanity."

This third effect is shown not only in Astrophil's actions but also in his words, for Astrophil constantly chooses the more material sense of a word, thinking to deplete it of its spiritual meaning. A simple example occurs in sonnet 1:

> Loving in truth, and faine in verse my love to show,
> That the deare She might take some pleasure of my paine:
> Pleasure might cause her reade, reading might make her know,
> Knowledge might pitie winne, and pitie grace obtaine.

The skillfull use of the figure *gradatio* leads up to the climactic word "grace," which here can only mean "favor," or even "sexual union," but at this point in the sequence we are hardly in a position to accuse Astrophil of indecorous suggestions or even of misappropriating a theological term. Nevertheless, the insinuation is there, as it is in sonnet 77.[20] After a partial "blazon" of looks, face, presence, grace, hand, lips, skin, words, voice, conversation, he concludes:

[They make] me in my best thoughts and quietest judgement see,
That in no more but these I might be fully blest:
Yet ah, my Mayd'n Muse doth blush to tell the best.

The *blazon* is partial because it omits details of a fleshly nature, as we shall. see by comparing it to Spenser's *Amoretti,* Sonnet 64, and *Epithalamion,* stanza 10. Spenser includes eyes, forehead, cheeks, lips, breast, paps, neck,

And all her body like a pallace fayre,
Ascending uppe, with many a stately stayre,
To honours seat and chastities sweet bowre.

Sidney's blazon anatomizes an animated conversation, hand gestures included. We can only assume then that the "best" is Stella's body, undescribed, but clearly present in Astrophil's imagination.

The same leveling of experience to the physical occurs in sonnet 76. After an absence Stella appears to Astrophil.

She comes, and streight therewith her shining twins do move
    Their rayes to me, who in her tedious absence lay
    Benighted in cold wo, but now appeares my day,
The onely light of joy, the onely warmth of *Love.*
She comes with light and warmth, which like *Aurora* prove
    Of gentle force, so that mine eyes dare gladly play
    With such a rosie morne, whose beames most freshly gay
Scortch not, but onely do darke chilling sprites remove.

Stella, his sun, has come like Aurora, to light his world and warm his spirits, but as his day increases in light and heat, he complains of the heat, "it burnes," and then turns in the concluding couplet to a desire that "my sunne go downe with meeker beames to bed." The image continues the progress of the sun of Astrophil's world, but he wants those burning beams to be meeker in "bed." Astrophil is not referring to the sun sinking in the west; the bed he is suggesting is his own, and the meekness he requires is Stella's submission to him. But a curious transference occurs in the poem to make the image blatantly sexual. In line 9 Astrophil remarks: "But lo, while I do speake, it groweth noone with me," transferring the basic metaphor, the daily progress of the sun (Stella-Aurora) from east to west, to Astrophil. Alan Sinfield suggests that the line is bawdy, comparing it to Mercutio's comment in *Romeo and Juliet,* 2.4.108: "For the bawdy hand of the dial is now upon the prick of noon," and to Barnabe Barnes's imitation of this sonnet, which is worth quoting for its clarification and simplification of the metaphor.

> When with the Dawning of my first delight,
>   The Daylight of love's Delicacy moved me;
>   Then from heaven's disdainful starry light,
>   The Moonlight of her Chastity reproved me.
> Her forehead's threatful clouds from hope removed me,
>   Till Midnight reared on the mid-noctial line;
>   Her heart whiles Pity's slight had undershoved me;
>   Then did I force her downward to decline
> Till Dawning daylight cheerfully did shine;
>   And by such happy revolution drew
>   Her Morning's blush to joyful smiles incline.
> And now Meridian heat dries up my dew;
>   There rest, fair Planets! Stay, bright orbs of day!
>   *Still smiling at my dial, next eleven!*[21]

Barnes makes his goddess-planet-woman "downward to decline" to his wishes. The noon dries up his dew, but still he smilingly can look at his dial, now not at noon, but at eleven, which should have been some comfort for the male ego.

Sidney's pun for Astrophil is more deceptively decorous, but equally physical:

> My heart cries 'ah,' it burnes, mine eyes now dazled be:
> No wind, no shade can coole, what helpe then in my case,
>   But with short breath, long lookes, staid feet and walking hed
>   Pray that my sunne go downe with meeker beames to bed.

The referent of "it" in the phrase "it burns" is to say the least, ambiguous, referring either to his sun, which burns him or to his own tumescence, or to both. The "short breath" and "long lookes" of line 13 suggest some kind of imaginative sexual excitement, but the "staid feet" and "walking hed" are perplexing, in spite of their obvious opposition. I think that "walking hed" is Astrophil's *penis erectus* and will support my contention by reference to sonnets 65 and 72. In 65 Astrophil concludes his address to Cupid:

> Since in thine armes, if learnd fame truth hath spread,
> Thou bear'st the arrow, I the arrow head.

In context Astrophil is saying that Cupid bears arrows and he bears the wound of the arrowhead of love, but as Ringler points out, the Sidney arms are *or, a pheon azure,* that is an azure arrowhead on a gold background. This in itself is a suitably complex image for Sidney's wit, but it gets complicated if we consider the middle lines of sonnet 72:

> I must no more in thy sweet passions lie;
> *Vertue's* gold now must head my *Cupid's* dart.

As discussed above, Astrophil has made a decision to abandon Desire, which has become indistinguishable from "my pure Love," but as I suggested above, this intellectual decision leads only to the dastardly kiss stolen from the sleeping Stella and the self-recrimination for not taking more of Song II. The ambiguity of these central lines suggests a devious reason for Astrophil's decision. "Lie" can mean either "rest in" or "tell untruths," both of which Astrophil has done, but to goldleaf Cupid's dart with Vertue's gold is absolute subterfuge. On the surface Astrophil means that he is simulating the golden arrows of Cupid that bring true love, but this prophylactic simulation of true love only disguises the fact that Astrophil has assimilated Cupid's dart as an attribute of himself, with the obvious phallic implications.

Sonnet 73, immediately following Song II, is a most skillful evasion of responsibility for the kiss he has just stolen.

> *Love* still a boy, and oft a wanton is,
> School'd onely by his mother's tender eye:
> What wonder then if he his lesson misse,
> When for so soft a rod deare play he trie?

The logic of the comparison is: Cupid is only a boy but sometimes wanton. This wanton boy is so because he is schooled only by his mother's tenderness. No wonder he misses the lesson she is trying to teach him when her treatment of him is so soft. That is what Astrophil thinks he is saying, but even then he is blaming Venus's "tender eye" for condoning a juvenile delinquency that will excuse both Cupid and himself. The implication is that Stella's beauty is the cause of Astrophil's transgression, but the *elocutio* of the fourth line suggests another kind of feigning excuse: Love is only a boy. He is safe, "when for so soft a rod deare play he trie," i.e., when he tries dear (deer, venereal) sport with so soft a penis. In this first quatrain Astrophil blames Venus's laxity; in the second he blames his indiscretion on Cupid's incapacity.

> And yet my Starre, because a sugred kisse
> In sport I suckt, while she asleep did lie,
> Doth lowre, nay, chide; nay, threat for only this:
> Sweet, it was saucie *Love,* not humble I.

The brilliance of this evasion of responsibility should not blind us to the kind of skillful feeling with which Astrophil can deceive. In the ninth and final stanza of Song IV Astrophil commits another of his phallicities:

> Wo to me, and do you sweare
> Me to hate? But I forbeare,
> Cursed be my desines all,
> *That brought me so high to fall:*
> *Soone with my death I will please thee,*
> 'No, no, no, no, my Deare, let be.'

The seeming self-abnegation of the underlined verses is undercut by the undertone of phallic height brought high and then low and the promise to please Stella with the *petite Morte* of orgasm, although in Astrophil's demented state he may mean a kind of lady of Shalott demise. In any event, in her constant refusal of his blandishments Stella is not hoodwinked.

Sonnet 56 is characteristic of the way in which Astrophil turns ordinary meanings to his sexually starved purposes.

> Fy, schoole of Patience, Fy, your lesson is
> Far far too long to learne it without booke:
> What, a whole weeke without one peece of looke,
> And thinke I should not your large precepts misse?
> When I might reade those letters faire of blisse,
> Which in her face teach vertue, I could brooke
> Somewhat thy lead'n counsels, which I tooke

As of a friend that meant not much amisse:
    But now that I, alas, do want her sight,
What, dost thou thinke that I can ever take
In thy cold stuffe a flegmatike delight?
No, Patience, if thou wilt my good, then make
    Her come, and heare with patience my desire,
    And then with patience bid me beare my fire.

Astrophil's annoyance at and contempt for what he terms the "schoole of Patience" is another witty rejection of virtue. Patience is traditionally a branch of the cardinal virtue fortitude, a virtue in which he is singularly lacking. He cannot learn the "large precepts" of Patience without the book open before him, and he can sustain those "lead'n counsels" only when the book of Stella's face is present to teach him virtue. Unfortunately, she is not present to help him with his lesson of patience, and therefore he cannot stomach the cold and moist *(flegmatike)* humour "in [her] cold stuffe." His conclusion is a bargain with patience to bring Stella to him to patiently hear his desire and then to bid him bear his hot desires, the assumption being that she is the better teacher of patience. But that is a rather lame conclusion for Astrophil's spirited and heated attack. The conclusion gains much in dramatic force, however, if we read "beare" as "bare," that is, show himself to her. What more could any lover ask or hope to be told? The pun is, needless to say, outrageous, as Sidney undoubtedly intended.

The sequence is studded with such inphallicities. One poem, early in the sequence, has caused difficulty to editors and critics. Sonnet 36 compares Stella to a conqueror of a town, beginning a new assault.

STELLA, whence doth this new assault arise,
A conquerd, yelden, ransackt heart to winne?
Whereto long since, through my long battred eyes,
Whole armies of thy beauties entred in.
    And there long since, *Love* thy Lieutenant lies,
My forces razde, thy banners raisd within:
Of conquest, do not these effects suffice,
But wilt new warre upon thine own begin?
    With so sweete voice, and by sweete Nature so,
In sweetest strength, so sweetly skild withall,
In all sweete stratagems sweete Arte can show,
That not my soule, which at thy foot did fall,
    Long since forc'd by thy beames, but stone nor tree
    By Sence's priviledge, can scape from thee.

Max Putzel's note in his edition is undoubtedly correct in suggesting "that the *new assault* of line 1 is the singing of a song, a point largely obscured by the battle metaphor of the octave."[22] Stella has assaulted him so often through the eyes that this song, attacking him through the ears, is a new kind of assault on his love. Putzel is equally correct in seeing that the battle metaphor of the octave projects itself forcefully into the total meaning of the sonnet. The usual assumption is that Stella is beginning a new assault, having already *long since* won the town that Astrophil has become, and that interpretation fits in quite well with Putzel's suggestion, but the force of the siege metaphor is more complicated, including a bawdy meaning that complements the meaning that Putzel suggests as the primary one.

I think that the assault is on the part of Astrophil, who wonders how in his conquered condition this new assault can *arise* on his part. Ringler finds difficulty in "My forces razde, thy banners raisd within" and comments: "Miss Wilson emended to 'fortress' because 'you cannot raze forces or raise banners within them'; but forces can be 'razed,' that is destroyed or swept away (*OED* 5), and the banners are 'rais'd' within the castle of the lover's heart."[23] This is no real explanation of the crux. Astrophil means both "razed" and "raised," that is, his forces have been previously razed by Stella's conquest but that conquest has raised his sexual forces, which are now ready for the new assault. Astrophil's strategy is, of course, to put the blame for the new assault on Stella: "But wilt new warre upon thine owne begin?" Even more difficult than the "razde" crux is the syntax of the last three lines. Apparently the meaning is: that not only my soule but also stones and trees cannot escape your conquest, that is, neither rational nor vegetable soul can escape your influence. Nevertheless, the locution is strange, and the unusual strength of those four monosyllables "That not my soule" suggests another opposition than "stone or tree," an opposition unstated but implied—the flesh, in which case, the phrase "By Sence's priviledge" would apply to the raised forces, that is, the involuntary privilege granted to the senses, which escapes the conquest already made upon his soul.

The phallic impudence of Astrophil's erected wit is particularly apparent in sonnet 45:

> Stella oft sees the verie face of wo
>   Painted in my beclowded stormie face:
>   But cannot skill to pitie my disgrace,
> Not though thereof the cause her selfe she know:
> Yet hearing late a fable, which did show
>   Of Lovers never knowne, a grievous case,
>   Pitie thereof gate in her breast such place

That, from that sea deriv'd, teares' spring did flow.
    Alas, if Fancy drawne by imag'd things,
Though false, yet with free scope more grace doth breed
Then servant's wracke, where new doubts honor brings;
Then thinke my deare, that you in me do reed
    Of Lover's ruine some sad Tragedie:
    I am not I, pitie the tale of me.

Astrophil's jealousy of the unnamed lovers, who move Stella's pity, is a literary boobytrap for his expectations. He carefully sets up an opposition between the "grace" granted their "imag'd" and therefore "false" passion and his own "verie face of wo / Painted," an art form that appeals to the eyes and not to the ears, for which he suffers "disgrace." By the end of the sonnet he has willingly, and falsely, given himself up ("I am not I") to become the words he speaks ("pitie the tale of me") in a vain effort to secure the grace of the unnamed lovers. He has lost the ability to distinguish between a response to literature and a response to life. Logically he has been hoist on his own petard, but Astrophil's unremitting passion surmounts even such logical defeat by blatantly punning on the word "tale," for which he would willingly substitute "tail," a word that he has become in the course of these sonnets, an object that he has elevated in his thoughts to be the principal definition of his being.

The dissociation of Astrophil's being and his growing concentration on his sexual desires as the central issue of his fable to Stella is matched by his hybris, Ascham's fourth effect derived from Plato. Ascham's rendition of Plato's term *hybris* restricts it to "a proud disdainfulness of other good men in all honest matters." Ascham could not envision that Astrophil would carry his hybris to the ultimate deification of his idol, blasphemy. Once more Sidney undercuts his plangent hero, and of this latter type of undercutting Song I is a perfect example.

III

The poem has been unjustly neglected by the critics, presumably because of the extravagance of the praise, unusual even for Astrophil's heady rhetoric. The poem is circular, in that the first and ninth stanzas are identical. Each stanza begins with two lines of question, which are answered by the last two lines. The third line is identical throughout:

Doubt you to whom my Muse these notes entendeth,
Which now my breast orecharg'd to Musicke lendeth?
To you, to you, all song of praise is due,
Only in you my song begins and endeth.

The self-conscious smugness of the question should infuriate the reader who has been barraged by unceasing praise of Stella for the preceding sixty-three sonnets. Astrophil is so "orecharg'd" that the sonnet form will not contain his passion and he bursts into song. But what is the purpose of that rhetorical question? And is the question addressed to Stella or to the reader? In either case the answer to the question is, of course, "Stella," as Astrophil's triumphant answer in lines 3 and 4 should assure us both of his intense devotion and the circularity of his argument mirrored by the circularity of his poem. The reader, however, should see that Astrophil's lyrical outburst is nothing else than blasphemy. Only to God all song of praise is due; only in God do we begin and end. Astrophil is both infatuated and fatuous. Sidney was neither of these, and in his case we need not rely on the putative intelligence and learning of the "Elizabethan reader," that most chameleon commodity of literary criticism, because Sidney has told us in his other works how he viewed the relationship of poetic utterance and Christian belief.

In the *Defense of Poesy,* describing the three most general types of poetry, he writes: "The chiefe, both in antiquitie and excellencie, were they that did imitate the unconceiveable excellencies of God. Such were *David* in his Psalmes; *Salomon* in his song of songs, in his *Ecclesiastes,* and *Proverbes.* *Moses* and *Debora* in their Hymnes; and the wryter of *Jobe* . . . against these none will speake that hath the holie Ghost in due holy reverence. . . . And this *Poesie* must be used by whosoever will follow S. *Paules* counsaile, in singing Psalmes when they are mery, and I knowe is used with the frute of comfort by some, when, in sorrowfull panges of their death bringing sinnes, they finde the consolation of the never leaving goodnes."[24] Sidney is referring to Paul's advice in Ephesians 5, which it might be well to quote since no modern editor of the *Defense* has seen fit to give so much as a reference:

> Be ye therefore followers of God, as dere children,
> And walke in loue, euen as Christ hathe loued vs, and hathe giuen him self for vs, *to be* an offring and a sacrifice of a swete smelling sauour to God.
> But fornication, & all vnclennes, or couetousnes, let it not be once named among you, as it becommeth Saintes,
> Nether filthines, nether foolish talking, nether iesting, which are things not comelie, but rather giuing of thankes.
> For this ye knowe, that no whoremonger, nether vncleane persone, nor couetous persone, which is an idolater, hathe any inheritance in the kingdome of Christ, & of God.

Let no man deceiue you with vaine wordes: for [of] suche things
    commeth the wrath of God vpon the children of disobedience.
Be not therefore companions with them.
For ye were once darkenes, but are now light in the Lord: walke as
    children of light,
(For the frute of the Spirit *is* in all goodnes, and righteousnes, and
    trueth)
Approuing that which is pleasing to the Lord.
And haue no fellowship with ye vnfruteful workes of darkenes, but
    euen reproue them rather.
For it is shame even to speake of ye things, which are done of them
    in secret.
But all things when they are reproued of the light, are manifest: for
    it is light that maketh all things manifest.
Wherefore he saith, Awake thou that slepest, & stand vp from the
    dead, & Christ shal giue thee light.
Take hede therefore that ye walke circumspectly, not as fooles, but
    as wise,
Redeming the time: for the dayes are euil.
Wherefore, be ye not vnwise, but vnderstand what the wil of the
    Lord is.
And be not drunke with wine, wherein is excesse: but be fulfilled
    with the Spirit,
Speaking vnto your selues in psalmes, and hymnes, and spiritual
    songs, singing, and making melodie to the Lord in your hearts,
Giving thankes alwaise for all things vnto God euen the Father, in
    the Name of our Lord Iesus Christ,
Submitting your selues one to another in the feare of God.
                         (Eph. 5:1–21, Geneva version)

Sidney's reference to verse 19 of this chapter, I think, is not restricted to
the muscularious merriment of hymn-singing, as I hope the extensive quotation will prove. This chapter of Ephesians is one of the crucial passages
of Paul's epistles in establishing the principles of hierarchy in medieval and
Renaissance society. Sidney could not have been unaware of the import of
his allusion, to the metaphors of light and dark, to the overriding allegiance of man to God, of the further consequence of this allegiance, the
obedience of the wife to the husband. Milton used this passage as the biblical source of his "He for God only, She for God in him." I am not suggesting for a moment that Sidney had this chapter in mind as he wrote *Astrophil and Stella,* although it is a source remote. I do want to suggest that it

does provide a context for his comments about the Psalms and about his understanding of what I have called the blasphemy of Astrophil's answer to his rhetorical question in Song I.

Sidney's reverence for the Psalms as divine praise extended to his translating a good portion of them into English meters, to make them available to English readers. The translation was completed by the Countess of Pembroke after his death, but the part that he assuredly did bears strong metaphorical resemblance to metaphors used in *Astrophil and Stella* and to the argument that I would like to present about the nature of Astrophil's witty eroticism. Sidney's metrical version of Psalm 10 is a strong case in point:

> Why standest thou so farr,
> O God our only starr,
> In time most fitt for thee
> To help who vexed be!
> For lo with pride the wicked man
> Still plagues the poore the most he can:
> O let proud him be throughly caught
> In craft of his own crafty thought!
> For he himself doth prayse,
> When he his lust doth ease,
> Extolling ravenous gain:
> But doth God' self disdain.
> Nay so proud is his puffed thought
> That after God he never sought,
> But rather much he fancys this
> That Name of God a fable is.
> For while his wayes do prove,
> On them he sets his love:
> Thy judgments are too high
> He cannot them espy,
> Therefore he doth defy all those
> That dare themselves to him oppose,
> And sayeth in his bragging heart,
> This gotten blisse shall never part.

It is interesting to note that the author of *Astrophil and Stella* compares God to "our only starr," especially so since it is Sidney's addition to the psalm. The Genevan version of verse 1 reads: "Why standest thou farre off, o Lord, & hidest thee in *due* time, *even* in afflictions?" Sidney's paraphrase reads almost like a gloss on the figure of Astrophil I am trying to present. The proud man of the psalm has turned away from the proper song of praise and has substituted an idol of his own making for the true God. The gloss to the Genevan version is uncompromising in its condemnation of such action: "The wicked man reioyceth in his owne lust: he boasteth when he hathe what he wolde: he braggeth of his wit & welth & blesseth himselfe, and thus blasphemeth the Lord."

Sidney's technique in Song I is to choose descriptive details that apply to Stella only as self-seeking, demented hyperbole, the very extravagance of which turns the reader to the only One to whom they rightly belong:

Only for you the heav'n forgate all measure	8
Onely by you *Cupid* his crowne maintaineth	12
Onely to you her Scepter *Venus* granteth	16
Onelie through you the tree of life doth flourish	20
Onely at you all envie hopelesse rueth	24
Only of you the flatterer never lieth	28
Only with you not miracles are wonders.	32

This litany of praise, when applied to Stella, is crass. What unwillingly sought-after woman would want to be reminded that she is the "tree of life"? Clearly Astrophil is rushing his thoughts through to hoped for success. One could, I suppose, accept the Cupid and Venus praises in the same way we accept the mythological extravagance of sonnet 13, but it is more satisfactory to acknowledge that human desire (Cupid) and beauty (Venus) are both maintained and surpassed by God, the beginning and end of all creation, through whom the tree of life really does flourish. It also seems an odd choice of praises to introduce envy and the flatterer into a verbal evocation of desire, envy and flattery being perversions of human desire and verbal truth. Envy is hopeless with God as his object because God is all and transcendent; flattery cannot lie about God because he is ineffable. Ringler suggests that the enigmatic last answer is really an inversion, that is, "only with you miracles are not wonders," a suggestion that makes perfect sense if one is urging the reader to see beyond the one addressed to Another One.

The idolatrous blasphemy of the answers is duplicated in the questions that form the first two lines of each stanza. Here the poetic technique is that of the riddle, in which one is asked a question about a thing but is given only the attributes of that thing. One might almost say that the riddle is the ultimate test of metaphor: all of the vehicle (to use I. A. Richards's terminology) is presented to the reader, and the test is to find the tenor, the concept or substantive that unites them. Sidney devised a formulaic pattern (who hath the eyes, lips, feet, breast, hand, hair, voice) followed by relative clauses that further complicate the description of the attributes. There seems to be no pattern to the ordering of the physical details, which is perhaps another indication of the disordered mind of Astrophil. He cannot get Stella straight. In fact, the whole poem can be seen as a dismemberment of Stella. The first question sets the problem.

> Who hath the eyes which marrie state with pleasure,
> Who keepes the key of Nature's chiefest treasure?

Immediately, other questions arise. What is the meaning of the marriage of "state" with "pleasure"? What have "eyes" to do with this marriage? What is the "key" of "Nature's chiefest treaure"? What is "Nature's chiefest treaure"? With the circularity of doubt that constitutes the poem none of these questions can be answered with any ready certainty. Let us begin with the last question. Nature's chiefest treasure for Astrophil is Stella, and she perforce must be the keeper of the key to herself, but in what sense are we the readers to understand this conundrum? If the "who" of the question is the lady who keeps the key to nature's chiefest treasure, then it is her portion to unlock or disclose that treasure to Astrophil, an unmistakably physical act of submission. But then we must ask, as we should with Astrophil's abjurations of virtue, philosophy, and morality of friends in the sonnets preceding this song, what is Nature's chiefest treasure? In sonnet 7 Stella's eyes are Nature's "chief work"; but I think it would be naive of us to think that that is the answer that Astrophil's "breast orecharg'd" would expect. The object of this "song of praise" is unusually crass even for Astrophil. The riddle turns on our seeing that what is ostensibly praise is in fact a kind of prurient, fawning sensuality that dehumanizes its subject by turning it into an idol, a "sex object," in modern parlance. Or we might recall an earlier manifestation of the same phenomenon in Pygmalion's fevered fantasies of the life his desires have inspired in his created idol.

Katherine M. Wilson has reminded us that "taken seriously sonnet talk would be blasphemous,"[25] and that is certainly the case with Song I. Astrophil is taking himself seriously, and unfortunately so have the critics. In each of the riddling questions unless we are persuaded by Astrophil's rare logic we will see that the hyperbole applies only to the ineffable fullness of God, the Creator, and is ultimately demeaning to the creature. Would any Christian reader not have answered the riddle, "Whose grace is such, that when it chides doth cherish" with Paul's advice to the Ephesians:

> So oght men to loue their wiues, as their owne bodies: he that
> loueth his wife, loueth him selfe.

Astrophil and Stella: A Radical Reading

For no man euer yet hated his owne flesh, but nourisheth & cherish-
eth it, euen as the Lord *doeth* the Church.

(Eph. 5.28–29, Geneva version)

One need not even seek the biblical sources of other riddles:

Who long dead beautye with increase reneweth 22
Who makes a man live then glad when he dieth 26

No satisfactory glosses of the lines I have quoted have been given by Sidney scholars; for the most part they are ignored in all modern editions—
presumably because Astrophil's praise is accepted as right and proper.

IV

In fact, the songs have played no part in modern critical commentary on
Sidney's sonnet sequence.[26] Only the numerologists have given them their
rightful place in the structure of the poem, but they understandably but
unfortunately do not talk about their meaning. In Song I, as I have tried to
prove, Astrophil breaks out into a song idolatrous and blasphemous. In
Song II Astrophil steals that kiss from his sleeping Stella, already discussed. Song III is a praise of the power of music. Song IV is the colloquy
between Astrophil and Stella, in which she refuses his advances with her
constant, "No, no, no, no, my deare, let be." Of the group of five Songs
V–IX, only the narrative Song VIII has elicited comment, but the substance of that group of songs is the key to the desperate meaning that Sidney intended. It is not enough to rely on the narrative content of Songs II,
IV, and VIII and to relegate the other lyrical outbursts to earlier poems included to fill out the sequence. Fill out what? Poets of Sidney's stature do
not fill grab-bags of scraps. This used to be the answer to the bewildering
array of tales that form the middle books of Spenser's *Faerie Queene,* but it
is not so. Songs V, VI, and VII are of major importance in determining the
meaning of Astrophil's struggle with Stella.

Song V is the second longest song in the sequence. It is a simple vilification of Stella for her "change of lookes" in sonnet 86, the preceding poem,
and attempts to undo all the praise he has heaped on her in the preceding
92 poems, and its text is the final three lines of sonnet 86:

Use something else to chast'n me withall,
Then those blest eyes, where all my hopes do dwell,
No doome should make one's heav'n become his hell.

And it is hellish vilification that he resorts to.[27] The poem is a one-sided lover's quarrel. The first five stanzas are a legalistic brief of all the benefits he has conferred on Stella through his love as expressed in his poetry. The sixth stanza introduces the true subject of the poem: revenge for his injured feelings:

> Revenge, revenge, my Muse, Defiance' trumpet blow:
> Threat'n what may be done, yet do more then you threat'n.
> Ah, my sute granted is, I feel my breast doth swell:
> Now child, a lesson new you shall begin to spell:
> Sweet babes must babies have, but shrewd gyrles must be beat'n.

Astrophil's infernal heroics masks a basic childishness, which he transfers immediately by making his idol Stella into a child to be whipped into shape. Succeeding stanzas introduce a crescendo of vilifying names: she is ungrateful, a thief, a murderer, a tyrant, a rebel, a witch, and finally a devil (presumably the one presiding over his private hell):

> You then ungratefull thiefe, you murdring Tyran you,
> You Rebell run away, to Lord and Lady untrue,
> You witch, you Divill, (alas) you still of me beloved,
> You see what I can say; mend yet your froward mind,
> And such skill in my Muse you reconcil'd shall find,
> That all these cruell words your praises shall be proved.

The irony of this stanza, and the whole process of vilification, is that he has used virtually every one of these terms as praises of Stella in earlier poems: ungratefulness (31), murdering, thief (applied to Love, 20), tyrant (2, 47), rebel (5).

Song V is the low point of Astrophil's songs of praise, and it introduces the reader to two songs that have perplexed the critics mainly because, as in Song V, they are determined to make Astrophil into the lover as hero. Song VI is a debate between beauty and music, which both Ringler and Putzel think is between Stella's beauty and her music.[28] I think that the debate has broader implications for the sequence and that the debate is between Stella's beauty and Astrophil's music, that is, between Stella as object and Astrophil as poet. It is in the long tradition of debates about the primacy of the ear or the eye as the primary or highest sense. To reduce the poem to a debate over whether Stella is more beautiful or sings more beautifully is to narrow our reading as in sonnet 36 (see p. 157). The logic of the poem is more complicated. Beauty is to the eye what music is to the ear. That is the start, but Astrophil writes poems and songs about the beauty of Stella's eyes, thus introducing a third and particularizing item into the basic equation, and the opening lines of the poem complicate the equation even further by bringing in the reader's response:

> O you that heare this voice,
> O you that see this face,
> Say whether of the choice
> Deserves the former place:
> Feare not to judge this bate,
> For it is void of hate.

The directive of these opening lines is clearly aimed at the reader, who can only hear the voice or see the face through the words of the poems he has been reading. The final line of the stanza equally clearly refers obliquely to the vilification of Song V and in characteristic Astrophilic manner contradicts what he has just said.

If we read the poem simply as another poem with Astrophil as "barker," we diminish its impact. Our training in finding "dramatic situations" for poems falsifies the moral intent of many Renaissance poems. Once more we as readers are placed in a situation created by Astrophil's words. In particular we should be aware of the abstraction of the diction.

> This side doth beauty take,
> For that doth Musicke speake.

Are we to see a scene in court with various parties taking sides? Are we to see the divided apprehension of Astrophil as "This side" and "that"? or are we to understand a generalized debate on the power of visual images and that of words? The poem is inconclusive in its findings, and as with most debate poems the reader must already know the moral answer to the riddle if the poem is to sit with any certainty in his mind. In this case Astrophil is presenting a well-known argument about the primacy of either hearing or sight, but he presents the argument in terms of the agent (beauty-music) rather than of the sense perceiver (eye-ear) except for the first stanza quoted. The abstraction of the debate reaches a climax in the seventh stanza:

> Musicke doth witnesse call
> The eare, his truth to trie:
> Beauty brings to the hall,
> The judgement of the eye,

THOMAS P. ROCHE, JR.

> Both in their objects such
> As no exceptions tutch.

Not Stella's song but "Musicke"; not Stella's beauty but "Beauty" calls in, not the Court's nor Astrophil's ear or eye but "The Eare" and "The judgement of the eye." The putative dramatic or pictorial quality of the poem becomes abstract and generalized. The real dramatic impact comes from the conflict of ideas, and here once more Astrophil's presentation of the facts must be called into question.

Renaissance psychology is unremittingly clear on the facts that the senses are mere receivers of perceptions, not judges, and that the "common sense" is the receiver only of these sense impressions and thus cannot be, as Astrophil suggests, an "arbiter" of this debate:

> The common sence, which might
> Be Arbiter of this,
> To be forsooth upright,
> To both sides partiall is.

The debate must be referred to the proper mental faculty, the reason, and this Astrophil even in his benighted condition does in the last stanza:

> Then reason, Princesse hy,
> Whose throne is in the mind,
> Which Musicke can in sky
> And hidden beauty find,
> Say whether thou wilt crowne,
> With limitlesse renowne.

The sudden change to the second person pronoun prepares us for the transition to the seventh song, which is not the words of Astrophil but the words of reason, following the example of Petrarch in *Canzoniere* 119. The seventh song leads us from the realm of philosophy and virtue that Astrophil's sonnets have tried to disparage and keep at bay into that very citadel of enigmatic clarity. Song VI has taken the debate of beauty and words as far as it can go in Astrophil's perverted apprehension. Song VII is another outburst of Sidney's poem that brings the reader into that realm of integrity that Astrophil has been playing with throughout the sequence through a glass darkly. The poem begins:

> Whose senses in so evill consort, their stepdame Nature laies,
> That ravishing delight in them most sweete tunes do not raise.

These heptameter lines of the seventh song could not be spoken by Astrophil. They occupy a central place in the sequence, as I shall demonstrate, and they are too critical and acute an assessment of Astrophil's condition for him to make in his own voice. The syntax of the lines is complex and confusing, but they may be paraphrased: who have senses in such bad harmony and make songs to their stepdame Nature that most sweet tunes do not raise in them ravishing delight? The lines are clearly a question, not a statement, and are parallel with the question of the first lines of the second stanza:

> Who have so leaden eyes, as not to see sweet beautie's show,
> Or seeing. . . .

The parallel is not only syntactical but also continues the debate of the preceding poem by having stanza one deal with music and stanza two deal with beauty (ear and eye). The conclusion of stanza one proceeds logically to develop the argument:

> Or if they do delight therein, yet are so cloyed with wit,
> As with sententious lips to set a title vaine on it:
> O let them heare these sacred tunes, and learne in wonder's schooles,
> To be (in things past bounds of wit) fooles, if they be not fooles.

The lines develop not only an argument but a picture of one, whose senses are in "evill consort / . . . so cloyed with wit / As with sententious lips to set a title vaine on it: / To be . . . fooles." The image projected is that of Astrophil, who has been called "fool" by his muse (1), by Morpheus (32), by Cupid (53) and by himself (43, 83, Song II), whose wit so pleases him that he puts it in opposition to will (4), reason (10), Stella (12) and himself (33, 34). Reason seems in these lines to be describing Astrophil's predicament, and in doing so she also seems to be suggesting that there are two kinds of songs (stepdame Nature's lays and sacred tunes) and two kinds of fool ("To be . . . fooles, if they be not fooles"). The tradition of two kinds of fools is derived from I Corinthians 3. 18–19: "Let no man deceiue himself. If anie man among you seme to be wise in this worlde, let him be a foole, that he may be wise. For the wisdome of this worlde is foolishnes with God: for it is written, He catcheth the wise in their owne craftines." The man who is wise in the things of this world is a fool in the eyes of God; he must die to the things of this world and become a fool of God, suffering God's will to be done. The distinction lies in one's attitude toward God and the things of the world. Nature becomes a stepdame only when one has in mind a heavenly Father and a spiritual home. To perceive naturally is to perceive only partially. Stepdame Nature's lays must be heard as sacred tunes in order for the reader to understand them truly. One must hear not only the letter but the spirit.

A similar kind of opposition is developed in the second and third stanzas. The progression in the second stanza is from "leaden eyes" that do not perceive beauty, to "wodden wits" that do not know the worth of beauty, to "muddy minds" that knowing are not in love with beauty, to "frothy thoughts" of those lovers who are easily moved to another object. The stanza ends by advocating that these four kinds of deficient perceivers of beauty amended their ways:

> O let them see these heavenly beames, and in faire letters reede
> A lesson fit, both sight and skill, love and firme love to breede

The progression of the images from "leaden" to "frothy" do not include Astrophil's particular kind of idolatrous devotion but expands the vision of the deficiency of human lovers, as a speech of Reason should.

The third stanza is an attempt to amalgamate the two kinds of love and the various oppositions that have occurred in Songs VI and VII.

> Heare then, but then with wonder heare; see but adoring see,
> No mortall gifts, no earthly fruites, now here descended be:
> See, do you see this face? a face? nay image of the skies,
> Of which the two life-giving lights are figured in her eyes:
> Heare you this soule-invading voice, and count it but a voice?
> The very essence of their tunes, when Angels do rejoyce.

The voice of reason tells of something in ordinary perception that is beyond even her ken: nature gives us only an "image of the skies," a "figure." The upshot of Reason's speech is that there is in fact no opposition between the senses as the sixth song suggested if we trace the lineage of the senses back to their ultimate source. Eye and ear are one, as are beauty and music if we could but see them truly in their fleshly manifestations, "when Angels do rejoyce." The perception is never a request for a denial of natural existence but a true apprehension of the reality of what human love and nature is in terms of its source. Sidney, in the *Defense,* is speaking of these things in his passage on the golden world of the poets and the erected wit and infected will of poet and reader, but "these arguments will by few be understood and by fewer granted." The double vision that is required of Christian readers, that is, the proper use of their stepdame Nature and their proper use of that nature to their true allegiance to God is the subject of Sidney's depiction of Astrophil. Song VII leads us to a vantage point where we are urged to take a proper view of the worth and wonder of humanity and to assess the fevered desires of Astrophil.

The increasing abstraction and distancing of Astrophil's plight in Songs VI and VII lead to the most dramatic depiction of the love affair in Song VIII. Only after the song of Reason in Song VII can we come with any certainty of approach to the only third-person narrative of Song VIII, the longest poem in the sequence. Song VII insists that we view Astrophil's problem outside the frame of his own editorializing wit, and Song VIII, the only song in the sequence to receive any real critical attention, is especially different from all the other songs and sonnets in that it is a third-person narrative. It is as if Reason's Song VII has taken us into another realm where we may observe the story that the plangent lover has been glossing in a new way, from a different perspective, in which for the first time Stella's responses are fully enunciated.

Stella's responses to Astrophil are all but forgotten in the hyperbolic onslaught of Astrophil's rhetoric, but they, more than the arguments of virtue, reason, or friends, present the case for positive Christian morality. The first important statement occurs in sonnet 62 and explains the simple oppositions we have been noting.

> Late tyr'd with wo, even ready for to pine
>   With rage of *Love*, I cald my Love unkind;
> She in whose eyes *Love*, though unfelt, doth shine
> Sweet said that I true love in her should find.
>   I joyed, but straight thus watred was my wine,
> That love she did, but loved a Love not blind,
> Which would not let me, whom she loved, decline
> From nobler course, fit for my birth and mind:
>   And therefore by her Love's authority,
>   Willd me these tempests of vaine love to flie,
> And anchor fast my selfe on *Vertue's* shore.

Sidney's strategy in this sonnet is to play with two meanings of the word "love." Stella speaks of a love that is not blind (6), a love considerate of the merits and possibilities of the other (7–8), a love based in virtue (11); Astrophil hears of a love that is blind and naked, of a love that exists in the flesh and extends itself whenever it can. The two loves described are the most common of Christian metaphors. They are the *caritas* and *cupiditas* that St. Augustine taught to the world of the Middle Ages and Renaissance as the two faces of human love. The juxtaposition of the two loves gives added point to the colloquial disappointment of line 5: "I joyed, but straight thus watred was my wine." Astrophil hopes that Stella's declaration of "true love" in line 4 will bring the heady intoxication of wine, a hope soon watered by the sobering expansion of meaning (6–11). But the homely image of the disappointingly watered wine of Stella's reply gives Sidney the opportunity to outwit his creation through an irony that Astrophil is not allowed to understand. Watered wine is a disappointment physically, but spiritually water and wine symbolize the Eucharist, the food of charity. The water that Stella's words add to Astrophil's wine is nothing less than the possibility of his spiritual regeneration into charity, a possibility that he unknowingly rejects in the almost patronizingly witty conclusion of the sonnet.

> Alas, if this the only mettall be
> Of Love, new-coind to helpe my beggery,
> Deare, love me not, that you may love me more.

Astrophil thinks that he has made a point here with his witty and falsely gracious abjuration of her kind of love so that she may fall into the trap of his kind of love, but although he can see that two definitions of love are at stake, he understands them both in terms of the goal of his desire only. His is the true love; hers can be merely active cruelty or passive fear, soon to be conquered by his superior love and wit.

Stella's voice is next heard in Song IV, again refusing Astrophil's demands with her understated but comprehensive "No, no, no, no, my dear, let be," a point to which we will return later, but her most extended exposition of her reaction to Astrophil occurs in Song VIII, the longest poem of the sequence and the only one in third-person narrative. Sidney plans the scene carefully.

> In a grove most rich of shade,
> Where birds wanton musicke made,
> May then yong his pide weedes showing,
> New perfumed with flowers fresh growing,

> *Astrophil* with *Stella* sweete,
> Did for mutuall comfort meete,
> Both within themselves oppressed,
> But each in the other blessed.

> Him great harmes had taught much care,
> Her faire necke a foule yoke bare,
> But her sight his cares did banish,
> In his sight her yoke did vanish.

The poem has been most often understood as a lover's tryst which the May-time setting of the first stanza would tend to support, but in view of the development of both Astrophil's and Stella's speeches (stanzas 8–16, 19–25, respectively) a more important consideration is the nature of the "mutuall comfort" they are seeking. We know without a doubt why Astrophil is there, but Stella's presence needs some explanation. Why should a married woman meet in a secluded place a young man who loves her, especially if her marriage is a "foule yoke"? The obvious answer is of course adultery, but that, the poem assures us, is not the answer. At the opposite extreme to this answer is one that Sidney might have used if he had been writing a different poem: Stella could have been turned into a Boethian Lady Philosophy to guide Astrophil to the proper path of virtue. The fact of the matter is that Stella is neither erring woman nor allegorical figure. Her presence in that "grove most rich of shade" is most comparable to those ladies in Book VI of *The Faerie Queene* who with the best intentions find themselves in rather murky moral situations that harm their social reputations but not their inner virtue. Stella is unhappy. She knows that Astrophil is unhappy, but it must be remembered that the poem states that only "In *his* sight her yoke did vanish." She meets him for that mutual comfort that grows out of the charitable love she has tried to explain to him in sonnet 62, but the possibilities of the situation are immediately exploited by Astrophil:

> There his hands in their speech, faine
> Would have made tongue's language plaine.   (65–66)

Stella's response to this "pass" has been often misinterpreted as a teasing half-acceptance, an interpretation that Sidney did not intend. To understand the extreme delicacy of Stella's response we can compare it to Fulke Greville's imitation in *Caelica, 75:*

> Philocel, if you love me,
> For you would beloved be,
> Your own will must be your hire,
> And desire reward desire.
> Cupid is in my heart sped,
> Where all desires else are dead.
> Ashes o'er love's flames are cast,
> All for one is there disgraced.
> Make not then your own mischance
> Wake yourself from passion's trance,

THOMAS P. ROCHE, JR.

And let reason guide affection
From despair to new election.   (95–106)

Caelica's rather testy Lady Philosophy is giving sound advice, advice that
Stella will give to Astrophil in Song XI, but here in Song VIII her response, although it has the immediate effect of staying Astrophil's advances and dampening his hopes, is compassionately gentle:

> Then she spake; her speech was such
> As not eares but hart did tuch:
> While such wise she love denied,
> As yet love she signified.

> 'Astrophil' sayd she, 'my love
> Cease in these effects to prove:
> Now be still, yet still beleefe me,
> Thy griefe more then death would grieve me.   (69–76)

Sidney sets the stage for her response by once more invoking the two loves
of sonnet 62: she is denying Astrophil his cupidity but is at the same time
signifying charity. It is wrong to read lines 71–72 as if Stella were merely
restraining her passion for Astrophil. She is quite clear that her love for
him cannot be tested in the ways he has proposed. She then cites in five
conditional statements her love for him, ending:

> If thou love, my love content thee,
> For all love, all faith is meant thee.   (91–92)

It is very significant that Sidney wrote Song VIII as third-person narrative,
for if Astrophil related this episode to us, we would be convinced that he
had lost the battle but won the day, and that is indeed the point that Sidney is making as the final two stanzas of Stella's response makes clear. She
does love him:

> Trust me while I thee deny,
> In my selfe the smart I try.
> Tyran honour doth thus use thee,
> Stella's selfe might not refuse thee.

She does want him and "might not refuse" him if it were not for "Tyran
honour." Stella's reply is the triumph of reason over passion, a triumph
that converts her desire to the charity she is now offering Astrophil. Critics have universally given Stella's voice too little credit. "Tyran honour" is

read as "I would if I could," but this reading does a disservice both to Stella and to sixteenth-century morality. "Honour" is the operative word; "tyran" is her mere concession to Astrophil's obsession, her grace to the grieving lover. Stella's love for Astrophil is one of Sidney's most brilliant strokes. It serves two purposes. It removes Stella immediately from the category of proud and aloof sonnet lady so that Astrophil will be forced to reconsider his lost possibilities in the knowledge that he might once have won his goal, just as in sonnet 33 he ruefully surveyed the possibilities lost through his own failure of initiative. It also serves as an exemplum of the proper discipline of the passion of desire by reason, which she serves up to Astrophil as the conclusion to the long string of conditional statements:

> Therefore, Deere, this no more move,
> Least, though I leave not thy love,
> Which too deep in me is framed,
> I should blush when thou art named. (96–100)

The blush would come, not only from embarrassment about her passion but also from the attendant dishonor.

Stella has presented a case that Astrophil cannot refute either on the basis of his or her definitions of love. She has made her triumph over passion and has learned to offer him charity. He has been overcome by passion and cannot comprehend what Stella's love means. His reaction is a retreat to the pastoral world in Song IX, the last of the central group of songs. He is left alone in the false Eden he has created for himself and is playing the role of Colin Clout in the January and December eclogues of Spenser's *Shepheardes Calender:*

> Go my flocke, go get you hence,
> Seeke a better place of feeding,
> Where you may have some defence
> From the stormes in my breast breeding,
> And showers from mine eyes proceeding.

Within the conventions of pastoral poetry Astrophil is simply abdicating his responsibility and indulging himself in self-pitying incomprehension of his situation:

> Yet alas before you go,
> Heare your wofull maister's story,
> Which to stones I els would show:
> Sorrow onely then hath glory,
> When tis excellently sory.

The humor of the poem may have been lost on the sheep, as it has on the critics. The sudden recall of the flock to hear his story is only to keep Astrophil from giving sermons to stones.[29] That sorrow should have any glory is surprising enough, but that it must be "excellently sory" to gain this reward shows Astrophil at his wonted task of overachieving. The picture he gives of his love for Stella is ludicrously inappropriate:

> *Stella* hath refused me,
> *Stella* who more love hath proved,
> In this caitife hart to be,
> Then can in good eawes be moved
> Toward *Lamkins* best beloved.

Even if we grant Astrophil his comparison of mother love, I am not certain that ewes do in fact single out particular lambs for especial affection. He is equally ignorant of what Stella has told him in Song VIII.

> Why alas doth she then sweare,
> That she loveth me so dearely,
> Seeing me so long to beare
> Coles of love that burne so clearely;
> And yet leave me helplesse meerely?
>
> Is that love? forsooth I trow,
> If I saw my good dog grieved,
> And a helpe for him did know,
> My love should not be beleeved,
> But he were by me releeved.

Argument from analogy is the weakest form of argumentation, as Sidney undoubtedly knew, which is probably why he allowed Astrophil this unfortunate excursion into animal imagery.

From this point on in the sequence Astrophil retreats to memory for his only satisfactions, for his Stella is absent. Song X is a deliberate sexual fantasy, which he sends off to persuade the absent Stella:

> Thought see thou no place forbeare,
> Enter bravely every where,
> Seaze on all to her belonging;
> But if thou wouldst garded by,
> Fearing her beames, take with thee
> Strength of liking, rage of longing.

> Thinke of that most gratefull time,
>   When my leaping hart will clime,
>   In my lips to have his biding,
>   There those roses for to kisse,
>   Which do breath a sugred blisse,
>   Opening rubies, perles deviding.
>
> Thinke of my most Princely power,
>   When I blessed shall devower,
>   With my greedy licorous sences,
>   Beauty, musicke, sweetnesse, love
>   While she doth against me prove
>   Her strong darts, but weake defences.
>
> Thinke, thinke of those dalyings,
>   When with Dovelike murmurings,
>   With glad moning passed anguish,
>   We change eyes, and hart for hart,
>   Each to other do imparte,
>   Joying till joy make us languish.

This unabashed exercise in sensuality ends in the recall of the thought:

> My life melts with too much thinking;
> Thinke no more but die in me,
>   Till thou shalt revived be,
> At her lips my Nectar drinking.

Sidney allows Astrophil one more sight of Stella. Song XI is a dialogue between the two.

> 'Who is it that this darke night,
>   Underneath my window playneth?'
> It is one who from thy sight,
>   Being (ah) exild, disdayneth
>   Every other vulgar light.
>
> 'Why alas, and are you he?
> Be not yet those fancies changed?'

Being assured of his unswerving devotion, she must resort to the conventional arguments to conquer desire: absence (11), time (16), new beauties (21), reason (26), wronged love (31). Stella's list of correctives resemble Caelica's already quoted, but the suggestions are delivered more gently. To no avail. Astrophil's wit is still about its old tricks of seizing on the outer senses of Stella's words and using them to support his own desires. Since he will not, or cannot, grasp the reasonableness of her arguments, she must resort to an angry dismissal lest the neighbors see or hear them:

> 'Well, be gone, be gone I say,
> Lest that *Argus* eyes perceive you.'
> O unjustest fortune's sway,
> Which can make me thus to leave you,
> And from lowts to run away.[30]

Where reason fails, prudence prevails, and Astrophil is left, disgruntled and unenlightened, contemplating an empty window (105, 106), and totally impervious to Stella's classical allusion.

Juno sent Argus, a hundred-eyed monster, to guard Io, a love of Jupiter's, whom he changed into a white heifer to escape the anger of the jealous Juno. Seeing Io's unhappiness, Jupiter sent Mercury to kill the monster and is reconciled to Juno on condition that she allow Jupiter to return Io to human shape. Stella's allusion suggests that she is the Io in this situation, with Lord Rich assigned the role of the jealous Juno. Her dismissal of Astrophil precludes the possibility of her seeing Astrophil in the role of Mercury, who got control of the monster through the power of his music. Sidney does not leave Astrophil a chance of winning such control, and the sequence ends in the despairing night world of sonnet 108.

Astrophil, as I hope I have made abundantly clear, in allowing his reason to let his erected wit free rein, has succumbed to the indulgence of the "sleep of the senses." He has become demented; he is no longer in control of his desires; he does not understand what Stella tells him. The flagrant logical and moral inconsistencies of his words push him closer and closer to the despair that finally engulfs him at the end of the sequence. Sidney consistently gives him verbal victories, all to no avail, but beneath the surface of lover's bravado Sidney provides a subtext in the elaborate disposition of the poems, and even parts of poems, that assert Sidney's complete control of this outburst of mad love.

VI

A brief consideration of the external features of the formal structure of *Astrophil and Stella* will enable us to understand better the disposition of the poems and possibly allow us to see the structure that Sidney intended. The 1598 edition of the poem included 108 sonnets and 11 songs, interspersed with apparent irregularity in the manner of Petrarch. All of the sonnets are conventional fourteen-line sonnets except that six (1, 6, 8, 76, 77, and 102) are hexameter rather than pentameter. The songs are written in iambic (I, III, V, VI, VII) or trochaic (II, IV, VIII, IX, X, XI) meter and range in length from 18 to 104 lines. As with Petrarch the apparent artlessness of the arrangement on closer examination reveals an artistry and ingenuity that organizes the substantive chaos of the individual poems into a coherent unity. The order of the poems is:

Sonnets 1–63	(63)
Song I	
Sonnets 64–72	(9)
Song II	
Sonnets 73–83	(11)
Song III	
Sonnets 84–85	(2)
Song IV	
Sonnet 86	(1)
Songs V–IX	(5, or 63 stanzas)
Sonnets 87–92	(6)
Song X	
Sonnets 93–104	(12)
Song XI	
Sonnets 105–08	(4)

The sonnet groups range from the largest group of 63 sonnets to the single sonnet 86, on either side of which are groups of 9, 11, and 2 sonnets (64–85) and of 6, 12, and 4 sonnets (87–108). The songs follow a more complicated but similarly formal pattern. The total number of stanzas in the songs is 108, corresponding to the number of sonnets. The stanza total of the unbroken block of Songs V–IX is 63, repeating the number of the unbroken block of sonnets 1–63, producing the following symmetry:

63 sonnets	(1–63)
1 song	(I)
25 poems	(64–85, II, III, IV)
1 sonnet	(86)
63 stanzas	(V–IX)
24 poems	(87–108, X, XI)

Alastair Fowler, who has done the most extensive work on the symmetries of *Astrophil and Stella,* presents the following resume of the formal structure:[31]

THOMAS P. ROCHE, JR.

I	II	III	IV	V–IX	X	XI
63	9	11	2	1	6	12	4
63		22		1		22

From this simple and irrefutable pattern he constructs a series of elaborate and related symmetries, which he relates to the mannerist habit of "making assymetries generally contribute to a complex symmetry, which remains completely, if obscurely, harmonious." Fowler then proceeds in the best mannerist tradition to reveal layer after layer of assymetrical symmetries in the songs through an examination of meters, lines in stanza, number of stanzas and line totals:

Song	I	II	III	IV	V	VI	VII	VIII		IX	X	XI
Meter*	*i*	*t*	*i*	*t*	*i*	*i*	*i*	*t*		*t*	*t*	*t*
Lines/stanza	4	4	6	6	6	6	6	4		5	6	5
No. stanzas	*9*	*7*	*3*	*9*	*15*	*9*	*3*	7	*9*	10	10	8	9
Line total	*36*	*28*	*18*	*54*	*90*	*54*	*18*	*28*	*36*	40	50	48	45
	e	*d*	*c*	*b*	*A*	*b*	*c*	*d*	*e*			

* *i* = iambic; *t* = trochaic

The chart (italics added) shows a recessed structure, typical of the forms of triumphal entry with the triumphator in the central position. Song V occupies the central position, provided Song VIII is divided into three parts: setting (7 stanzas), Astrophil's requests (9 stanzas), and Stella's response (10 stanzas). Fowler is quick to point out that Song V is not the only "structural centre," centrality being shared by Song VI by virtue of its being the central poem of the eleven songs and "containing the central lines of the whole array," and by Song VII, which owes its centrality to the "13 song parts that result from dividing Song VIII." He might have accounted for the centrality of VII by combining the last forty lines of VIII (not used in his calculation) with the fifty lines of Song IX, so that another recessed structure appears in that block of Songs V–IX.

V	VI	VII	VIII		IX
90	54	18	28	36	40	50
90	54	18	54		90
a	b	C	b		a

Fowler points out as possible coincidence that the line total of III and V, IV and VI, and V and VII equals 108, the number of the sonnets; the probability of coincidence is lessened if we consider that the same line total is achieved by adding *b* and *b* and *C* and *a*.

Sidney is clearly relying on the number 108 to serve some structural and symbolic purpose; poets paid him mute tribute by adopting the number 108 as a structural device in their poems.[32] Sidney's choice of 108 has been given a most ingenious and convincing explanation by Adrien Benjamin as reported by Fowler. There can be no doubt that Sidney's Stella was Penelope Devereux Rich, the daughter of the first earl of Essex.[33] Sometime after her marriage to Lord Rich (probably in the spring of 1581), Sidney metamorphosed her into his Stella, always keeping in mind that other chaste Penelope in Homer, who by keeping her suitors at bay for twenty years became the type of chaste married love. Homer in the first book of the *Odyssey* tells that Penelope's suitors whiled away their time in a game, similar to the Elizabethan game of bowls. Homer's simple account received greater elaboration from the scholiasts Athenaeus and Eustathius, whose comments found their way into Sir Thomas Browne, who describes the "prodigal paramours" at their game of Penelope: "For being themselves an hundred and eight, they set fifty four stones on either side, and one in the middle, which they called *Penelope,* which he that hit was master of the game." As Fowler comments, "Thus the absence of a 109th or Penelope sonnet-stone from Sidney's sequence confesses Astrophil's failure as a lover."

In spite of the brilliance of Fowler's and Benjamin's explanation of the significance of 108 for the structure and meaning of *Astrophil and Stella,* a simple question arises: why does the sequence contain 119 poems instead of 108? The answer, as I suggested earlier, is to be found again in the Homeric story. We are not meant to see Astrophil as just another suitor but as the inversion of the wise and wary Ulysses returning to his chaste wife. The 119 poems are meant to symbolize the ten years of Ulysses's journey home: the total number of poems is one short of the number of months of that epic voyage (120). I do not want to push the Ulysses analogy too far because Sidney is no more explicit about Ulysses than he is about Penelope, neither explicitly mentioned in the text of the poems. I do think, however, that the group of poems 84–85, Song IV and 86 may be a covert allusion to the return of Ulysses. This sequence of poems, which concludes one of the major blocks I find, is one of the more tentatively narrative sections. Sonnet 84 addresses a highway through which Astrophil is approaching Stella. Sonnet 85 focuses on a house in which Astrophil will seize on his treasure. Song IV is the meeting of Astrophil and Stella, who refuses his advances. Sonnet 86 complains of "this change of lookes," and introduces the block of Songs V–IX that sends Astrophil into his despairing decline.

The ninth song has two details that suggest further Odyssean analogies. Ulysses returns to Ithaca and is received by the swineherd Eumaeus. If it is not a pastoral retreat, it is still not home, and Ulysses must move from the country to the town where his palace is. On the way he meets his old dog Argus, who recognizes him and dies (*Odyssey* 17). I have already spoken of the false Edenic world that Astrophil has created for himself in this Song IX. In the second stanza Astrophil laments (emphasis added):

> Merry flocke, such one forego,
> Unto whom mirth is displeasure,
> Only *rich* in mischiefe's treasure.

Surely this is another reference to Lord Rich as in sonnets 35 and 37, part of that riddle of sonnet 37 and the reason that not even "*Nestor's* counsel can my flames alay" in sonnet 35. This love is an inversion, an invasion of Lord Rich's marriage to Penelope, but Astrophil sees himself as rightfully dispossessed in the next stanza of Song IX (emphasis added):

> Yet alas before you go,
> Heare your wofull maister's story,
> Which to *stones* I els would show:
> Sorrow onely then hath glory,
> When tis excellently sory.

It might seem appropriate to have Astrophil turn from his sheep, like the despondent Colin Clout in Spenser, to stones, but I think that the stones referred to here are an explicit reference to the stones of the Penelope game, especially since the line about the stones in the fourth stanza is the fourth time the number 108 is repeated. Hence the "Sorrow that hath only glory," which is not to be, occurs in the fourth 109th line of the line number of the songs.

The fifth and final such occurrence is in the last stanza of the eleventh and final song:

> 'Well, be gone, be gone I say
> Lest that *Argus* eyes perceive you.'
> O unjustest fortune's sway,
> Which can make me thus to leave you,
> And from lowts to run away.

The Argus eyes to which Stella refers have always been interpreted as the eyes of the monster set to watch Io, but I think that Sidney is playing another trick on Astrophil. Argus is the dog who first recognizes Ulysses on his return, and Stella may be saying that this false suitor may be recognized by the faithful hound of Ulysses as the false suitor he is, playing with his 108 stones to win the Penelope game. The possibility is further enhanced by the reference to a dog in the eighth stanza of Song IX:

> Is that love? forsooth I trow,
> If I saw my good dog grieved,
> And a helpe for him did know,
> My love should not be beleeved,
> But he were by me releeved.

This stanza says explicitly what a deceitful Ulysses would say on his return about the dog that was not his.

Many readers will be unwilling to accept both Fowler's and my readings of the numbers 108 and 119 as symbolically significant parts of the meaning of the sequence. For them the jump from number as quantitative measure to number as meaning will be too great. Fowler points out one instance in which Sidney is almost explicit about his strategy:

> For this division [of Song VIII into three parts] we have some verbal warrant, since the lyric concludes with the statement 'my song is broken.' Referring primarily, of course, to Astrophil's grief, this statement secondarily alludes to Song VIII's being broken off just before the twenty-seventh stanza needed for a line total of 108. (Unbroken, VIII would have brought the Songs' stanza total to 109, hitting the Penelope stone and making Astrophil 'master of the game.')[34]

The lines Fowler refers to are:

> Therewithall away she went,
> Leaving *him* so passion rent,
> With what she had done and spoken,
> That therewith *my* song is broken.

The shift from third to first-person pronoun is important in that it would appear to be Sidney speaking *in propria persona*, showing the control he has over his creation. Such a reading suits well my earlier suggestion that Song VII is the answer of Reason to the debate of Song VI. That is, both VII

THOMAS P. ROCHE, JR.

and VIII take us outside the narrating voice of Astrophil to a more objective stance to view the situation.

Fowler's brilliant but short account of the numerological complexities of *Astrophil and Stella* does not deal with several problems that require further elaboration: the organization of sonnets 1–63; the hexameter sonnets, and the meaning of the sequence as a poem.[35]

Fowler rightly points out that the first sixty-three sonnets form a symbolic unit based on the ancient notion of the Grand Climacteric year 63, a crisis of both mind and body.[36] The sequence of these sonnets begins with a total misapprehension of basic rules of rhetoric (the inversion of *inventio, dispositio, elocutio* discussed above)[37] and ends with a misapplication of the rules of grammar ("For Grammar sayes . . . that in one speech two Negatives affirme"). The sequence of sonnets 1–63 thus reverses the traditional order of the trivium (grammar, logic, rhetoric) in the same way that sonnet 1 reverses the order of rhetorical composition, logic being misapplied throughout the entire sequence. Although Astrophil seems to think that both 1 and 63 are significant triumphs in his pursuit of love, we as readers should know that he has turned the ordinary process of education in using words upside down. Grammar playing as rhetoric is illogical. The midpoint of this sequence of sonnets is sonnet 32, the invocation to Morpheus, another inversion, in that Astrophil is asking for a kind of sleep that will further delude his already deluded senses.

The sequence proceeds to a second invocation of the muses at sonnet 55, another inversion of traditional knowledge, in which Astrophil refuses the support of the muses to write his poems. Sonnet 55 is also the midpoint of the 108 sonnets, and as Fowler points out, would have been the Penelope stone if the sequence had been carried out successfully for Astrophil.[38] The symmetry for the entire sequence of sonnets is:

1–31	32	33–63	64–85	86	87–108
31	1	31	22	1	22

This symmetry becomes more complicated, but more convincing, if one wants to emphasize the structural importance of sonnet 55:

1–31	32	33–54	55	56–63	64–85	86	87–108
31	1	22	1	8	22	1	22
31	1	22		31		1	22
a	b	c		a		b	c

It seems to be significant that sonnet 86 is the thirty-second sonnet of the second half.

This interlocking elaboration of the groupings of sonnets around the songs is further complicated by the placement of the hexameter sonnets: 1, 6, 8, 76, 77, and 102. Fowler's presentation of the placement of the songs in *Astrophil and Stella* among the 108 sonnets seems to me convincing and right, but why should Sidney have chosen to begin his sequence with an hexameter sonnet and why place other hexameter sonnets throughout the sequence at the places he did? Could it be that Sidney is trying to tell us that Astrophil is at sixes and sevens? I think it is. To insert songs or any forms other than the usual fourteen-line pentameter sonnet in sequences was common from the time of Dante and Petrarch, but to vary the expected pentameter sonnet is Sidney's innovation. Certainly to begin his sequence with a hexameter sonnet was meant to alert the reader to an undertaking less than ordinary. Whether that reader followed the signs of metrics and placement of poems is another question which remains for us, since none of Sidney's contemporaries commented on the structure of his poems.[39] My earlier comment that Sidney wanted the reader to see that Astrophil was at sixes and sevens was not idly posited, for I think it will lead us into an understanding of why the hexameter sonnets were placed as they are. The second and third hexameter sonnets (6 and 8) frame the seventh sonnet "When Nature made her chiefe worke, Stella's eyes," introducing the theme of black eyes as beautiful, as light, as all. Sonnet 6, "Some Lovers speake when they their Muses entertaine," deals with previous literary treatments of love; sonnet 8, "Love, borne in *Greece,* late fled from his natiue place," gives a genealogy of love and his present residence in Stella. I cannot believe that a Renaissance reader familiar with the hexameral tradition from Genesis to Du Bartas would have been unaware that two hexameter sonnets, themselves anomalies, surrounding a seventh sonnet, beginning "When Nature made her chiefe worke, Stella's eyes," was flying in the face of traditional knowledge that God created for six days, and "the seventh daye he rested from all his worke, which he had made" (Genesis 2.2). Even placing the responsibility on "stepdame Nature" as in sonnet 1 and Song VII, would not have dissuaded those readers from realizing that Astrophil was not seeing through to the origins of things, not getting his numbers straight. Astrophil, in the first line of the seventh sonnet, is talking about creation at one remove.

The other hexameter sonnets 76, 77, and 102 are also parts of symmetries. Sidney calls attention to the significance of the hexameter sonnets in the structure by using the same rhyme pattern for sonnets 1 and 77, 8 and 76.[40] It may also be significant that 76 and 77 are the twenty-second and twenty-third sonnets of the second 54, calling further attention to the patterns of 22 and 23 we have been observing. There are also 32 sonnets from 77 through 108. Sonnet 102, the last of the hexameter sonnets, is the seventh poem from the end of the sequence, balancing sonnet 7, placed between two hexameter sonnets, 6 and 8. The Penelope number (108) occurs again if we count the sonnets and songs, counting VIII as three parts, between sonnet 7, framed by two hexameter sonnets, and 102. There are also 108 stanzas and sonnets between 77 and 102.[41] Sidney may also have made 76 and 77 hexameters to show a connection between Song I and Song VII, the song of blasphemy and the song of reason, I and VII being equidistant from the two sonnets in question.

The complexities of the numerical patterns I have been suggesting should not make us forget that in spite of the overlapping symmetries a basic structure does emerge, which supports the reading I gave the sequence at the beginning of this essay. I suggested that a formal division could be made as follows: 63 sonnets (1–63), Song I, 25 poems (64–85), one sonnet (86), 63 stanzas (V–IX), 24 poems (87–108): 63/1/25/1/63/24. The repetition of the climacteric number seems to me important. Most of the studies of *Astrophil and Stella* are postulated on the assumption that Astrophil changes dramatically as the sequence progresses. They try to demonstrate the progress of the lover through various stages of love, but neither these stages nor when they occur is agreed upon.[42] My reading of Sidney's poem is based on a different assumption: there is no progress in this sonnet sequence. Astrophil is sadly in love in sonnet 1 and sadly in love in sonnet 108. All the intervening sonnets and songs are recapitulations of the same crisis: human desire and its effects. As Rosemond Tuve remarks, "We meet the Beast in a thousand guises and recognize him each time for the first time."[43] One might almost say that in English sequences there is not progression, only regression into the selfish nightworld of desire unfulfilled. The crises occur again and again and are met with the same response:

> So while thy beautie drawes the heart to love,
>   As fast thy Vertue bends that love to good:
>   'But ah,' Desire still cries, 'give me some food.'[44]

These lines are literally at the midpoint, or heart of the whole sequence. All that comes before and after is mere descant and recapitulation. No progress is possible; no reasonable outcome can be expected. The Penelope stone is absent from the beginning, hence the 24 rather than 25 poems at the end of the sequence. Whether in song or sonnet Astrophil repeats his crises, by invoking Morpheus (32) or renouncing the Muses (55) or grammar rules (63), by observing "changed looks" (86) or by retreating into a false pastoral world (Song IX). Once the desire is codified into idolatrous blasphemy (Song I) there is no hope that the voice of reason (Song VII) will be understood, and Astrophil must sing his way to a "conclusion in which nothing is concluded."

Princeton University

APPENDIX
Numerological Structure of Sidney's *Astrophil and Stella*

1	33	Song I	Song V
2	34	64	Song VI
3	35	65	Song VII
4	36	66	Song VIII
5	37	67	Song IX
6 hexameter	38	68	87
7	39	69	88
8 hexameter	40	70	89
9	41	71	90
10	42	72	91
11	43	Song II	92
12	44	73	Song X
13	45	74	93
14	46	75	94
15	47	76 hexameter	95
16	48	77 hexameter	96
17	49	78	97
18	50	80	98
19	51	81	99
20	52	82	100
21	53	83	101
22	54	Song III	102 hexameter
23	55 invocation of muse; midpoint of 108	84	103
24		85	104
25	56	Song IV	Song XI
26	57	86 32nd sonnet	105
27	58	of second 54	106
28	59		107
29	60		108
30	61		
31	62		
32 Morpheus, midpoint of 1–63	63		

NOTES

1. The 1591 edition, first quarto, contains 107 sonnets (37, the sonnet punning on Lord Rich's name, omitted) and ten songs (XI omitted). The order of the poems is different in that 55 and 56 are reversed, and the ten songs appear as a block at the end of the sonnets. The many verbal differences are cited in William A. Ringler, Jr., ed., *The Poems of Sir Philip Sidney* (Oxford: Oxford University Press, 1962), to which edition all further citations of the poems are made. Ringler's excellent discussion of the textual history of the poems is on pp. 447–57.

2. Thomas Nashe, preface to *Syr P. S. His Astrophel and Stella* (1591; rpt. Menston-Scolar Press, 1970), Sig A.3.

3. Alastair Fowler, *Triumphal Forms* (Cambridge: Cambridge University Press, 1970), 175–76. See also note 32.

4. *The Prose Works of Sir Philip Sidney*, ed. Albert Feuillerat (Cambridge: Cambridge University Press, 1912–1926), vol. 3, p. 20.

5. For example, Leonora Leet Brodwin, "The Structure of 'Astrophel and Stella,'" *MP* 67 (1969), 25–40, in a very perceptive study leaves Astrophil in a thoroughly untenable situation: "In the first section [1–35], Astrophel sought a virtuous resolution of the conflict between *ideal reason* and desire caused by a love which had no hope of reciprocation. In the second section [36–86], Astrophel's internal struggle is displaced by the 'new warre' of *external* struggle with Stella following upon her unexpected show of favor to him. This wrecks the *virtuous* resolution toward which he had struggled so painfully in the first section and leaves him in the third section [87–108], with no *moral armor* against the unrelieved despair *caused* by Stella's final rejection of his love" (p. 27, emphasis added). I do not accept the *virtue* of Astrophil's dilemma. With Anne Romayne Howe, "Astrophil and Stella: Why and How?" *SP* 61 (1964), 150–69, I can recognize much poetic talent in Astrophil but no virtue. I do not want to restructure the sequence as she would, nor do I want to divide the persona of Astrophil into pure and impure persuasion as does Richard A. Lanham, "*Astrophil and Stella:* Pure and Impure Persuasion," *ELR* 2 (1972), 100–15. James J. Scanlon, "Sidney's Astrophil and Stella: 'See what it is to love' Sensually!" *SEL* 16 (1976), 65–74, is closer to the points I want to make, but I would like to trace Sidney's use of sonnet themes back to pre-Bembo sources, since Neoplatonism tends to becloud the basic Christian issues at stake. A reading closer to mine is Alan Sinfield, "Astrophil's Self-Deception," *EIC* 28 (1978), 3–17.

6. *Some Longer Elizabethan Poems*, ed. A. H. Bullen (Westminster: Archibald Constable, 1903), pp. 321–22. Alexander Craig, another follower of Sidney, makes the same point: "*So haue I in middest of my modest Affections, committed to the Presse my vnchast Loue to Lais, that contraries by contraries, and Vertue by Vice, more cleerely may shine*" ("To the Reader," *Amorose Songes, Sonets, and Elegies* [1606], Glasgow: Hunterian Club Publications, No. 5 [1873], p. 11). The basic critical issue is whether one achieves the moral purpose of literature by writing strict doctrine or by slyly using ironic techniques while implying the opposite. The most ancient and common version of the issue is whether Ovid was a lewd or a moral poet. In recent scholarship the problem has been debated on the meaning of Andreas Capellanus's *De amore*. See D. W. Robertson, Jr., "The Subject of the *De amore* of Andreas Capellanus," *MP* 50 (1953), 145–61. An interesting example of the problem, roughly contemporaneous with Sidney, is Robert Greene's *Vision* in which the supposedly dying author reflects on his own literary practice and has both Chaucer and Gower tell a tale on how to drive out jealousy, Chaucer taking the ironic, witty route and Gower taking the straightforward moral route. Greene describes the business of the true writer not "in painting out a goddesse, but in set-

ting out the praises of God; not in discovering of beauty, but in discovering of virtues, not in laying out the platforms of love, nor in telling the deep passions of fancy, but in perswading men to honest and honorable actions, which are the steps that lead to true and perfect felicity." (*Life and Works of Robert Greene, MA,* ed. A. B. Grosart, 15 vols. [1881–1886], vol. 12, p. 189). The further irony of Greene, very lively, writing about his death and repentance, deserves further study.

7. For example, see David Kalstone, *Sidney's Poetry, Contexts and Interpretations* (Cambridge, Mass.: Harvard University Press, 1965), p. 178.

8. For a different interpretation of the star imagery, see Ruth Stevenson, "The Influence of Astrophil's Star," *TSL* 17 (1972), 45–57.

9. See note 26.

10. The phrase "daily unbidden guest" seems to me to foreshadow Milton's "worthy bidden guest" of *Lycidas* 118, derived from Matthew 22:8: "Truely the wedding is prepared but they which were bidden were not worthie."

11. Text and translation from Loeb edition, ed. and trans. Frank Justus Miller.

12. On the identification of Stella with Penelope Lady Rich, see Ringler, *Poems of Sir Philip Sidney,* pp. 440–47 and Hoyt H. Hudson, "Penelope Devereux as Sidney's Stella," *Huntington Library Bulletin* 7 (1935), 89–129; Jack Stillinger, "The Biographical Problem of *Astrophel and Stella,*" *JEGP* 59 (1960), 617–39; and Ephim G. Fogel, "The Mythical Sorrows of Astrophil," *Studies in Language and Literature in Honour of Margaret Schlauch* (Warsaw: Polish Scientific Publishers, 1966), 133–52. I cannot accept A. C. Hamilton's suggestion of strong autobiographical impulse in the sequence (*Sir Philip Sidney: A Study of His Life and Works,* Cambridge: Cambridge University Press, 1977, pp. 80–86).

13. See final section of this essay.

14. *The Schoolmaster* (1570), ed. Lawrence V. Ryan (Ithaca, N.Y.: Cornell University Press, 1967), pp. 62–63.

15. Ibid., p. 64.

16. Ibid., pp. 68–69.

17. Ringler, *Poems of Sir Philip Sidney,* p. 459; Kalstone, *Sidney's Poetry,* pp. 124–30.

18. Thomas Wright, *The Passions of the Minde in Generall,* intro. Thomas O. Sloan (1604; rpt. Urbana: University of Illinois Press, 1971), Sigs D^V–D2 (pp. 34–35).

19. Ringler, *Poems of Sir Philip Sidney,* p. 478. For a full treatment of Sidney's misuses of grammar, see Margreta de Grazia, "Lost Potential in Grammar and Nature: Sidney's *Astrophil and Stella,*" *SEL* 21 (1981), 21–35.

20. See Alan Sinfield, "Sexual Puns in *Astrophil and Stella,*" *EIC* 24 (1974), 341–55. I think we would have to agree that one reader's pun is another's poison. On the relation of sonnet 1 and 77. see note 41.

21. Ibid., p. 344; Barnabe Barnes, *Parthenophil and Parthenophe: A Critical Edition,* ed. Victor A. Doyno (Carbondale, Ill.: Southern Illinois University Press, 1971), p. 16 (sonnet 23).

22. Max Putzel, ed., *Astrophil and Stella* (Garden City, N.Y.: Doubleday, 1967), p. 166.

23. Ringler, *Poems of Sir Philip Sidney,* p. 473.

24. Sidney, *Defense,* ed. Feuillerat, *Prose Works of Sir Philip Sidney,* vol. 3, p. 9. Most modern editors follow the Olney and Penshurst texts which read "James," a reference to James 5.13; later folios read "Paul," a reading that should at least have a hearing.

25. Katherine M. Wilson, *Shakespeare's Sugared Sonnets* (New York: Barnes and Noble, n.d.), p. 34.

26. The one exception I have found is James Finn Cotter, "The Songs in *Astrophil and Stella,*" *SP* 67 (1970), 178–200. Our basic disagreements will be apparent; our readings are fundamentally different even when we seem to agree on individual points.

27. It seems to me significant, as I shall try to show in the last section, that sonnet 86 is important as a structural referent. Its final rhyme word *hell* is meant to support the kind of allusive reading I have been suggesting as a means of giving a Christian context to Sidney's poem. The word *hell* appears four times in the sequence, three of those times as rhyme words: in 2.14: "While with a feeling skill I paint my hell"; in 74.7: "And this I swear by blackest brook of hell, / I am no pickpurse of another's wit"; and the present example of the last line of sonnet 86. The fourth occurrence is line 83 of the fifth song. Putzel comments on Song V in his edition of *Astrophil and Stella* (p. 193) as to "tone and burden" and finds it "unrelated to any other poem." Then relying on Ringler's regress to earlier Arcadian composition, Putzel seems to me to beg the question of artistic integrity, of which Sidney was a master: when a poem does not match one's exceptions as to tone, throw it back into the court of juvenilia.

28. Ringler, *Poems of Sir Philip Sidney*, p. 485; Putzel, p. 195.

29. In addition to being the dullest of listeners, these hapless stones may be a covert allusion to the stones of the Penelope game, which Fowler and others find as the structural basis of the sequence. See Fowler, *Triumphal Forms*, p. 175 ff.

30. For Argus reference see *OA* 8, in Ringler, pp. 20–22.

31. Fowler, *Triumphal Forms*, pp. 175–80.

32. See note 3. The 109 (or 110) poems of *Caelica* with their numerous borrowings from Sidney is probably an acknowledgement of praise from Fulke Greville, Sidney's closest friend. It may also be of significance that Sidney's Song VIII is the one hundred eighth poem in *England's Helicon* (1600). Whether the compilers of anthologies were also numerologists is a question that should be looked into. The fact that the word *love* is used precisely 108 times *in the sonnets* suggests the degree of ingenuity expended on the composition of sonnet sequences.

33. See n. 12.

34. Fowler, *Triumphal Forms*, p. 178.

35. On the meaning of the sequence Fowler writes: "For the authors of many sequences of love sonnets mannered their eroticism with a cool deliberation, arranging individual sonnets — themselves often ardently passionate yet highly structured — in intricate symmetrical patterns or according to relatively *recherché* number symbolisms." On sonnets 1–63: "Now by Sonnet lxiii *Astrophil and Stella* has certainly reached a critical phase of heightened intensity, marked in the form by interposition of lyrics, in the narrative by Astrophil's outbursts of passion, by his dishonourable suggestion of Song VIII and by his consequent loss of Stella." On the alignment of the stanza totals of the Songs (I–IV = 28; V–IX = 63; X–XI = 17): "The number 28, a 'perfect' number, signified virtue: 63 denoted a life crisis: and 17 was a familiar Pythagorean number symbolic of misfortune and grief." As for the number of the whole songs, 11, it signified both transgression and grief." On the pair of 22 sonnets surrounding sonnet 86: "We find a symmetry about Sonnet lxxxvi, the sonnet concerned with a 'change of looks' in Stella the 'sweet judge,' who thus occupies a central seat of judgement in the formal structure in the midst of numbers signifying chastity (22, 22)." Especially for those who find numerological symbolism unconvincing, some further correlation between the numbers and the text is required (Fowler, *Triumphal Forms*, pp. 174–77).

36. In *Triumphal Forms*, p. 176, Fowler cites the 63 sonnets of Constable's *Diana* (1592) and Drayton's *Idea* (1619). The number is the product of 7 (body) × 9 (mind). The complexities of the climacteric are spelled out in Thomas Wright's appendix to *The Passions of the Minde in Generall* (1604), *A Succinct Philosophicall declaration of the nature of Clymactericall yeeres, occasioned by the death of Queen Elizabeth*, Sigs A3–C3.

37. See Ringler, *Poems of Sir Philip Sidney*, pp. 458–59, 478.

Astrophil and Stella: A Radical Reading

38. The fact that 55 and 56 were reversed in 1591 seems to me of little importance.

39. See James J. Yoch, "Brian Twyne's Commentary on *Astrophel and Stella,*" *Allegorica* 2 (1977), 114–16. Twyne's comment on 63, I think, supports Ringler's suggestion and my reading of that sonnet. "His loue Stella saide, no, no, whenes he concludes yt accordynge to gramer rules 2 negatiues make an affirmatiue."

40. Fowler cites Benjamin's suggestion of a correspondence between sonnets in the first and second half, e.g., 22 and 76 (*Triumphal Forms,* p. 177). Other possible hints of structure from similarity of form and rhyme scheme occur in 1 and 77, 3 and 61, 4 and 62, 5 and 75, 8 and 76. See Ringler, *Poems of Sir Philip Sidney,* pp. 570–71.

41. One might by including 77 come to the total of 109, that is, the suitors plus the Penelope stone, or winning the game. I could accept such a count if one read the "winning" as a further delusion on Astrophil's part. Fowler's observation (*Triumphal Forms,* p. 178n.) that the line total of the songs is 545 (or 5 × 109) seems to fit in the same category of symbolism, general and supportive of the basic symbolism but not determinative or decisive for the structure. The five 109s occur at IV.27, V.82, VIII.9, IX.14, and XI.45. Fowler does not mention that IX.14 immediately follows the lines: "Heare your wofull maister's story, / Which to stones I els would show." See my explanation of these lines above and sonnet 36.13 and Song III.3, 6, 13, 14. I can make no relationship between the hexameter sonnets and the hexameter songs III and V. I have also not been able to work out the possible division of the sequence into 17 groups of 7 poems each, 17 being an unlucky number. Sidney may also have made 76 and 77 hexameters to show a connection between Song I and Song VII, the song of blasphemy and the song of reason, I and VII being equidistant from the two sonnets in question.

42. In response to the proposed tripartite division of the poem by earlier critics A. C. Hamilton in his article, "Sidney's *Astrophel and Stella* as a sonnet sequence," *ELH* 36 (1939), 59–87, makes both a poignant and witty assessment of the critical situation: "Since critics have placed the end of the first section of Sidney's poem variously at sonnets 32 [Buxton], 40 [Rudenstine], 43 [Young], and 51 [Ringler], one may fairly conclude that it does not possess 'a clearly discernible three-part structure'" (p. 66). This absolutely astute assessment of the situation does not prevent Hamilton from throwing his hat in the ring with a new tripartite structure of 1–35, 36–71, Song II–108, with strong arguments to enforce the dramatic or narrative development of the persona of Astrophel [sic]. Hamilton's division of the sequence did not deter others from dividing up the sequence in different ways. Leonora Leet Brodwin ("The Structure of *Astrophel and Stella,*" *MP* 67 [1969], 25–40) suggests a division 1–35, 36–86, 87–108. Ruth Stevenson ("The Influence of Astrophil's Star," *TSL* 17 [1972], 45–57), reverting to Young, divides it 1–43, 55–Song 9, 85–108. Andrew Weiner ("Structure and 'Fore Conceit' in Astrophil and Stella," *TSLL* 16 [1974], 1–25) decides on a five-part structure: 1–20, 21–45, 46–68, 69–Song VII, Song VIII–108; and B. F. Harfst ("*Astrophel and Stella:* Precept and Example," *PPL* 5 [1969], 397–414) urges the seven-part structure of a classical oration. Weiner's justification is that we are dealing with a "dynamic process and not a static definition" (p. 1). I think that Sidney would not have understood the dynamic of the process. Not one of these critics acknowledges what Sidney wants us to see Astrophil doing to himself: verbal talent in the service of desire defeating itself through its own cleverness and basic desire.

43. Rosemund Tuve, *Allegorical Imagery* (Princeton, N.J.: Princeton University Press, 1966), p. 108n.

44. Ringler, *Poems of Sir Philip Sidney,* poem 71.

JOHN HOLLANDER

Observations on a Select Party

*B*Y THE "select party" of the title of these brief remarks, I might be taken
to refer to the membership of the Spenser Society, or even to the slightly
more select subset of that membership who have been pouring out the
wine without restraint or stay. In fact the "select party" has to do with a
Spenserian vision of the American poetic genius, as I shall shortly disclose;
I hope, at any rate, that a matter of cisatlantic repercussions is sufficiently
peripheral to Spenser as to be appropriately postprandial.

The presence of Spenser in modern American literature has been problematic. Henry Miller was quoted in an obituary as having said that he
could not finish City College because he was unable to get through *The
Faerie Queene*. Although we should say that he was referring to a different
text from ours—indeed, probably to the text of the way the poem was
taught, and to an emanation of asexual (and never punned-upon) quaint-
ness wich modernist nonreaders of Spenser ascribed to the poem for so
long—this was by no means the *ad hoc* objection of one of our most unwittingly Ariostan of writers. Our own modern—or rather, postmodern—
Spenser, Spenser for the person who has not only read Joyce, but who is in
quest of *Ulysses'* true genre of romance is the revisionary poet and master
of parody, allusion, self-reference and all of the other modes which
modernist poetic had claimed as exclusively its own. But in our modern
American poetry, when Spenser's shade appears, it is like the return of the
repressed. When the *Prothalamion* refrain is apparently mockingly quoted
in *The Waste Land*, the added line, a rhyming alexandrine, in fact, completes not the neoclassic triplet, but a suppressed Spenserian stanza above
it—"Sweet Thames, run softly till I end my song, / Sweet Thames, run
softly, for I speak not loud or long." The allusion anxiously echoes more in
Spenser than it sets out to deflate. Our greater poet, Wallace Stevens,
whose echoes of Shelley, Keats, and Milton suggest that his attitude toward their precursor might be very different from Eliot's, propounds a
beautiful Spenserian moment in the third part of *Notes Toward a Supreme
Fiction*, the mystic marriage, on "the ever-hill, Catawba":

> At noon it was on the mid-day of the year
> Between a great captain and the maiden Bawda.

This was their ceremonial hymn: Anon
We loved but would no marriage make. Anon
The one refused the other one to take.

It is not only that Catawba is an "ever-hill" of the tribe of Arlo and Aci-
dale, but revised by a later reason, made "of what we see clearly / And
have seen, a place dependent on ourselves." For we hear the very covert
encoding of a Spenserian close in his own blank-verse lines as an injunction
to consider the mode of fable being recounted here.

But it is Henry Miller's dismissal which leads more directly to our select
party. Certainly the almost Atlantic expanse which separates the genres of
novel and romance, as Richard Chase characterized them in the opening
sections of his very influential book on the American novel, was once no
wider than the narrow stream across which Cervantes sent the Don and
Sancho, in unwitting and triumphant quest, not manifestly of more belated romance, but of the new novel. In arguing for the primacy of romance in nineteenth-century American fiction, Chase articulated what has
become a characteristic position among Americanists; and alas, in not
mentioning Spenser, and implicitly foreshortening the history of prose romance, he was doing so as well. Unlike F. O. Matthiessen, who could at
least arguably invoke Pearl in *The Scarlet Letter* as "the perfect type of Spenserian characterization, which starts with abstract principles and hunts for
their proper embodiment," a good deal of American literary history has
left Spenser's name alone, or to mere casual mention.

And yet Hawthorne, whose first book purchase in youth was *The Faerie
Queene* and who named his daughter Una, is far more obviously Spenserian in many of his short stories and sketches than in the larger romances.
From the early "The Hollow of the Three Hills," with its naturalised Temple of the Heart and its attachments; through tales like "Drowne's
Wooden Image" with its splendid assimilation of the Pygmalion legend to
the conceit in Michelangelo's sonnet about freeing a sculptural form from
its imprisonment in the implicit; the inverted echoes of the music in the
Bower of Bliss in "Young Goodman Brown"—"every . . . voice of the un-
concerted wilderness . . . mingling and according with the voice of guilty
man in homage to the prince of all"—not to speak of the flickering in and
out of local allegory in the name of the hero's spouse, Faith; the transformation of Despair's cave in "Dr. Grimshawe's Secret" (in an early draft,
Hawthorne notes "a chamber which when I think of it seems like entering
a deep recess of my own consciousness, a deep cave of my nature . . .
[Compare it with Spenser's Cave of Despair. Put instruments of suicide
there"]) and in "The Man of Adamant," as well as of both the House of

Alma and Mammon's Cave in "The Hall of Fantasy" in these and many other instances, it is not merely Spenserian character (Archimago as Mark Van Doren saw him in Chillingworth) or—as dissertations are beginning to argue—locale or figuration of place and space and object which are themselves shadowed in Hawthorne's narratives. It is, even more, a matter of the very structure of Spenserian episode itself: the shaping of a phase of a quest, the avowal of an apparent typological or quasi-figural connection between persons or representations and a self-imposed mandate—on the part of a story's central figure—to search out the authenticity of the connection. In stories like "The Christmas Banquet," and particularly "The Hall of Fantasy"—the sort of less-than-narrative "sketch" which we tend to neglect, or to write off as insufficiently sharp satire—the triumphal forms of Spenserian processional array themselves become the format of the story.

The most neglected of these pieces by Hawthorne has been the one called, indeed, "A Select Party." It recounts an entertainment given by "a man of fancy" at one of his castles in the air. The castle itself has been quarried out of clouds "which had hung brooding over the earth, apparently as dense and ponderous as its own granite, throughout a whole autumnal day." The visual effect of the completed exterior seeming to the owner to be too gloomy and gothic, he resolved to gild it, but "a flood of evening sunshine of the air . . . gathered up and poured abundantly on the roof and walls, imbued them with a kind of solemn cheerfulness; while the cupolas and pinnacles were made to glitter with the purest gold, and all the hundred windows gleamed with a glad light, as if the edifice itself were rejoicing in its heart."

This palace of the imagination, whose meteor-lit hall is described in a subsequent paragraph, then becomes the scene for a procession of invited guests. It is easy to see why Mark Van Doren could write off stories such as this as failed Swiftian satire: the first guest, arriving "with old-fashioned punctuality" looks to be a figure of Time himself, but is thereafter identified as Time's twin brother, a journalistically proverbial Oldest Inhabitant; he is followed by a string of other personified cliches, such as Nobody, Monsieur On-Dit, the Wandering Jew, the Clerk of the Weather, and so forth. But then there follows a sort of Triumph of Dream, clearly modeled on the Mask of Cupid: a crowd "of shadowy people with whom the Man of Fancy had been acquainted in his visionary youth," hoped-for friends, companions, and a "beautiful dream-woman who would become the helpmate of his human toils and sorrows" arrives, but are quickly seen to be "fantastic maskers, rendering heroism and nature alike ridiculous by the grave absurdity of their pretensions to such attributes." Then appears, "with a movement like a jointed doll, a sort of wax figure of an angel, a creature as cold as moonshine, an artifice in petticoats, with an intellect of pretty phrases and only the semblance of a heart, yet in all these particulars the true type of a young man's imaginary mistress." This Laura-Stella-Celia-Delia-Idea is followed by another train of impossibilities: phantasms from his childhood, such as "a deformed old black woman whom he imagined as lurking in the garret of his native home, and who, when he was an infant, had once come to his bedside and grinned at him in the crisis of a scarlet fever."

But the procession then yields momentarily to more trivial, satirical hypostatizations again: "an incorruptible Patriot; a Scholar without pedantry; a Priest without worldly ambition . . . and a Poet who felt no jealousy toward other votaries of the lyre." And yet all this has been a preliminary procession, for there finally arrives "a young man in poor attire, with no insignia of rank or acknowledged eminence" but with "a high, white forehead, beneath which a pair of deepest eyes were glowing with warm light. It was such a light as never illuminates the earth save when a great heart burns as the household fire of a grand intellect." This figure, perilously balanced between profoundly solemn mythmaking and the papier-mâché troping of the easy satirist, is that of the American Genius, and the tone in which he is described has all of the double-edged ambivalence of a defended poetic anxiety: "The noble countenance which should be distinguished by a halo diffused around it passes daily amid the throng of people toiling and troubling themselves about the trifles of a moment and none pay reverence to the worker of immortality." Hawthorne means this even as he means to mock it, and the American Genius, whether in the form of an epic poem or assuming a guise altogether new as the spirit itself may determine, we are to receive our first great original work." (We must remember that this passage is being written perhaps at the same moment as those in Emerson's "The Poet" which it seems to echo, mockingly and affirmatively at once.)

The parade concludes with some more tinsel fictions (Davy Jones and the like) and, finally, the figure of Posterity itself. What makes the procession in the Hall of Trope so remarkable is the structure and placement of the figures of the trivial and the profound, the phasmata of ordinary language and the slyly shaded object of Hawthorne's own true devotion, placed almost in the middest of his tales. Furthermore, the entire select party now repairs to the rest of the castle—to the galleries lined with "a multitude of ideal statues, the original conceptions of the great works of ancient or modern art, which the sculptors did but imperfectly succeed in putting into marble; for it is not to be supposed that the pure idea of an immortal creation ceases to exist; it is only necessary to know where they are deposited in order to obtain possession of them." Similarly, the castle's library is almost a Borgesian one, containing the completions of all the world's great unfinished books: "Here were the untold tales of Chaucer's Canterbury Pilgrims; the unwritten cantos of the Fairy Queen; the conclusion of Coleridge's Christabel; and the whole of Dryden's projected epic on the subject of King Arthur."

That Spenser's name alone is suppressed in this catalogue is hardly surprising, and I take that suppression not to be of the type of Professor Chase's, but rather of the type of Milton's in *Il Penseroso,* when, after invoking Chaucer's unfinished *Squire's Tale* as the sole example of romance (probably because of its fulfillment in *FQ* IV) he mentions only what "great Bards beside / In sage and solemn tunes have sung / Of Tourneys and of Trophies hung, / Of Forests and enchantments drear, / Where more is meant than meets the ear." Sage and serious Spenser's name does not meet the ear, and instead, the following line ("Then night oft see me in thy pale career"), the only hypermetrical one in *L'Allegro* and *Il Penseroso,* fills in for the name of the Bard with a kind of reduced version of the Spenserian stanza ending—not two rhyming tens and a twelve, but two rhyming eights and a ten.

In suggesting that Hawthorne's story (sandwiched in between "The Birthmark" and "Young Goodman Brown" in *Mosses from An Old Manse*) is in structure, and in mythopoetic intent, a vagrant core canto from what we might call "*FQ* Book A, or The Legend of America," I seem to fly in the face of critics of Hawthorne who consider this sketch an instance of chatty satire and mild. But in fact I was directed to it by a critic of Hawthorne who seized on it as "the sweetest and sublimest thing that has been written since Spenser wrote," who compared it to any canto of *The Faerie Queene,* and who associates the figure of the Master Genius in the procession of guests with his own prophecy of the coming of "the literary Shiloh of America."

This critic was Herman Melville, writing in 1850 of how "genius, all over the world, stands hand in hand, and one shock of recognition runs the whole circle round." And the lesson, I suppose, is not only that American poets in verse, as in the prose of romance, are a more select party than Americanists. Nor is it only that Concord read Spenser—and Marvell and Dryden and Donne—more profoundly and authentically than St. Louis, or Hailey, Idaho, those most kindly nurses of Anglo-American modernism. I think that it is more a matter of prose romance itself; of the "fayned colours" of American fable shading a true case of Spenserian mythmaking; and of the bold, but I hope not too bold, suggestion that prose

romance from Mary Shelley to Thomas Pynchon (and I hope beyond) begin to come more under the scrutiny of our own select party, by which, of
course, I invoke, challenge, and toast our present company.

Yale University

NOTE

This paper was delivered at the Spenser Luncheon, held at the annual meeting of the Modern Language Association, Houston, Texas, 1980.